The Mustache Gang
Battles the Big Red Machine

# The Mustache Gang
# Battles the Big Red Machine

## *The 1972 World Series*

JOHN G. ROBERTSON *and*
CARL T. MADDEN

McFarland & Company, Inc., Publishers
*Jefferson, North Carolina*

RECENT WORKS OF INTEREST AND FROM MCFARLAND

Amazin' Upset: The Mets, the Orioles and the 1969 World Series (by John G. Robertson and Carl T. Madden, 2021); Hockey's Wildest Season: The Changing of the Guard in the NHL, 1969–1970 (by John G. Robertson, 2021); When the Heavyweight Title Mattered: Five Championship Fights That Captivated the World, 1910–1971 (by John G. Robertson, 2019); *Too Many Men on the Ice: The 1978–1979 Boston Bruins and the Most Famous Penalty in Hockey History* (by John G. Robertson, 2018); *The Games That Changed Baseball: Milestones in Major League History* (by John G. Robertson and Andy Saunders, 2016); *A's Bad as It Gets: Connie Mack's Pathetic Athletics of 1916* (by John G. Robertson and Andy Saunders, 2014); *The Babe Chases 60: That Fabulous 1927 Season, Home Run by Home Run* (by John G. Robertson, 1999; paperback 2014); *Baseball's Greatest Controversies: Rhubarbs, Hoaxes, Blown Calls, Ruthian Myths, Managers' Miscues and Front-Office Flops* (by John G. Robertson, 1995; paperback 2014)

ISBN (print) 978-1-4766-8860-2
ISBN (ebook) 978-1-4766-4616-9

LIBRARY OF CONGRESS AND BRITISH LIBRARY
CATALOGUING DATA ARE AVAILABLE

Library of Congress Control Number 2022035730

Front cover: Gene Tenace of the Oakland A's
(Doug McWilliams/National Baseball Hall of Fame and Museum)

Printed in the United States of America

*McFarland & Company, Inc., Publishers*
*Box 611, Jefferson, North Carolina 28640*
*www.mcfarlandpub.com*

To the players, managers and coaches
who made the 1972 World Series so compelling and
to the baseball writers and broadcasters
who covered that Fall Classic so well.
In both cases their professionalism
has stood the test of time.

# Acknowledgments

It always takes many helpful people for a book such as this one to reach fruition. Accordingly, special thanks go to the following people:

- Mark Satterstrom, who provided us with copies of the original NBC radio broadcasts of each of the seven 1972 World Series games along with select games from that year's National League Championship Series and American League Championship Series;
- John Horne of the National Baseball Hall of Fame for his assistance in providing photographs for this book;
- Chris Eckes, of the Cincinnati Reds Hall of Fame, for kindly providing photographs and valuable information about the 1972 Reds;
- Linda Parker of the *Pittsburgh-Post Gazette*'s licensing department for granting us permission to reprint that newspaper's October 23, 1972, editorial about the recently concluded World Series in its entirety;
- Dr. Laura Neal, for her medical insights pertaining to Reggie Jackson's severe hamstring injury in the deciding game of the ALCS that unfortunately kept him out of the 1972 World Series and Mike Andrews' alleged shoulder injury in the 1973 World Series;
- The good folks, whoever they are, who maintain the fantastic Retrosheet, baseball-reference.com and baseball-almanac.com websites. They (the people and those websites) are godsends;
- Major League Baseball for providing collections of video highlights and some abridged games from the 1972 postseason on YouTube.

# Authors' Notes

Although it was seldom done in the North American sports media in 1972, we have made a point of including (or at least trying to include) the proper accents on players' first and last names wherever needed, such as Pedro Borbón, Dave Concepción, César Gerónimo, Ramón Hernández, Ángel Mangual, Gonzalo Márquez, Tony Pérez, Manny Sanguillén and others. Accents are indeed part of the correct spellings of those names. If some accents were missed in this text, those omissions were unintentional.

Although the names of the MLB divisions were sometimes presented as "Eastern" and "Western" in newspapers and other print media of the time, the correct terms—as verified by MLB.com and other baseball reference sites—were "East" and "West." That is how they appear in this text.

# Contents

# Introduction

"It was a World Series between a pair of upstart teams, the Oakland Athletics and the Cincinnati Reds, teams that would win the next five baseball championships, but it was so much more than just a thrilling Series in which six of the seven games were decided by one run. It was a World Series that brought baseball into the modern world, and what a world it was. The turbulent '60s had ended, a decade of drugs and hippies, of psychedelic music and protest over a war in Southeast Asia that had divided the country. The world was now changing—and the new order was not much better than the old."[1]—Bob Hertzel

When scholarly baseball fans gather to talk about great World Series from the past, the discussion often turns to the famous, thrill-packed 1975 Fall Classic between the Cincinnati Reds and Boston Red Sox or 1947's back-and-forth, intercity struggle between the New York Yankees and Brooklyn Dodgers as the best of the bunch. Other candidates for the greatest World Series ever contested include 1912 (a matchup between the New York Giants and Boston Red Sox that, remarkably, took eight games to decide a best-of-seven affair), 1955 (when "next year" became "this year" to frustrated Brooklyn fans as the Dodgers finally upended their great October rival, the Yankees), and 1957 (when the Milwaukee Braves won their only World Series title against—who else?—the New York Yankees). The seven-game Fall Classics of 1909, 1924, 1926, 1931, 1940, 1946, 1962, 1985, 1986, 1991, and half a dozen more recent World Series justifiably merit honorable mentions too.

For some reason, however, the terrific 1972 World Series is often overlooked. Consider the following: Six of the seven games contested by the Oakland A's and Cincinnati Reds that October were decided by a single run. Two of the games ended in spectacular fashion. Moreover,

1

there were plenty of memorable talking points generated throughout those mighty struggles. Furthermore, both teams' lineups featured a bevy of future Hall of Famers; among them were the two managers. The 1972 World Series certainly did not lack star appeal—as least retroactively. Altogether, its absence from most fans' lists of fondly remembered Fall Classics is quite perplexing.

Perhaps it was just the year. Nineteen seventy-two had more than its fair share of negatives, including the Watergate burglary that eventually led to Richard Nixon resigning the presidency and the Nicaraguan earthquake that killed 10,000 people. Old staples in American culture seemed to be vanishing. CBS canceled Arthur Godfrey's radio show after 27 years. *Life* magazine ceased publication after 36 years. But change brought new classics. The musical *Grease* made its stage debut in 1972. *M*A*S*H* first hit the airwaves on CBS in September, as did a revised remake of the game show *The Price Is Right* hosted by Bob Barker. Still, movies and television programs in general were becoming noticeably edgier and less uplifting. Fictional antiheroes were becoming just as common as make-believe heroes.

Certainly there were positive milestones in sports in 1972. Jockey Bill Shoemaker, at age 41, won his 555th career stakes race to eclipse Eddie Arcaro's lifetime record of 554. A 24-year-old Swedish pole vaulter, Kjell Isaksson, set a new world record in his specialty, successfully attaining a height of 18'1" at a meet in Austin, Texas, on April 8. (A week later Isaksson surpassed that record by another inch and a quarter. On June 12, he improved it again by half an inch. On July 2, Bob Seagren would set a new world mark, obliterating Isaksson's standard by three full inches in the American Olympic trials in Eugene, Oregon.) Nevertheless, the world of sports seemed especially hard hit that year. The Summer Olympics in Munich, West Germany, should have been fondly remembered for the sensational performances of American swimmer Mark Spitz and Soviet gymnast Olga Korbut. Instead, it is the lasting impression of the terrorist attack at the Olympic village—in which 11 Israeli athletes and officials were killed—that remains at the forefront of many minds.

That same year's Davis Cup final, contested in a Cold War atmosphere on a clay court in communist Bucharest, Romania, almost turned into a disgraceful sham because of blatantly corrupt officiating. Under adverse conditions, Wimbledon champion Stan Smith won the clinching match for the United States against Ion Țiriac in five sets. (Because of the unfavorable and hostile setting, some tennis historians have called Smith's dramatic win the most impressive performance by an American athlete in any international sport ever.)

Politics seemed to intrude in all international sports. The Winter Olympics in Sapporo, Japan, did not feature a Canadian hockey team, a glaring omission from the country that produced 97 percent of the National Hockey League's players in 1972. Canada's amateur hockey poohbahs had abruptly bolted from the International Ice Hockey Federation in 1970. They could not comprehend why the IIHF's definition of amateurism allowed for communist-bloc athletes who trained together for 50 weeks per year—but not for a few former North American ex-pros, reinstated as amateurs, who worked regular jobs and merely played hockey as a hobby.

Major League Baseball took its share of knocks too. The grand old game lost some of its old-timers from previous eras: Gabby Hartnett, Dizzy Trout, Zack Wheat, Pie Traynor, among others. Baseball also endured the sudden and shocking deaths of people who should have had decades more to live: Gil Hodges, Jackie Robinson and Roberto Clemente.

A labor dispute caused Opening Day to be delayed and, subsequently, made cynics out of thousands of previously unshakable loyal fans. Attendance fell just about everywhere. Only one of the four MLB divisional races in 1972 was close. The National Football League was becoming the premier choice of more and more American sports fans. Baseball, it was said by critics, was too slow-paced, too cerebral for the fast-moving 1970s. ABC's Howard Cosell opined that baseball was better suited to 19th-century America. Even in 1972, however, the World Series had more than a fair share of glamor attached to it. One could still see newspaper advertisements, such as one that appeared in a Pittsburgh daily, proclaiming in large letters, "It's World Series Time! Watch All the Games on a New Color TV." Similarly, a full-page in the *Fredericksburg Free Lance-Star* advertised a "World Series Furniture Sale" at a local store where shoppers could find "sure hits in sensational values."

Despite its knocks, baseball showed its resiliency, as it has often done throughout its glorious history, when it most needed a boost. The postseason activities of 1972 featured easily the most competitive confrontations since MLB expanded to its four-divisional setup in 1969. Every postseason series went the maximum number of games. Thrills abounded. (There were black marks too, most notably a horrible bat-throwing incident by Oakland's Bert Campaneris in the second game of the American League Championship Series.) The culmination of the 1972 MLB season was a finely played, thoroughly entertaining, seven-game World Series between two solid and superb teams.

During Game Six, announcer Monte Moore stated unequivocally on NBC Radio that the 1972 MLB postseason was the greatest ever.

Granted, 1972 was only the fourth season in the modern era in which the two major leagues had expanded postseason play to anything other than World Series games, so Moore was choosing from a very small sample size. But half a century later, it could be argued that Moore's superlative has stood the test of time.

Decide for yourself. It is time to revisit that terrific, underappreciated 69th Fall Classic of the modern era, as well as the abridged season and the two league championship series that led up to it.

# — 1 —

# Labor Dispute

## *Lost Games, Lost Faith*

"The idea of a union for major league baseball players seemed odd to the average American. That it would ever think to go on strike would be considered sacrilege. In 1972, the fledgling Major League Baseball Players Association would take that risk and forever change the fans' perception of the game—and its players. Until this time, fans held the view that to play big-league ball was a privilege, something that transcended the commonalities that other, less glorified lines of work offered."[1]—*thisgreatgame.com*

"But what about Marvin Miller, executive director of the MLBPA? Does his high-priced salary continue, or is he, too, taken off the payroll? And if not, does he really care how long the strike lasts and how long Joe Fan is without baseball?"[2]—Jack Hugerich, *Schenectady Gazette* sports editor

On April 1, 1972, Major League Baseball was faced with its first players' strike. (Some cynics saw symbolism in the date being April Fools' Day.) The unprecedented labor disruption erased the first week and a half of the season. Baseball resumed 13 days later when major league owners and players agreed on a $500,000 increase in pension fund payments. The owners also promised to add salary arbitration to the Collective Bargaining Agreement. Most teams lost anywhere from six to eight games from their usual 162-game schedule. The Houston Astros and San Diego each played only 153 games—nine fewer than normal. No one could foresee it at the time, but the team most adversely affected by the truncated schedule would be the Boston Red Sox.

Professional baseball had been played openly since 1869. Over the next century, the players who made their livelihoods from the game, for the most part, generally realized they were treated no worse or no better by the men who paid their wages than the average American employee elsewhere and were not especially militant for too long. Because of the nature of the sport, however, an MLB player was a chattel; he could be bought, sold and traded at his employer's whim. Certainly, players had rebelled occasionally in the past. The failed Players' National League (PL) of 1890 was the best example of ballplayers trying to free themselves from the hated reserve clause. It was a nifty little portion of a standard player's contract that bound him to his club indefinitely—thus severely hampering him from selling his services to the highest bidder. The PL collapsed under a tidal wave of red ink after just one season of challenging the primacy of the other two major leagues in existence at the time—the National League and the American Association.

It was not until 1954 that a union—the Major League Baseball Players Association—was founded. It did not have much clout in its early days, however. For several years, the MLBPA was run by a representative of the MLB owners—some observers might say a puppet of the establishment. Players received a small handful of benefits, but hardly anything substantial. By the middle of the 1960s, the players were becoming a little more worldly about such things as finances, pensions, and workers' rights. They began to realize they were not reaping many of the benefits of America's national pastime at its highest level. A renowned labor lawyer, Marvin Miller, was hired in 1966 by the players to run their union. Miller became nationally known in the 1950s for being a key figure in the United Steelworkers' Union. He later augmented his reputation as a highly competent labor official during John F. Kennedy's administration. His history of success showed that Miller was not a man to be trifled with. The baseball owners were very wary of what the MLBPA could be under Miller's stewardship.

At first, Miller focused on only small issues with the owners. Even so, the owners seldom budged on any of them. This only served to embolden the ballplayers and foster resentment, convincing them that Miller was the right man to head their previously docile union. It also gave the impression that the owners generally feared Miller and his hardcore union beliefs. The end result was that the players gradually became more and more militant in their demands with management. A strike during the 1969 season was barely averted. When 1972 rolled around, discussions for a new labor contract between MLB and the MLBPA were not going especially well.

There was one major point of contention in the spring of 1972: The players desired an increase in their pensions equivalent to three years' worth of inflation. The owners flatly refused to consider such a concession, wrongly believing that the players would not dare strike over what they perceived to be small potatoes. Miller also had serious doubts whether the players would really stage a walkout. Nevertheless, barely one week before the scheduled Opening Day games on April 5, the 48 player reps—two from each of the 24 MLB clubs—during a meeting in Dallas, surprised the sports world by voting to strike. The vote was overwhelming: 47–0 with one abstention. (Miller did not publicly name the rep who declined to vote, but it later came to be known that the abstainer was Wes Parker of the Los Angeles Dodgers. He could not bring himself to vote in favor of a strike because he had just bought a new house and was worried about how he would make the payments on it if he was not being paid to play baseball.) Reggie Jackson, one of the Oakland player reps, was quite militant in his outlook. "Goddammit, there are just times when you've got to stand up for your rights,"[3] he shouted at his colleagues. The general MLBPA membership voted 663–10 in favor of strike action. No further preseason games were played after March 31.

One of the two Boston Red Sox reps, Gary Peters, spoke on behalf of the strikers. He declared, "We were forced into doing what we did. If we had gone any other way, it would have ruined our association. We would like to think that the owners will believe that we are serious now."[4] Commissioner Bowie Kuhn spoke tersely and briefly to the media, offering a totally different viewpoint. "Obviously," he said, "the losers of the strike action taken tonight are the sports fans of America. Beyond that, I will have no statement to make at this time."[5]

A group of professional athletes walking away from their sport in a labor dispute was uncharted territory in America. Atlanta Braves owner Bill Bartholomay defiantly told the media that "every effort will be made to field a team for Opening Day—even if it means using minor leaguers."[6] This drastic move did not occur. MLB ballparks were desolate places on April 5—what should have been Opening Day 1972. One widely circulated news photo showed an attendant for the Baltimore Orioles, sitting alone in the home team's clubhouse, idly playing solitaire on an equipment crate to pass the time.

In his syndicated column that ran on April 4, Jim Murray penned some blunt advice directed at the striking ballplayers:

> If the men who ... drive trains, or pick up garbage go on strike, the Republic is in trouble.
> If the guys who hit home runs, throw no-hitters, steal bases or write columns go on strike, it's doubtful the White House would go on all-night sessions.

> The first law of a general strike is indispensability of the strikers. Lepidop-terists can strike and influence only the butterfly-net industry. A strike of automobile-makers is crippling. A strike of automobile racers is not.[7]

From April 1 to April 13, the MLB players established a precedent by refusing to suit up for work. Eventually, after some contentious nego-tiations, on April 10 the owners agreed to contribute an extra $500,000 to the MLBPA pension fund and, as an added goodie, included salary arbitration to the Collective Bargaining Agreement. (Interestingly, the owners had an $800,000 surplus in the pension fund! Apparently, this surfeit was a revelation to a few of them.) The owners estimated they had lost $5 million in ticket revenues when their ballparks were vacant. A total of 86 games were removed from the MLB regular-season schedule. They were never rescheduled because the owners steadfastly refused to pay any player salaries for the period of the strike—something the play-ers demanded.

Ballplayers were not making obscene salaries in 1972. Only two Cincinnati Reds were known to be earning six-figure salaries. Some even held offseason jobs. (Oakland outfielder Joe Rudi, for example, who would star in the World Series that autumn, supplemented his income during the winter by selling insurance out of his house. His teammate, pitcher Blue Moon Odom, worked in a Georgia liquor store to make ends meet.) Not surprisingly, however, the unprecedented disruption to the baseball season did not sit well with the average MLB fan who con-cluded that modern ballplayers had become greedy ingrates.

When the 1972 season finally got underway, attendance was noticeably down everywhere. Crowds on the rescheduled Opening Day were markedly smaller than usual, a 40 percent drop from the previ-ous year. Players were routinely booed for a long time by those disillu-sioned but diehard fans who did buy tickets. Fan bitterness lingered well into the season. Overall, in 1972, there was an eight percent decline in attendance throughout MLB compared to 1971. Few MLB games drew more than 20,000 spectators. Attendance frequently dipped to four fig-ures in many locales. Five MLB teams drew fewer than 700,000 fans for the season. The strike probably alienated more than a few would-be supporters of the newly christened Texas Rangers. (The second incar-nation of the Washington Senators had just been transplanted to the Dallas-Fort Worth area.) The nascent Rangers only had about 663,000 souls buy tickets for their home games—only marginally more than the 655,156 fans the unfashionable 1971 Senators drew to Robert F. Ken-nedy Stadium in the team's final campaign in DC. Even worse was the turnout in Milwaukee where the Brewers barely surpassed the 600,000 mark.

One baseball history website has lamented the 1972 strike and its impact thusly:

> Fans would never look at the players quite the same way again, even if the players were still at an enormous disadvantage to the fat cats who ran the game. For they now saw ballplayer greed in the context of their own lives, working jobs without glory and often with less pay. And like a slap in the face, they had endured the insulting inconvenience of having the National Pastime stolen from them for a week.[8]

An article in the April 22 issue of *The Sporting News* seemed to agree. The weekly's assistant managing editor Oscar Kahan declared, "Letters to [our periodical] and to papers all across the country showed that public opinion was overwhelmingly on the side of the owners. An amazing number of fans swore they never would attend another game. It remained to be seen whether they would carry out their threat."[9]

MLB had clearly lost some of its luster. However, as Joel Zoss and John S. Bowman wrote in their history of the National League,

> It was only one of many indications that the traditional immutability of Major League Baseball was beginning to bend to the realities of modern life. Imagine the ballplayers of 50 years earlier striking for medical benefits and salaries of over $100,000 a year.[10]

Despite the shine of America's national pastime being dulled somewhat by the unprecedented players' strike, the 1972 MLB season quickly proceeded as if nothing too significant had happened in the first two weeks of April. Baseball fans would be rewarded for their patience with a brilliant and highly memorable postseason.

# The Swingin' A's

## *Unshaved, Unloved ... but Superb*

"In 1971, while playing for the Washington Senators, I was called into manager Ted Williams' office after a night game in Minnesota. [He said], 'We've traded you to Oakland. You've hit 50 home runs over the past two seasons for me and they need a power-hitting first baseman. This is a helluva break for you.'"[1]—Mike Epstein

"Their common foe was always Charles Oscar Finley. If the A's players sometimes fought with one another as well as their opponents, the bond most of them shared was a loathing of the A's irascible, overbearing, pompous, manipulative, scheming, cantankerous, bombastic, often prevaricating, but flamboyant, creative, forward-thinking, and inventive owner."[2]—Oakland A's historian Chip Greene

The Oakland Athletics were the descendants of one of the most storied of American League franchises. The Philadelphia Athletics were one of the original eight clubs that participated in the AL's inaugural season in 1901. Strangely, the man who owned the club in the early 1970s, Charles O. Finley, seemed to want to distance his A's from their colorful past. In fact, when the 1972 MLB season began, the team had quietly but officially changed its name to the "Oakland A's."

Of course, the nickname "A's" had long been used interchangeably with the more formal "Athletics," dating back to the team's early professional days when baseball scribes—particularly newspaper headline writers—needed a nifty way to shorten the name. According to Bill Libby, the author of the book *Charlie O and the Angry A's*, Finley went as far as to ban the old Athletics nickname from being used by any player or team employee. That assault on tradition was a bit of a shame. The Athletics were a team steeped with a history that dated back more than a century. It was not always a tapestry of excellence, but it was certainly revered baseball history, nevertheless.

The nickname "Athletics" for a Philadelphia-based ball club predates the 20th century by decades. An amateur team calling themselves "the Athletic Baseball Club" was in existence in the City of Brotherly Love at least as early as 1860. They soon became a dominant outfit. In 1871, another incarnation of the Philadelphia Athletics was a charter member of the first professional baseball league, the National Association (NA) which began play in 1871. In fact, they were the circuit's pennant winners that very first season, compiling a fine 21–7 record to cop the flag.

The NA barely survived five rocky seasons, with teams coming, going and folding in mid-season with great rapidity. Only the Boston Beaneaters, New York Mutuals and Philadelphia Athletics fielded teams throughout the NA's entire shaky run. When the National League was founded in 1876, a team calling itself the Philadelphia Athletics was one of the initial eight clubs. They finished dead last—and were expelled from the league by incoming president William Hulbert for failing to make a late-season road trip. There was no Philadelphia entry in the NL in 1877. Philadelphia would not return to the NL until 1883. The new club was called the Quakers. They would change their name to the Phillies in 1890.

Meanwhile, in 1882, the American Association (AA) declared itself a major league. It was dubbed the "Beer and Whiskey League" by its detractors. Unlike the NL, it sold intoxicating libations at its parks and had the temerity to break the Sabbath by playing games on Sundays. A Philadelphia club calling itself "the Athletics" was part of that loop. They finished second in their inaugural campaign and won the pennant the following year. Mediocre and worse seasons followed the AA version of the Athletics until they dropped from the scene in 1890. The AA gave up its major league status in 1891 and the Philadelphia Athletics name was dormant for another decade.

In 1901, the financially successful Western League changed its name to the American League, declared itself a major circuit, and operated as a rival to the quarter-century-old NL. One of its eight charter clubs was ... the Philadelphia Athletics. A former catcher named Connie Mack was given 25 percent ownership of the club and appointed himself as the team's manager. Mack and his family would eventually acquire full ownership of the franchise.

Mack stayed on as the club's manager for a remarkable 50 years, setting all sorts of records in the process for games won, games lost, and just about every other statistic linked to managerial longevity.

Mack never wore a uniform while managing. Instead, he always donned a civilian business suit and whatever type of chapeau that was in style at the time. Positioning his outfielders with gentle waves of his scorecard, slowly but assuredly the courtly Mack became something of a national institution and the personification of what was good, solid and wholesome about professional baseball. His Athletics (often abbreviated to A's in newspapers and baseball periodicals) fluctuated between greatness and comic ineptness throughout the years. His two best teams were the bunch that won every AL pennant but one from 1910 to 1914 and the crew that won three straight flags from 1929 to 1931. The former team was replete with Hall of Famers and featured the famed "$100,000 infield" of Stuffy McInnis, Eddie Collins, Jack Barry and Home Run Baker.

The latter assemblage got the better of the formidable New York Yankees of Babe Ruth, Lou Gehrig and company for three consecutive seasons. Mack's 1931 A's featured Al Simmons, Jimmie Foxx, Mickey Cochrane, Max Bishop, and the fiery Lefty Grove, a surly and thoroughly dominant southpaw pitcher who amassed a fabulous 31–4 record.

Oddly, the A's were never enormous box office draws at picturesque Shibe Park in their two Philadelphia heydays despite their talented lineups and multiple championships.

The money-conscious Mack was often forced to sell his best players to stay financially solvent. The aging Mack stepped down as manager—not exactly by his own choosing—after the 1950 season just before his 88th birthday. By that time, the Athletics were clearly lagging behind the NL Phillies in local popularity and were hemorrhaging money. Jimmie Dykes, who was the A's first post–Mack manager,

Connie Mack was synonymous with the Philadelphia Athletics, managing the team from 1901 to 1950. His long tenure with the A's made him a national figure. No man in baseball was held in higher esteem than Mack (Library of Congress).

**One of the first great baseball palaces to be built in the 20th century, Shibe Park was the home of the Athletics from 1909 until the club's departure from Philadelphia in 1954 (Library of Congress).**

painted a dismal image of things in his autobiography. He noted, "The club was sinking into the quicksand of financial catastrophe."

Indeed, only 304,666 fans watched A's home games in 1954—an average of fewer than 4,000 per game. That season was the franchise's last in Philadelphia.

A new ownership group headed by Arnold Johnson moved the team to Kansas City in 1955 but kept the "Athletics" moniker as an homage to the club's past. (Ninety-two-year-old Connie Mack reputedly turned ashen when he learned about the A's impending move to Missouri.) Despite the passage of nearly 70 years, as of 2022, the long-departed Athletics still have won more championships (five World Series) than any other Philadelphia team from the four major North American team sports.

Johnson firmly believed there was nothing wrong with the A's franchise that a few million dollars wisely spent could not fix. Nevertheless, the fortunes of the Athletics did not improve much in the 13 years they spent playing before generally small crowds in Missouri. As a novelty, they drew nearly 1.4 million fans to home games in 1955 and slightly above one million in 1956. (Breaking the seven-figure barrier was something that never occurred in any of the team's 54 years in Philadelphia.) After that, it was an annual struggle to draw crowds to Municipal Stadium. Mediocre or worse on-field products created fan apathy. The Athletics never finished better than sixth place while in Kansas City. Slightly more than 528,000 home fans bought tickets in 1965 to see an A's club that lost 103 games. After another last-place finish in 1967, few tears were shed when owner Charles O. Finley uprooted the once-proud Athletics from Missouri and replanted them in Oakland, California, for the 1968 season.

Finley, who ran a Chicago-based insurance company, bought the A's in 1960 at age 41; he had unsuccessfully tried to buy the team in 1954. Ken Burns' PBS *Baseball* documentary described Finley as "an old-fashioned, autocratic owner with revolutionary ideas."[3] In his autobiography, Oakland pitcher Jim (Catfish) Hunter likened Finley to P.T. Barnum—a man always coming up with novel and outlandish ways of promoting his team and sport "whether baseball liked it or not. And back in the late 1960s and early 1970s, it did not."[4] In a retrospective piece written in 2010, baseball historian Bob Hertzel penned, "Charles O. Finley, was as much a protester in the world of baseball as any anti-war hippy was in the real society."[5]

Finley was not one to hesitate in making radical changes. He replaced the A's long-standing elephant logo with a mule.

Furthermore, he acquired a live mule as a team mascot, named it Charlie-O, and proudly paraded it across the outfield prior to home games at Municipal Stadium. A herd of sheep once happily grazed on a hillside beyond the outfield wall. In 1963, Finley decked out his team in a new and garish color combination: Kelly green, Fort Knox gold, and wedding-gown white. Mickey Mantle of the New York Yankees was both unimpressed and appalled. He thought the A's revised uniforms were garishly effeminate. "They should have come out of the dugout on tippy-toes, holding hands and singing,"[6] he told *Baseball Digest*.

Finley liked to micromanage every detail about his team—from the color of their uniforms to the music played by the team's organist. Harried office employees quit in exasperation at an alarming rate. The club's 60-year history in the AL did not mean much to its owner. Finley seldom referred to his club as the Athletics anymore—merely the A's. Other aspects of baseball tradition were also not carved in stone, either. Finley thought the covers on baseballs should be bright orange rather than white and that the diamond's foul lines and bases should be more colorful, too. His fellow owners disagreed. Finley also liked the idea of a "designated pinch hitter" to bat throughout the game for pitchers. By 1973, enough AL owners did agree with him on

**Charles O. Finley poses with Charlie-O. The mule was the Athletics' mascot from 1965 until its death in 1976. Finley, an outspoken advocate for the designated-hitter rule, was full of radical marketing concepts. Among them were the use of orange baseballs in exhibition games and paying his players $300 bonuses to grow mustaches (National Baseball Hall of Fame and Museum).**

that radical idea. Finley also was a great believer that the first, second, sixth and seventh games of the World Series be played during the daytime on the weekends to attract young viewers and that weekday games should be played at night to attract the biggest possible television audiences.

Knowing a good thing when he saw it, during the Beatles' American tour in 1964, Finley persuaded the Fab Four to forego a planned day off and add a lucrative one-night stop in Kansas City on September 17. Lucrative was the key word: John, Paul, George and Ringo were paid $150,000 for the show—an unbelievable amount of money at the time for a single concert. The special tickets for the event featured Finley in a Beatles wig and featured the following optimistic quote: "Today's Beatles fans are tomorrow's baseball fans." Alas, few Beatles fans—or anyone else, for that matter—took the Kansas City A's to their hearts. When Finley announced he was moving the team to the west coast for the 1968 season, Missouri senator Stuart Symington publicly stated, "Oakland is the luckiest city since Hiroshima."[7] Only about 5,300 people bothered to show up for the last Athletics home date in 1967—a doubleheader versus the Chicago White Sox. The A's won both games. A promising 21-year-old pitcher named Catfish Hunter threw a 4–0 shoutout in the nightcap.

Attendance did not improve much for the newly relocated Oakland A's—but the team's performance certainly did. Gradually the A's acquired the pieces to be a very competitive outfit by improving their farm system. The players often squabbled amongst each other in the Oakland clubhouse, but Reggie Jackson, Joe Rudi, Bert Campaneris, Sal Bando, Dick Green and others provided the day-to-day strength to turn the A's into pennant contenders for the first time since the early 1930s. Jim (Catfish) Hunter, Vida Blue, Johnny (Blue Moon) Odom, and Ken Holtzman combined to form a reliable and stellar pitching staff. In 1968, the last year before MLB split into four divisions, Oakland finished in sixth place in the 10-team AL with a respectable 82–80 mark—and they were only four games out of third place. In both 1969 and 1970, Oakland finished in second place in the new AL West division. Things were looking up for Charlie Finley's squad.

The Swingin' A's (a term that appeared on the team's official logo in 1972) were a unique bunch in professional baseball. As a publicity gimmick, Finley paid his players $300 apiece if they would grow mustaches by Father's Day. This was utterly foreign in recent MLB times. To the best of anyone's recollection, the last MLB player to have sported facial hair was Wally Schang—way back in 1914. (Coincidentally, Schang was a catcher for the Philadelphia Athletics that year.) Most of Finley's A's good-naturedly accepted the idea. Relief pitcher Rollie Fingers certainly had the most noticeable mustache on the squad, one that curled upward at its edges. It made him look akin to a villain from an 1890s melodrama. Of course, Finley liked it—and gave him an additional stipend to offset the cost of mustache wax. The A's were also notable for the numerous varieties of uniforms. Players never quite knew which combination of cap, jersey, undershirt and socks they would find in their clubhouse stalls before any given game.

Nineteen-seventy-one was a breakthrough year for Oakland. New manager Dick Williams was at the club's helm. (He replaced John McNamara who had won 89 games in 1970, but McNamara was constantly battling with Finley about the owner's meddling in managerial decisions. Remarkably, Williams became the 11th man to manage the A's in 11 years!) According to Eric Aron who wrote Williams' SABR biography,

Dick Williams was regarded as one of baseball's premier managers and turnaround artists. He was only the second skipper to win pennants for three different teams—Boston, Oakland, and San Diego. As a rookie manager in 1967, Williams led the Red Sox from ninth place the year before to the World Series. Both personally and tactically, he took a no-nonsense, aggressive approach, which electrified several teams that he managed.[8]

Finley hired Williams as the man to guide the talented A's to the elusive divisional title. "I want a 25-man baseball team to represent the A's," the team's owner told *The Sporting News*. "We're going to have unity in 1971 under the leadership of Dick Williams."[9] He succeeded—with plenty of room to spare. Whether or not it was because of team cohesion or despite its absence is a matter of debate. The A's famously battled amongst each other throughout their championship seasons. According to Jim (Catfish) Hunter's autobiography, Reggie Jackson and Mike Epstein nearly came to blows in the clubhouse late in the 1972 season in a dispute over an allotment of *free* tickets to the A's home games in the ALCS. (Hunter broke up the fight before it began, much to the displeasure of several A's who wanted so see Epstein deck Jackson!) Years later Williams would recall that he was a particularly good fit on such a feisty club:

> This team was basically 25 versions of me. They didn't care about their appearance (we looked like damn hippies) or their deportment (we fought like sailors) or their safety (we led the league in Games Played with Death Threats Hanging Over the Players' Heads). The score after nine innings was their only interest; the rest of their world was like recess. So, when I looked at them, it was like looking in a mirror.[10]

Williams was never especially popular with his players, but he knew what he was doing—and he did it well. One biographer stated that Williams "struck a visceral chord" with the Oakland players that won their collective respect. In a 2002 interview, second baseman Dick Green said, "I played for 11 or 12 managers, and as far as liking managers, [Dick Williams] was near the bottom of that list, maybe at the very bottom. But he was the smartest baseball man I played for."[11]

Despite losing 8–0 to Washington on Opening Day 1971, starting out 2–4, and being outscored 40–24 in those six games, Oakland won the AL West for the first time. They compiled an excellent 101–60 record, comfortably finishing 16 games ahead of the ascending, second-place Kansas City Royals, one of the four 1969 MLB expansion teams.

The A's were stealthily becoming a very good baseball team. "Watching them play was like watching a boa constrictor eat," noted Bay Area sports journalist Ray Ratto decades later. "They didn't win 11–1; they'd win 3–2. They'd just slowly choke you—and they did it day after day—so it dawned on people awfully late that this was a juggernaut in the making."[12]

The losing pitcher on that Opening Day was Vida Blue who did not last two innings against the Senators. That result was an aberration. Blue quickly put that early setback behind him and enjoyed a dream season: 312 innings pitched, a 24–8 won-lost record, a 1.82 ERA, and eight shutouts. He also became the main gate attraction for the A's in 1971. Other teams took advantage of Blue's rapid rise to fame, too. New York held a special "Blue Tuesday"—complete with blue-colored scorecards in the programs—on a night he pitched. It drew the biggest weekday crowd in three years to Yankee Stadium.

Blue won both the AL's Cy Young Award and its MVP Award in 1971. Interestingly, the Cy Young Award voting was very close; Blue barely edged out Detroit's Mickey Lolich who had won 25 games. However, Blue finished far ahead of teammate Sal Bando in the AL MVP voting. He was so dominant in 1971 that *CBS Evening News* devoted a five-minute segment to Blue and his pitching exploits on its Saturday, June 26 broadcast. (CBS chose a good game to film Blue in action. The night before he had been thoroughly dominant in tossing a complete-game, 7–0 shutout over Kansas City in which he struck out 12 Royals, walked only one man, and allowed just five hits. The win raised Blue's seasonal record to 16–3.) Kansas City manager Bob Lemon could only admire the young man who had utterly dominated his team. "God gave [Blue] a good arm and he's taking advantage of it," he said. "Who knows how many games he might win? The way he's pitching right now, he might never get beat."[13] Three weeks later, Blue was the AL's starting pitcher in the MLB All-Star Game in Detroit. He was credited with the win in the AL's 6–4 victory.

As his win total and reputation grew throughout the summer of 1971, Blue was besieged by media wherever he went. Flattering comparisons to Sandy Koufax were made. It was difficult for a 21-year-old to handle all the overwhelming attention and adulation, but the well-spoken Louisiana native did his best. Blue told one of his many interviewers,

> It's a weird scene. You win a few baseball games and all of a sudden you are surrounded by reporters and TV men with cameras asking things about Vietnam and race relations. Man, I'm only a kid. I don't know exactly who I am. I don't have a whole philosophy of life set down.[14]

The 1971 ALCS was a huge disappointment for the A's, however, as the defending champion Baltimore Orioles swept them in three straight games (5–3, 5–1, and 5–3) to advance to the World Series for the third consecutive autumn. Like the A's, the Orioles had also won 101 games in the regular season. Oakland batted just .229 as a team in the 1971 ALCS compared to the Orioles' .274. Sal Bando, Tommy Davis and Reggie Jackson had productive at-bats over the three games, but Joe Rudi, Bert Campaneris and Ángel Mangual did not. In contrast, only Frank Robinson (one hit in 12 at-bats) had a poor offensive series for the victors. After the seventh inning of Game One, the Orioles never trailed at any time in the ALCS. Gayle Montgomery, a reporter for the *Oakland Tribune,* described the scene shortly after the A's 1971 season came to a disappointing conclusion to Game Three:

> The bunting was hung by the grandstand with care, but all that was left were lonely little clumps of hard-nosed Oakland A's fans who stood around the Coliseum long after the 5–3 score was in—still reluctant to let go of the visions of sugar plums.[15]

"We were in awe just to be there," Gene Tenace admitted many years later. "Baltimore had been there. We weren't ready for them yet. It was a different story the next year."[16]

Nineteen-seventy-two brought another divisional crown to Oakland. Their 93–62 mark in the strike-shortened season was 5½ games superior to the second-place Chicago White Sox. (Oakland lost 25 one-run games in 1972. Thus, with a bit of luck, they easily could have won at least a dozen more.)

Joe Rudi, who hit .305, was the only Athletic regular in 1972 to bat over .300, but there were few weak spots in the Oakland batting order. Reggie Jackson hit .265 (and belted 25 home runs) while constantly swinging for the fences. First baseman Mike Epstein batted .270 and surprisingly led the A's in home runs with 26. (Epstein, who would never again attain double digits in homers, answered to the comical and politically incorrect nickname "Superjew." He had acquired it in the minor leagues—and he had fun with it. Epstein insisted that baseball scribes write it as one word, like Superman.) Shortstop Bert Campaneris was not much of an offensive threat. He batted just .240, but when he got on base, he was the club's biggest stolen base threat. He copped 52 bags to lead the AL. It was the sixth (and last) time Campaneris would be the most prolific base stealer in the junior circuit. No other member of the 1972 A's had more than nine thefts. Even 30-year-old journeyman Tim Cullen, in his final year in the majors, made a big contribution to the team's success. He hit .261 while playing in 72 games, mostly at second base. (During the Oakland glory years, second base was the most unsettled infield position. The A's employed 17 different second basemen in five seasons.) Right fielder Ángel Mangual batted .246, an acceptable average, but it was still 40 points down from his 1971 figure when he was named to the AL's All-Rookie Team. The weakest bats among the Oakland regulars belonged to catcher Dave Duncan (who hit just .218) and third baseman Sal Bando (who batted .236). Both were very sound defensively, however.

Oakland's starting pitching was again superb in 1972. The club posted 23 shutouts (although only 15 of them were complete games for the starters). Catfish Hunter had an excellent 2.04 ERA and notched 21 victories. Ken Holtzman—who remained conspicuously clean-shaven—managed 19 wins. Blue Moon Odom picked up 15. Given what happened to him on Thursday, January 6, the fact that Odom was playing baseball at all in 1972 was quite remarkable.

That afternoon, Odom's wife, Perrie, witnessed several youths breaking into a house near her mother-in-law's home in Macon, Georgia. She telephoned the police and her husband, who had an offseason job at a nearby liquor store. When the youths fled past the store, Odom gave chase and confronted them. One miscreant turned and fired shots at Odom. Hitting him twice: once in his neck and once in his side. The wounded Odom fell to the sidewalk. Perrie came upon the scene, put her husband into her car, and drove him to a hospital. Blue Moon had luck on his side—as much as any man who has been struck by two bullets has luck. Neither of his wounds turned out to be life-threatening and surgery was not required. Three days later, on January 9, he was released from the hospital and was in perfect health by the time spring training began in March. Shortly thereafter, two suspects, aged 16 and 17, were arrested. A third culprit was later taken into custody. Odom identified all three of them at their trial.

"I was thinking I would never pitch again after that first shot," Odom commented to a baseball writer. "After that second shot, I thought it was all over."[17]

The man widely perceived to be Oakland's best pitcher, Vida Blue, the 1971 AL MVP, had a surprisingly poor 1972. He was just 6–10—but he had sat out for a month in a highly publicized contract dispute. During the offseason, Blue had traveled to Thailand, Spain, Okinawa, Vietnam and other locales over the space of 15 days to entertain American troops with Bob Hope. (Cincinnati catcher Johnny Bench was also part of the group.) "Being the only black male on the trip meant that I was well received," Blue told *The Sporting News*. "After the show I would leap off the stage, shake hands and rap with the guys. I didn't just talk to black guys, of course. I tried to keep it integrated." Blue said a Hope one-liner about professional baseball routinely generated the most laughs: "Where else can you spend eight months on grass and not get busted?"[18] According to *TSN*, Blue was a quick learner and something of a showbiz natural. Within a very short time, he had memorized not only his lines for the comedy routines, but the lines of the entire ensemble for the whole show.

Picking up the slack from Blue's subpar 1972 was the superb Rollie Fingers, who accrued 11 wins coming out of the A's bullpen. (Williams had converted Fingers from a starter to a reliever in 1971; he would only make two more starts in a terrific 14-year MLB career that led to a spot in Cooperstown.) Two other relievers, Bob Locker and Darold Knowles, had six and five victories respectively. The A's had 42 complete games in 1972—a total that would once have been considered unsatisfactory at the MLB level—but was now becoming normal as managers began to use their relievers more and more as shut-down weapons rather than mere mop-up men. Dick Williams was only patient with his starters to a point. He smartly knew he had a quality bullpen he could turn to every day, if necessary, to hold any opposing club at bay.

Interestingly, the highest paid Oakland pitcher in 1972 was long gone by the time the postseason came along. Denny McLain, who had famously won 31 games for the 1968 Detroit Tigers, was picked up by the A's from Washington at the end of the 1971 campaign. It was thought McLain's presence would offset Vida Blue's sudden unexpected and prolonged absence. The fading McLain—whose 1972 contract paid him an eye-popping $75,000—failed miserably. He had just one win in his five starts for Oakland. McLain was sent to the minors on May 15, then traded to Atlanta on June 29 where his checkered MLB career quietly ended.

Despite the formidable A's of the early 1970s playing excellent baseball and Charlie Finley's endless publicity stunts, they never drew sizable crowds to the Oakland-Alameda County Coliseum, their home stadium that they shared with the NFL's Oakland Raiders. In fact, the team's attendance figures were downright disappointing. Only twice in the five-year period from 1971 through 1975, when the A's were the best club in the AL West, did they break the million mark. In 1973, they attained it just by a whisker as 1,000,763 fans passed through the turnstiles. In 1975, they did it with 75,000 spectators to spare.

In his autobiography, Catfish Hunter ruefully discussed the surprisingly poor attendance at A's home games year after year:

> That's the one thing that wasn't perfect about Oakland. For the first three or four years, we pretty much played by ourselves. Heck, we got outdrawn by a World Team Tennis match one night. It got so quiet at times that [Sal] Bando nicknamed the place the "Oakland-Alameda County Mausoleum." And it wasn't like Finley was just sitting on his hands. Hell, he spent more

than $1 million to create and install two computerized scoreboards. He held every promotional day known to man: Auto Industry Day, Farmers' Day (I did the hog-calling), Bald-Headed Man's Day. You get the picture.[19]

It was generally believed by baseball insiders that the Bay Area's sports fans were missing out on something quite special.

# The Cincinnati Reds

## *The NL's Emerging Powerhouse*

"The [1869 Red Stockings] were thus the first avowedly professional team in baseball history, a distinction that scholars insist on using to separate this mighty team from under-the-table schemers and gate-receipt communards who had preceded them."[1]—John Thorn, MLB's official historian

"When [Bob] Howsam became the general manager of the Cincinnati Reds in 1967, he wanted his team to have an image based on an identity that separated them from the times—something altogether separate from the hippies, the long-hairs and bra-burners who danced to that sitar music in the Summer of Love. He wanted a baseball team that would not terrify the good and decent family folk of Cincinnati. He decreed that every Reds player would wear his hair short, his uniform would be wedding-gown white, and his shoes tuxedo black. No one would wear a beard, of course. He wanted them to be, yes, a machine, a Big Red Machine...."[2]—Joe Posnanski, author of *The Machine*

While the true birthplace of baseball has always been a bit of a contentious mystery, there is no doubt that Cincinnati was the city where open professional baseball was born. In 1869, a group of enterprising businessmen in that Ohio city had the audacity to assemble the best ballplayers in the country, form an invincible team, and openly pay the athletes for their labors on the diamond. For at least a decade, the top so-called amateur ballplayers had quietly accepted payments and shares of the gate from top-tier games, but it was not until the Cincinnati Red Stockings came along that professional baseball was displayed for all to see.

After all, beginning in 1869, the governing body of the sport, the

National Association of Base Ball Players (NABBP), would begin to allow openly pay-for-play teams to operate within its membership.

Players for the Red Stockings were recruited from far and wide—only one actually called Cincinnati home. Most were youthful New Yorkers. English-born Harry Wright, age 34, captained the squad and patrolled center field.

His younger brother, George, the shortstop, was probably the most talented member of the team, at least judging by his whopping $1,400 salary. The Red Stockings would play home games occasionally, but would largely be a touring club, playing wherever they believed they could draw a crowd and demand the lion's share of the gate receipts.

Starting with a 45–9 romp on May 4 over another Cincinnati club—the Great Westerns—the Red Stockings rolled to an undefeated season beating fellow but overmatched NABBP clubs at least

In 1869, Harry Wright was the captain of baseball's first openly professional team—the famous Cincinnati Red Stockings. Wright organized and managed the team. He also played center field (Library of Congress).

57 times without suffering a single setback. The routs and winning streak made for fun reading in the Cincinnati newspapers, but not so much elsewhere. At the end of the fiscal year, the Red Stockings turned a tiny profit for the 1869 season of $1.39. Despite the paltry gain, professional baseball was here to stay—thanks to a Cincinnati-based baseball team. Club president Aaron B. Champion, a Cincinnati lawyer, proudly proclaimed at a season-ending banquet that he would rather hold his position with the Red Stockings than be president of the United States.

*Sporting Life*, a leading periodical of the day, recognized the

**An artist's depiction of the presentation of an enormous bat to the 1869 Cincinnati Red Stockings to commemorate their undefeated season (Library of Congress).**

impact of what had happened in that seminal summer from a business standpoint:

> Every magnate in the country is indebted to this man, Harry Wright, for the establishment of baseball as a business, and every patron for furnishing him with a systematic recreation. Every player is indebted to him for inaugurating an occupation by which he gains a livelihood; and the country at large for adding one more industry to furnish employment.[3]

In 1870, the Red Stockings, after adding two dozen more wins to their ledger, finally lost a game—8–7 to the Brooklyn Atlantics in 11 innings before 20,000 excited spectators—and their aura of invincibility was forever crushed. Interest in the club dramatically waned. The Red Stockings ceased operations when the winter winds came. The team's important contribution to baseball history was recognized a century later when MLB had a season-long celebration of 100 years of the professional game in 1969.

There was no Cincinnati entry in the first professional baseball league, the National Association, which operated from 1871 to 1875. When the National League was founded in 1876, a club calling itself the "Cincinnati Reds" was one of eight entrants. The Reds finished in the NL basement, with an awful 9–56 mark. They finished last again in 1877. In

1878 and 1879 the Reds were at least competitive, but in 1880 they plummeted to the bottom of the NL standings once again. To make a poor on-field product more appealing, that season the Reds began scheduling games on Sundays and selling beer at their Bank Street Grounds ballpark—direct violations of the NL's strict rules designed to encourage respectable people to buy tickets to ballgames. At the end of the 1880 season, no-nonsense NL president William Hulbert expelled the maverick Reds from the circuit.

The Red Stockings name was resurrected when a Cincinnati club was part of the rival American Association from 1882 to 1889. It won the AA pennant in its first year with a dominant record of 55–25. (Pitcher Will White accounted for 40 of the club's 55 wins!) Second-place finishes came in both 1885 and 1887, but there were no further AA championships in Cincinnati.

In 1890, the Reds rejoined the NL and they have been a member ever since. Success on the field was elusive for nearly 30 years. The first time the Reds won the NL pennant was in 1919. (Its roster included a bevy of colorful names familiar to Deadball Era baseball buffs, but they seldom ring too many bells with casual fans of today. Among them were Edd Roush, Morrie Rath, Heinie Groh, Sherry Magee, Ivey Wingo, Greasy Neale, Dutch Reuther, Hod Eller and Slim Sallee.)

The Reds also won the World Series that October—largely due to eight corrupted members of the opposing Chicago White Sox not trying especially hard to beat them.

During the Great Depression, attendance at Cincinnati home games dipped to dangerously low levels. In both 1933 and 1934, the Reds averaged fewer than 3,000 fans per game. This prompted the team to try something new and somewhat desperate: the first ever MLB night game. On May 24, 1935, the Reds edged the Philadelphia Phillies 2–1 under artificial lights. It was a resounding success at the box office as the game drew about nine times the typical number of fans to Crosley Field. Thus, the city that first instituted professional baseball also gave birth to night baseball in the majors.

Another 20 years went by before the Reds again captured the NL flag. It occurred in 1939 with players such as Frank McCormick, Bucky Walters, Paul Derringer, Billy Myers, Lonny Frey, Ernie Lombardi, Billy Werber and Ival Goodman. They were swept by the powerful New York Yankees in that year's World Series, but they won everything they could in 1940 by again hoisting the NL pennant and beating the Detroit Tigers in a hard-fought, seven-game World Series. It was the last World Series victory for the Reds until 1975 when Cincinnati featured Pete Rose, Johnny Bench, Joe Morgan and Tony Pérez—and white-haired manager George (Sparky) Anderson.

After the team's 1940 triumph, Cincinnati endured two decades of generally mediocre play. After the Second World War, they only occasionally finished above fifth place until they won their next NL pennant in 1961. (From 1953 to 1958 the Reds officially changed their nickname to Redlegs to avoid any perceived connection with communism! Many baseball writers simply ignored the new moniker and kept calling them the Reds. Happily, the team went back to its old, respected and traditional name in 1959.) Cincinnati lost the 1961 World Series in five games to the unstoppable New York Yankees of Roger Maris and Mickey Mantle. They lost all three of the games played at their home ballpark, Crosley Field.

Edd Roush was the center fielder for the 1919 Cincinnati Reds—a team that won the NL pennant and the tainted World Series. Roush compiled a .323 lifetime batting average. Having played 12 seasons in Cincinnati, Roush was feted as the greatest player in Reds history during the closing ceremonies for Crosley Field in 1970 (Library of Congress).

No other championship came to Cincinnati for another nine years, but the Reds were starting to load up with talent in the interim. Pete Rose joined the club as a second baseman in 1963 and would become Cincinnati's favorite son. Tony Pérez, a steady Cuban first baseman, became a mainstay on the Reds starting in 1965.

Johnny Bench, the best catcher of his era—and arguably the best backstop of all-time—arrived in 1967 and played 26 games. He became the team's full-time catcher the following season. As a child, Bench practiced signing his autograph because he knew in his heart that someday he would be a baseball star. His high school's valedictorian in Binger, Oklahoma, Bench oozed both intelligence and confidence. Bench was voted the NL MVP in 1970 when he was not quite 23 years old. In a retrospective article about Bench in 2018, Jon Wertheim of *Sports Illustrated* wrote, "Bench's right arm was worthy of U.N. weapons inspecting; he took as much pride throwing out baserunners as he did in launching balls over fences."[4]

Outfielder Bobby Tolan, possessing a quirky but effective swing, was acquired from St. Louis in 1969. Hard-hitting Lee May won a regular spot in the Cincinnati lineup in 1967. A new manager helped matters too.

Sparky Anderson replaced Dave Bristol as Cincinnati's field pilot following the 1969 season. He was just 35 at the time, but Anderson looked at least two decades older because of his weather-beaten, bronze face and prematurely whitening hair. Anderson had played seven years in Toronto for the International League's Maple Leafs. A local newspaper, the *Globe & Mail*, annually conducted a widespread poll of the circuit's managers on various topics. Anderson was voted the smartest player in each of his seven seasons in the IL. His high baseball IQ was so obvious that several of his own managers told Anderson he was destined to manage in the majors someday. By 1964 he was the player-manager in Toronto. He only lasted one unsuccessful season there, but by the end of the decade, Anderson was coaching in the majors.

As a third-base coach with the expansion San Diego Padres in 1969, Anderson did not garner much attention. He was certainly a mystery man in his new Ohio home later that year when the Reds acquired him. The *Cincinnati Post* reported his surprise hiring with the unflattering headline "Sparky Who?" The unknown Anderson would not be anonymous for long. In his nine seasons with the Reds, he would eventually manage 1,450 games and win 863 of them. Both figures are unmatched by any other Cincinnati manager in the team's long history.

In writing Anderson's SABR biography, Cindy Thomson penned, "George Lee (Sparky) Anderson was one of the great baseball men of all time in terms of success, integrity, and personality."[5] Anderson may have been the most approachable baseball star in history. In fact, he seemed more likely to engage a stranger than vice versa. He loved circulating among common people to talk about everyday things. A true everyman, Anderson lived the last four-plus decades of his life in a relatively modest home in Thousand Oaks, California. He never tired of chatting with the ordinary folks he encountered in banks, drug stores, or any other public venues. A fan was once surprised to see Anderson among the lumpen proletariat in a fast-food restaurant lineup and asked him why he was there. Anderson, in his typically unpretentious fashion, replied that he liked the place.

**Cincinnati manager Sparky Anderson was as prominent a member of the Big Red Machine as any of his players. Beloved by Red fans, Anderson was well respected by his charges too, despite being a tough taskmaster (courtesy Cincinnati Reds Hall of Fame).**

A sportswriter's delight, Anderson never gave one-word responses to journalists' queries. If one sifted through the double negatives and his awkward syntax, Anderson's quotes were replete with wonderful tidbits of wisdom and insights into baseball and life in general. Dan Ewald, who co-wrote Anderson's autobiography, noted, "A sharp writer, properly equipped with questions, could walk away with enough material to fill a column for the next couple of weeks."[6]

On the day he was hired to lead the Reds—Thursday, October 9, 1969—Anderson told the press, "I consider myself very, very fortunate to wind up with a club with so much talent [in] my first year as a manager in the major leagues."[7] This was quite true, but general manager Bob Howsam was quick to add, "[Sparky] has fine leadership qualities and the ability to get the most out of his players."[8] But with talent comes the pressure to succeed. In the October 25, 1969, edition of *The Sporting News*, Earl Lawson commented, "The firing of Bristol wasn't a big surprise. He had been expected to guide the Reds to a flag—just as Anderson is expected to do in 1970."[9] Anderson's salary for 1970 was $28,500.

In Anderson's first year at the helm, the Reds handily won the NL West in 1970, impressively accruing 102 wins and finishing 14½ games in front of the second-place Los Angeles Dodgers. Anderson completely agreed with the strict club rules for appearance and deportment of the Cincinnati players that came from the very top—and made sure they were always followed. He believed it fostered self-discipline that helped create good teamwork. Pete Rose recalled an incident a day before the Reds were about to fly to Pittsburgh for the first game of the 1970 National League Championship Series:

> Bench and I came [to Riverfront Stadium] with fresh haircuts. We had two guys on the team named Ted Uhlaender and Joe Hague. Sparky called me and Bench into his office and then sent the clubhouse guy for those two guys.
>
> They hadn't shaved in four days and it showed. Sparky was real [*sic*] nice. He said [to them], "Gentlemen, I just want to tell you that these two guys sitting in this office are very important to what we do in Pittsburgh. And you are, too. However, if you guys aren't shaved by the time the plane is ready to leave tomorrow, don't bother to show up because you aren't getting on."
>
> They didn't say a word. The both got up and walked straight to the bathroom and shaved immediately. Sparky made his point. He wasn't nasty, but he wouldn't have taken them. Little things like that mattered to him. That's why we respected him.[10]

In that 1970 NLCS, the Reds made short work of the Pittsburgh Pirates, winning it in three straight games by scores of 3–0, 3–1 and 3–2. After taking care of the Pirates in the minimum three games, Sparky Anderson looked forward to the upcoming World Series versus the Baltimore Orioles which would open in Cincinnati. He giddily told reporters, "Bring on those big, bad Birds! We'll beat 'em!"[11] The talented AL champions had other ideas, though.

In Game One, the Reds fell victim to a notoriously bad call in the bottom of the sixth inning. Plate umpire Ken Burkhart was caught horribly out of position, became entangled in a play at home, and called out Cincinnati runner Bernie Carbo even though Carbo had been tagged with an empty glove by Oriole catcher Elrod Hendricks. Carbo's run would have tied the game. What truly did the Reds in, however, was the stunningly spectacular World Series turned in by Baltimore third baseman Brooks Robinson, who starred offensively and put on the greatest sustained defensive performance ever seen in a Fall Classic. One Robinson fielding gem followed another. Baltimore won the first three games of the World Series, let Game Four slip away, but took the Fall Classic in five games. The better team had clearly won. At its conclusion, in a very sporting gesture, Sparky Anderson felt compelled to visit the Baltimore clubhouse and personally congratulate Robinson, the Series MVP, on national TV. The Reds may have lost the 1970 World Series soundly, but they looked to be an ascending outfit—and Anderson won many fans.

In 1971, Cincinnati surprisingly did not win the NL West. In fact, they only won 79 games and surprisingly fell into a fourth-place tie with the Houston Astros. Changes in personnel were on the horizon. General manager Bob Howsam pulled off the biggest trade in the club's history in November 1971. At the time, Cincinnati fans and local media generally thought their team had been fleeced. The Reds and Astros completed a deal which saw the right side of the Cincinnati infield go to Texas. First baseman Lee May and second baseman Tommy Helms were shipped to the Astros. May and Helms were homegrown Reds who were very popular with the fans. May had twice been on the NL All-Star team and had hit 133 home runs in the previous four seasons. Helms was named NL Rookie of the Year in 1966 and he had won two Gold Gloves. Another fan favorite, Jimmy Stewart, a versatile bench player, was included in the deal too.

It was a huge gamble. Howsam risked the wrath of Cincinnati fans by making this daring deal. "Imagine trading front-line players to a team in your own division," said one unnamed executive of another NL team. "Howsam must be getting ready to leave Cincinnati. If he doesn't leave on his own, the fans might run him out of town."[12]

Whom did the Reds acquire in the major trade? One player was 28-year-old second baseman Joe Morgan who had led the NL in triples in 1971. He had been an All-Star with the Astros, but he was not especially well known outside of Houston. He also allegedly had a bad attitude and was widely perceived as being arrogant. This accusation came from his Houston manager, Harry (The Hat) Walker, who accused Morgan of agitating Houston teammate Jim Wynn. "He stirred up Wynn and kept him upset," Walker claimed. "Morgan wasn't the easiest kind of guy to work with. He's had to fight all his life to get where he is. You can be aggressive, but you have to channel it in the right direction. He flared in the wrong direction and got others to follow."[13] Years later, both Morgan and Wynn would claim that Walker's problems with them were largely race-related. Anderson would eventually label Morgan as the smartest player he had ever managed. As for Morgan's talent, Anderson gushed, "That little man can do everything."[14]

Pete Rose became a big admirer of Morgan's speed on the basepaths. In the September 30, 1972, issue of *The Sporting News*, Rose said of Morgan, "That guy is amazing. Honestly, he can steal a base anytime he wants to. And he does it when every person in the ballpark, including the opposing catcher, knows he's going to steal."[15]

Cincinnati also picked up third baseman Denis Menke, whose bat was substandard, but he was a solid defensive player. Twenty-eight-year-old righthanded pitcher Jack Billingham was part of the deal, too. At the time, he possessed an unimpressive career won-lost record of 32–32. The Reds also picked up César Gerónimo, age 23, who had played only 169 MLB games in parts of three seasons without much distinction, and Bahamian-born Ed Armbrister, another 23-year-old who had not played a single game above AA ball. One person who thought the trade was excellent was Sparky Anderson, who excitedly proclaimed to anyone who would listen that Howsam's bold deal had just won the pennant for the Reds. Few listened, but Anderson was indeed correct. In one move the Reds picked up team speed which they had sorely lacked in 1971, a pitcher who would become Cincinnati's steady workhorse, and one of the most reliable utility players in the game. The parts for The Big Red Machine were methodically being assembled.

"We had talent; there's no question about it," Johnny Bench said years later. "I used to joke with Sparky that if he kept his feet in the aisle and didn't trip anyone, we'd make him a star."[16]

In 1972, Cincinnati returned to the top of the NL West, cruising home 10½ games ahead of the runner-up Los Angeles Dodgers, with 95 wins against just 59 losses. The Reds were underdogs, however, going into the 1972 NLCS. The very capable Pittsburgh Pirates, the champions of the NL East—and the defending World Series champions from 1971— were awaiting them.

# The AL East

## *1972's Only Competitive Divisional Race*

"In the annals of Red Sox history, the heartbreak of 1972 is rarely spoken of and often forgotten. It was a season that saw the Red Sox lose the American League East by a half-game, the byproduct of a strike-shortened season and the decision to not make up the games that had been missed. The 1972 season was essentially 'joined in progress.' Some teams played more games than others, resulting in an uneven number of games played around the league, a fact that would form the foundation for yet another Red Sox heartbreak."[1]—Red Sox historian Christopher D. Chavis

"High or low in the standings, the Detroit Tigers have always been a fighting baseball club, snarling and scrapping to the finish."—Frederick G. Lieb in his 1946 book *The Detroit Tigers*

In 1908, the Detroit Tigers won the American League pennant by half a game over second-place Cleveland. The Tigers finished the 154-game schedule, sort of, with a record of 90–63 and a .588 winning percentage. One postponed game—a rainout versus the Washington Senators—was never made up. The Naps (as the Cleveland club was called by the press in honor of their best player, Napoleon Lajoie) played their full slate of 154 games that year and finished with a 90–64 record—and were penalized for it. The American League simply declared that the 1908 season would end on Wednesday, October 6. No extensions for makeup games would be considered.

To modern baseball fans, this seems horribly unfair to Cleveland, a club that finished with a .584 winning percentage. Such a scenario would not be allowed to happen today. Detroit would have to play their 154th game of the season to even things up. The sporting public would demand it. In fact, following the 1908 season, both the NL and AL amended their rules to specify that all postponed games that could impact a pennant race would have to be contested. Obviously, the unsatisfactory conclusion to the 1908 season was the driving force behind the change.

It was actually a sensational three-team race in the AL in 1908. The Chicago White Sox were in the pennant chase until almost the very end. (By chance, the Tigers and White Sox faced each other in a three-game series in Chicago to conclude the season. The White Sox won the first two clashes 3–1 and 6–1, but Detroit won the critical third game, 7–0.) The loss by Chicago dropped them to 88–64, 1½ games back of Detroit, and third place. Cleveland played a three-game set against the Browns in St. Louis to conclude their 1908 schedule. The first game, a Sunday affair, ended in a 3–3 tie; it was called on darkness after 11 innings and had to be replayed as part of a doubleheader the next day. The Browns won the makeup game, 3–1. Cleveland won the second game of the twin bill, 5–3, and the next day's game too, 5–1, to finish half a game shy of Detroit.

What if Detroit had to make up that rainout versus Washington? What would have happened? It is only speculation, of course, but the Tigers—clearly the better of the two teams—had won 16 of the 21 games they had played against the Senators, a struggling seventh-place outfit. Washington ended September and entered October by losing 14 of 17 games, but the Senators had rebounded to win five straight contests to conclude their 1908 schedule. Could they have extended the streak to six with a victory over Detroit in a make-up game? No one will ever know. "There's no consolation in *if*,"[2] noted the *Cleveland Plain Dealer* in summarizing the disappointment in its city's baseball fans.

Oddly, the rules requiring that all postponed games that could be impactful seemed to be disregarded in the AL in 1935. Again the beneficiaries were the Detroit Tigers. Complaints were strangely few. Perhaps it was the sheer volume of unplayed games that made fans more willing to accept the incompleteness of the result—or perhaps it was the poor quality of the absent opponents. That season the Detroit Tigers finished atop the AL standings with a 93–58 record, three games ahead of the New York Yankees and their 89–60 mark. Thus, Detroit only contested 151 of their 154 games. Their three missed games were all against the last-place Philadelphia A's. New York played just 149 games in 1935. (The Yankees' five postponed games included one versus Boston, two versus Philadelphia and two versus Chicago.) Of course, had the Yankees won all five of those canceled games, they would have attained 94 wins. Similarly, just two Tiger wins out of the three Detroit postponements versus the AL's cellar dwellers would have mathematically clinched the pennant for the Tigers regardless of anything that New York did. The 22 games the Tigers and Yankees played against each other in 1935 resulted in 11 wins apiece.

The 1972 MLB season featured something very similar to 1908. A team won one of the four divisional titles by half a game. Remarkably, it was again the Detroit Tigers. This time it was the Boston Red Sox who were victimized by an imbalance in the schedule. The problem occurred because a week of games missed due to the players' strike in April were never made up during the season. Those games were cancelled—simply wiped from the slate. In three of MLB's four divisions it did not matter very much because the Cincinnati Reds and Pittsburgh Pirates won their divisions by double-digit margins. (The Oakland's A's won the AL West by 5½ games, so, although mathematically possible, it would have taken an extraordinary occurrence for them to be overtaken by the second-place Chicago White Sox had a full 162-game schedule been played.) However, at season's end in the AL East, Detroit was on top by the slimmest of margins. The Tigers had a record of 86–70 while the Red Sox were 85–70. In terms of winning percentage, the 1972 Detroit club finished on top by even a smaller margin than their 1908 ancestors did: .551 to .548.

Proving that baseball gods really do exist, there was high drama on the AL schedule: The Tigers and Red Sox finished the 1972 season playing a three-game set against each other at Tiger Stadium from Monday, October 2, to Wednesday, October 4. Boston entered the crucial series holding a half-game edge over Detroit, so the Tigers needed to win two out of three to take the AL East title. The same applied to Boston. For both clubs, the half-game lead/deficit was mathematically irrelevant.

In hyping the series, a United Press International story declared,

> The season has come down to winning two of the next three games for Boston and Detroit....
>
> But remember too what [Bowie] Kuhn and [Marvin] Miller did last spring when the national game was mired in its first baseball strike. They—the owners and the players—desperate to get on with the season, decided to cancel all the games up to the point of the settlement and have the teams play uneven schedules.
>
> The decision may cost Boston the AL East pennant.[3]

Detroit won Monday's game 4–1 as Mickey Lolich struck out 15 Red Sox in a superb and timely complete-game effort. Aurelio Rodríguez drove in three of the four Tiger runs with a homer and a pair of singles. The game was contested before "a screaming Tiger Stadium crowd of 51,518,"[4] as described by an unnamed Associated Press correspondent. They went home happy.

The October 2 game included a bizarre baserunning mishap that has gone down in infamy in Red Sox lore. In the top of the third inning, Boston was trailing the Tigers, 1–0. The Red Sox had one out with two runners on: Tommy Harper at third base and Luis Aparicio at first base. Carl Yastrzemski hit a ball to the deepest part of Tiger Stadium's vast center field that looked like it would be an easy triple. Harper scored, but the 38-year-old Aparicio, trying to score on the play too, fell as he rounded third base. Aparicio got up and retreated to third base—only to find that Yastrzemski was already there. Yastrzemski attempted to return to second but was tagged out in a rundown. (The botched play was kindly referred to as "a 420-foot double" in the Associated Press report in the next day's newspapers. The putout was scored 8–6–2–5.) Thus, instead of having a 2–1 lead with one out and a runner at third, Boston had only tied the game and now had two outs with Aparicio stationed at third base. The next Boston batter was Reggie Smith. He struck out looking to end the promising inning. Boston did not score again.

With a chance to clinch the division within their grasp, Detroit put away Boston with a 3–1 win in Tuesday's game. Boston had led 1–0 heading into the home half of the sixth inning, but Red Sox starter Luis Tiant could not keep the home team's offense shut down. The victory gave the Tigers an insurmountable lead of 1½ games with just Wednesday's matchup left on the schedule.

The game's decisive moment occurred in the bottom of the seventh inning. The score was tied 1–1 when, with one out, Detroit's Dick McAuliffe smashed a double. The red-hot Al Kaline was the next scheduled batter. Instead of intentionally walking Kaline, Boston manager Eddie Kasko opted to have Tiant pitch to him. Kaline drove in the go-ahead run with an RBI single. Kaline later scored an insurance run that same inning when Boston's Carl Yastrzemski mishandled an infield grounder at first base. When questioned about the strategy to pitch to Kaline in that situation, Kasko told the press, "We didn't want to put him on and get into the middle of the order with [Detroit's] lefthanders up. Kaline hit a bad, inside pitch on the handle, but it found a hole."[5]

"This is fun," a smiling Kaline told the press. "This is how the game should be played every day."[6]

Woodie Fryman was the winning pitcher for the Tigers. He was relieved in the bottom of the eighth inning by Chuck Seelbach who got a four-out save. Tiant was the losing hurler.

Another huge turnout, 50,653 fans, witnessed the game that clinched the AL East for the Tigers. AP baseball scribe Larry Paladino wrote, "The fans raced onto the field after the final out, mobbing the jubilant Tigers."[7] It was the Tigers' first championship of any sort since winning the 1968 World Series.

In what turned out to be a superfluous contest, Boston won the third game of the series, 4–1. The game took just two hours to play and, with the drama of the divisional title gone, only 21,956 people passed through the turnstiles at Tiger Stadium to watch it. Detroit pitcher Joe Coleman, a lanky right-hander gunning for his 20th win of the season, was instead handed his 14th loss. Boston righthander Marty Pattin— who had been a disappointing 2–8 at one point in the season—tossed a complete game for the win. He allowed only four hits to the Tigers. The victory gave him a respectable 17–13 record for 1972. Both teams liberally employed their second-string players in the meaningless game. If the Red Sox management thought that Kasko had blundered with his strategy in the game that eliminated Boston from the AL East title chase, they did not hold it against their manager. Kasko signed a new two-year contract shortly after the season ended—but he only lasted through the 1973 season.

Despite their 4–1 victory, there were no happy faces in the Red Sox clubhouse—and understandably so. In speaking with Harold Kaese of the *Boston Globe*, a sullen Carl Yastrzemski ruefully called the 1972 season's outcome the biggest disappointment of his career.

As was the case in 1908, there was no consolation in *if.*

# — 5 —

# The ALCS

## Comebacks, Blown Calls
## and a Thrown Bat

"You bet I was after him! There's no place for that kind of gutless stuff in baseball. That's the worst thing I've ever seen in all my years [in the game]. I would respect him if he went out to throw a punch, but what he did was the most gutless thing of any man to put on a uniform. It was a disgrace to baseball."[1]—Detroit manager Billy Martin on Oakland's Bert Campaneris throwing his bat at Tiger pitcher Lerrin LaGrow in Game Two of the ALCS

"Although replays show clearly that [George] Hendrick was out by two steps, umpire John Rice called him safe, later claiming [Norm] Cash had pulled his foot off the bag. Martin, Cash, and [Bill] Freehan went nuts. [Jim] Northrup actually told me that the call was so blatantly wrong that he even wondered if Rice was on the take."[2]—Tiger fan and baseball journalist Bill Dow recalling the controversial call made by the first-base umpire in Game Five

The Detroit Tigers entered the 1972 ALCS as the champions of the unfashionable AL East. In years to come, the AL East was often regarded as the strongest of any division in MLB. That was not the case in 1972. At one point in the season, Harold Kaese of the *Boston Globe* brazenly declared that no team in the AL East would be a worthy champion. (A seasonal recap article by Larry Claflin that appeared in *The Sporting News* stated, "What made the Red Sox a pennant contender? A weak division, of course...."[3]) Every club in the AL East seemed to struggle offensively. When the Baltimore Orioles faced the Detroit Tigers on July 1 on NBC's *Game of the Week* telecast, Curt Gowdy noted that the Orioles, who had won the last three AL pennants, were batting just .216 as a team but somehow were still very much in the running for the top spot in the AL East.

Despite the naysayers, the 1972 Tigers were a quality ball club. Their pitching staff was quite capable. Portly Mickey Lolich, a 32-year-old lefthander, was its brightest member. He won 22 games and pitched 327⅓ innings. (That lofty total represented a 10 percent decline from 1971 when he pitched 376 innings!) Typical of the era, Lolich completed 23 games. Joe Coleman, a 35-year-old righty, won 19 games while Woodie Fryman won 10. Altogether, the 1972 Tigers had a 2.96 team ERA.

The ageless Al Kaline was the face of the team. He batted .313 in the 106 games he played. That was his highest batting average since 1961. No other Tiger regular surpassed .262. Kaline, who had joined the Tigers as an 18-year-old in 1953, was at his best when it mattered most. Kaline seemed to star in every game during the final weeks of the 1972 regular season. Detroit certainly had experience on their side, with several key players being in their thirties. First baseman Norm Cash was 38. Second baseman Dick McAullife was 32 as was outfielder Jim Northrup. Catcher Bill Freehan was 30. Some key second-string players were up in years, too. Tony Taylor was 36. Tom Haller was 35. Gates Brown was 33.

The driving force behind the team was feisty manager Billy Martin. The former Yankee second baseman was in his second season as Detroit's field pilot. He had led the Tigers to 91 wins and a second-place finish in the AL East in 1971. Martin had previously guided the Minnesota Twins to a divisional title in 1969, and was hugely popular in Minneapolis, but he ran afoul of upper management and was dismissed after losing the ALCS to Baltimore in a sweep. It was a pattern that would continue throughout his tempestuous career.

Martin was not involved in baseball in 1970; he instead worked at KDWB, a Minneapolis radio station. According to newspaper reports that were prevalent throughout the 1972 ALCS, Martin and Oakland owner Charlie Finley were feuding. Apparently, Finley had intended to hire Martin to manage his club, but suddenly withdrew his offer based on negative reports he had received from the Twins about Martin's inability to be a good company man and follow direct orders. Over the years, any team that hired Martin indeed got a firecracker—but they also got a proven winner. In an interview a few months before his death in August 1975, ex-Yankee manager Casey Stengel was questioned about Martin's managerial abilities. Stengel, who had known Billy since his minor league days, told *The Sporting News*: "He's a good manager. He might be a little selfish about some things he does. He may think he knows more about baseball than anybody else—and it wouldn't surprise me if he was right."[4] Martin was earning a $65,000 salary from Detroit in 1972, a hefty sum for the time.

Versus Oakland in the regular season, the Tigers won just four of 12 games while being outscored 53–37. (In fact, in each of the four series the teams played, Oakland won exactly two out of three games.) Nevertheless, five of those dozen games were decided by two runs or fewer, with two of the contests requiring extra innings to determine a winner. Perhaps they were a harbinger of a closely fought ALCS.

The 1972 American League Championship Series, a best-of-five affair, opened at the Oakland-Alameda County Coliseum on Saturday, October 7. Typically for the underappreciated home team, a less than capacity crowd was on hand—far less. Just 29,566 people bought tickets to see the first game between the AL East champion Detroit Tigers and the hometown Oakland A's, winners of the AL West. Those who were in attendance saw a terrific ballgame. It was a battle of the aces between the clubs' best starters: Catfish Hunter of Oakland and Mickey Lolich of Detroit.

Norm Cash slammed a solo home run in the top of the second inning for the visitors. (Amusingly, moments before Cash's clout, NBC's Curt Gowdy had mentioned the Detroit first baseman had been in a home-run drought, not having connected for once since August 13.) In the bottom of the third inning, Oakland's Joe Rudi leveled the score. His sacrifice fly to center field easily brought home teammate Bert Campaneris who had walked with one out and moved to third base on Matty's Alou's bloop single to right field.

The game stood 1–1 after eight innings. Both starters were still pitching. After Detroit catcher Duke Sims led off the top of the ninth with a double, Oakland manager Dick Williams pulled Catfish Hunter from the game, replacing him with Vida Blue. Blue, who endured a hugely disappointing 1972 season after being named the 1971 AL MVP, had been relegated to the bullpen for the ALCS. He was not pleased with his demotion and was quite vocal about it to the media. Norm Cash came up next for Detroit and laid down a sacrifice bunt. It was fielded by A's third baseman Sal Bando who had anticipated the play. He made a decent throw to first base, but second baseman Ted Kubiak, who was covering the bag, misplayed it. Sims was safe at third; Cash was safe at first base—and there was nobody out. Oakland was in deep trouble.

Blue's outing was a short one. Manager Williams yanked him after just one batter. Rollie Fingers came out of the A's bullpen to attempt to squelch the Detroit rally. Billy Martin made a countermove. The Tiger manager sent Gates Brown to pinch hit for Willie Horton. Brown squandered his opportunity to be a hero. He harmlessly popped up in foul territory to third baseman Sal Bando. Jim Northrup fared even worse.

He grounded into an inning-ending, 4–6–3 double play. The A's had averted disaster; the game was still tied, 1–1.

Oakland quickly was set down in order in the bottom of the ninth by Lolich. Fingers, not a bad hitter at all for a relief pitcher—he had one home run and a .316 average in 19 at-bats during the regular season—made the second out. Obviously, Williams wanted to keep him on the mound as extra innings beckoned.

Both halves of the tenth inning were uneventful. Neither team managed to put a runner on base. The eleventh inning was chock-full of incidents, however. After Dick McAuliffe struck out, Al Kaline drilled a solo homer off Fingers that sailed over the left field fence in the top of the inning to give the visitors a 2–1 edge heading into the home half of the eleventh. "Kaline has done it again for the Tigers!" Curt Gowdy reported. "He carried them on his back the last two weeks. He's homered here in the eleventh, the 20-year veteran."[5] Duke Sims followed Kaline's homer with a triple, but the inning ended with Sims stranded on third base. The Tigers would rue not being able to tack on an insurance run.

Oakland refused to go quietly, however. The first two A's to come to bat in the bottom of the eleventh inning—Sal Bando and Mike Epstein—connected for base hits. Billy Martin opted to bring in Chuck Seelbach, a 24-year-old righty, to relieve the tiring Lolich. Oakland had runners at first and second base when Gene Tenace came to bat. (Blue Moon Odom was the lead runner, having entered the game as a pinch-runner for Bando. Mike Hegan was similarly running for Epstein.) Tenace's bunt toward third base was fielded nicely by Sims, the Detroit catcher. The throw to shortstop Eddie Brinkman covering third base beat Odom for a force out. Brinkman fired across the diamond in an attempt to nip Tenace at first base for a double play. The ball beat Tenace, but it pulled second baseman Dick McAuliffe off the bag and into foul territory. Nevertheless, McAuliffe had the presence of mind to put a swipe tag on Tenace. At least he thought he had. First-base umpire Nestor Chylak, who appeared to be fixated on McAuliffe's foot being off the bag rather than his attempted tag, called Tenace safe. Instead of Oakland having two outs and a runner at second, there was just one out with runners at first and second. McAuliffe and his Tiger teammates squawked loudly, but to no avail. It would not be the last time in the ALCS the Detroit club hotly disputed a call at first base.

Next up was a pinch hitter for second baseman Dal Maxvill, Gonzalo Márquez, a Venezuelan rookie who had come to bat just 21 times in 1972 but had managed eight hits. He promptly connected for a base hit to right field. Hegan was clearly going to score easily to tie the game, but right fielder Al Kaline spotted Tenace trying to advance to third base on Márquez's single. The play at third was going to be close—until it eluded Aurelio Rodríguez. Tenace, who had slid headfirst into third base, got to his feet and scampered home with the game-winning run. Kaline was charged with an error—perhaps unfairly. (Any sort of defensive miscue was a rarity for Kaline. At one point during the 1972 season he was riding a streak of 242 consecutive errorless games.) Oakland had won Game One, 3–2. They had managed 10 hits to Detroit's six. All the A's hits had been singles. Despite a very shaky eleventh inning, Rollie Fingers got credit for winning the ALCS opener. Mickey Lolich was the hard-luck loser. Chuck Seelbach was saddled with a blown save.

Game Two the next afternoon was an easy 5–0 win for Oakland. Before a slightly improved crowd of 31,088, Oakland broke open a 1–0 game with a four-run fifth inning. Blue Moon Odom pitched a terrific complete-game, three-hit shutout for the winners—but few people were discussing his dominant mound outing. Instead, most everyone was talking about an ugly incident involving Oakland's Bert Campaneris and Detroit pitcher Lerrin LaGrow that occurred in the home half of the sixth inning.

By the time Campaneris stepped up to the plate for the fourth time in the game, he had already had three hits in three at-bats. He had also scored two of Oakland's runs and had stolen two bases. LaGrow, the fourth Detroit pitcher of the afternoon, wasted no time in delivering a message to the speedy Oakland leadoff hitter. LaGrow drilled him solidly on the left ankle with a fastball. In the NBC broadcast booth, Tony Kubek barely got the words, "There's going to be trouble!"[6] out of his mouth before Campaneris infamously reacted: He violently flung his bat toward the mound. Even the hometown A's fans gasped at what they had witnessed.

The bat helicoptered, sailing over LaGrow who adroitly ducked to get out of its flight path. The malicious intent to injure the Detroit hurler was clear. (LaGrow would later describe the accuracy of the bat toss as "head high but off to the side."[7]) Both benches cleared. Billy Martin tried to get at Campaneris, but he was forcibly held back by three umpires. "Billy Martin is incensed!" Kubek told North America's baseball fans, "but Campaneris has every right to be mad also if they took away one of his best assets if they hit him in a bad spot. It looked like [it was] right in the ankle."[8] In the Detroit radio booth, both George Kell and Ernie Harwell were strangely nonplussed at what had happened.

"I'm no manager if I don't protect my pitcher," Martin insisted afterwards. Had it been a regular-season game rather than a key ALCS game, the incident probably would have sparked a major brawl. "Neither team could afford a fight," Martin rationally admitted after the game. "With the World Series so close, the [ALCS] winner could [not risk] injuries."[9]

Reggie Jackson commented, "I don't like Billy Martin because he plays tough, [but] I'd probably love him if I played for him. He stands up for his players."[10]

Plate umpire Nestor Chylak chose to eject both Campaneris and LaGrow. Martin was outwardly mystified by LaGrow's ejection. "I told Nestor it's the worst decision he ever made," the Tiger manager insisted. Martin further told reporters that Campaneris' action was "the dirtiest thing [I] ever saw in the game of baseball. No doubt about it: He's got to be suspended for the rest of the playoffs."[11]

Chylak later told reporters LaGrow had to be removed from the game even though the arbiter said he didn't think LaGrow had deliberately thrown at Campaneris. In a moment of pure candor, Chylak explained, "I threw the pitcher out to even things out—to keep the fans in their seats—so there wouldn't be any more incidents in the ballgame."[12] LaGrow maintained complete innocence, calling the hit-by-pitch "a misunderstanding." He said, "The pitch was low and inside. It just got away. I try to throw good, hard stuff inside."[13] Martin tried to back up his pitcher's view of things by curiously noting, "The only way it can be intentional is to throw high."[14]

In an interview conducted 30 years later, Joe Rudi opined, "Campy had run the Tigers ragged in the first two games, and when Martin gets his ears pinned down, he's going to do something about it."[15] Similarly, Mike Hegan had no doubts at all that Martin had ordered LaGrow to plunk Campaneris. "[Martin] wanted to light a fire under his ball club, and Campy was the guy they were going after because he was the guy who set the table for us. There's no question that Billy Martin instructed Lerrin LaGrow to throw at Campaneris."[16]

After the game, Martin shared this bit of insight with *Detroit Free Press* baseball writer Joe Falls:

> I don't know what that idiot [Campaneris] was thinking. He may have to talk to his psychiatrist to find out. You can bet your ass I was going out there for him. I'm not going to get after him now, but if there's ever another fight out there, I'm going out there and find him and beat the shit out of him.[17]

Afterwards the explanation Campaneris offered for his actions was incredible—in the literal sense of the adjective. "I [did not] try to hit him with the bat," Campaneris said with a straight face. "If [I wanted] to hit him, I [would] throw it more sidearm than overhand. I just [wanted] to warn him not to do that again to me."[18]

AL president Joe Cronin, who had the power to fine and suspend Campaneris for the duration of the ALCS, said, "The way I feel personally, any time you swing [sic] your bat at another ballplayer, it's something that doesn't belong in baseball."[19]

Campaneris himself knew he was going to be severely punished for his part in the incident. He offered this explanation: "My ankle hurt so bad. I knew he was going to throw at me, but people now tell me it's better to go and fight. I don't know. I just lost my temper."[20]

Campaneris' bat would probably fetch a considerable sum in the sports collectables market today. Alas, it is not available. Tiger utility infielder Ike Brown was so angry at Campaneris that he picked up the bat, smashed it into pieces, and threw the chunks of lumber in the general direction of the Oakland dugout.

Discussing the ALCS in *The Sporting News*, Ralph Ray wrote, "Detroit's old pros looked too old, except when they wanted to fight. And Oakland's young pros looked extra sharp with their bats and gloves, if not their fists. That's the way it went in the first two games...."[21] The Tigers only managed three hits off Blue Moon Odom in Game Two. A witty and punny one-word headline above the *TSN* box score read, "Punchless."

After the game, the A's flight to Detroit was delayed by a bomb threat. It turned out to be a hoax.

Before Game Three, Joe Cronin announced the AL had suspended Campaneris for the remainder of the ALCS and fined him $500—a hefty sum in 1972. If the A's managed to earn a World Series berth, Cronin left the decision about extending Campaneris' suspension through the Fall Classic to MLB Commissioner Bowie Kuhn. Kuhn decided to delay announcing any further discipline until the winner of the ALCS had been determined. The ALCS shifted to Detroit's Tiger Stadium where Game Three would be played on Tuesday, October 10, as would the fourth and fifth games (on Wednesday and Thursday), if necessary.

One newspaper, the *Baltimore Afro-American*, whose news stories were routinely presented within the context of race, ran a photo of Martin being restrained by the umpires. It wondered why Martin avoided a suspension for his role in the incident while Campaneris was banished from the rest of the ALCS.

In an unusual coincidence, Detroit lost their shortstop too. Slick-fielding Eddie Brinkman was ruled out for the season after x-rays showed he had a ruptured disc in his back. He was scheduled to undergo surgery on Friday—the day before the World Series would begin. The 30-year-old Brinkman had played in the first game of the ALCS, but he had sat out the second game due to back pain. Brinkman had had a superb 1972 at shortstop. Despite playing home games in a park featuring a natural dirt infield, Brinkman recorded a .990 field percentage to set an MLB record for his position. During one stretch he went 72 consecutive games without making an error

Perhaps the Campaneris-LaGrow incident did motivate the Tigers to play better. In Game Three, Detroit's 25-year-old righthander, Joe Coleman, struck out 14 Oakland batters—a new ALCS record—in pitching a complete-game, 3–0 shutout. Detroit catcher Bill Freehan had a home run and a double (and a sacrifice bunt!) to lead the Tiger offense. Like the two games in Oakland, Game Three did not sellout either, as slightly more than 41,000 fans saw the hometown Tigers stave off elimination. According to a story in the *Syracuse Post-Standard*, a reporter asked Coleman if his outing was the biggest game he had ever pitched. Coleman laughed at the silly question and replied, "Having come here from the Washington Senators, I guess this is the most important game I've pitched since I lost a high school playoff game."

Oakland manager Dick Williams tried his best to generate offense. He used 20 different players in a valiant attempt to get back in the game. It was all to no avail. The A's stranded 10 baserunners without bringing any of them across the plate. Despite setting a new ALCS strikeout record, Coleman did not think it was one of his better outings of 1972.

The *Oakland Tribune* reported that a few of the A's were so confident of a series sweep that they had checked out of their Detroit hotel before heading to Tiger Stadium. After Detroit won Game Three, they hastily checked back in.

Hal Bock, covering the ALCS for the Associated Press, wrote, "Joe Coleman made sure the A's didn't get the [series-clinching] victory on Tuesday. The hard-throwing pitcher worked out of frequent jams, allowing seven hits and pitching with men on base in all but two innings. His strikeout total kept bailing him out of trouble."[22] Coleman's 14 whiffs were two more than the previous high of 12 attained by Baltimore's Jim Palmer in the 1970 ALCS versus the Minnesota Twins.

Game Four took place the following afternoon. In one of the most thrilling postseason MLB games ever played, Detroit overcame a two-run deficit *in extra innings* to win 4–3 and force a series-deciding fifth game the following afternoon.

After nine innings, the game was tied, 1–1. Both runs came via solo homers. Detroit's Dick McAuliffe smacked one in the bottom of the third inning. (There was an element of luck to McAuliffe's round-tripper. Right fielder Matty Alou drifted back to the wall to make what appeared to be a routine catch, only to have the ball glance off the overhanging second deck. The ground rules at Tigers Stadium deemed such an occurrence—which happened frequently—to be a home run.)

Oakland's Mike Epstein homered in the top of the seventh, also to right field. There was no luck whatsoever involved in his line-drive smash; it left the playing field in a hurry. Oakland starting pitcher Catfish Hunter was pulled with one out in the bottom of the eighth inning and Detroit mounting a potential rally. Rollie Fingers replaced him and got out of a major mess thanks to a botched squeeze play. Detroit's starter, Mickey Lolich, made it through nine innings before being relieved.

Oakland looked like sure winners when they scored twice in the top of the tenth inning. Pinch hitter Gonzalo Márquez, as he had in Game One, singled. Matty Alou hit a double off the left field wall. Márquez was nearly thrown out at home plate by Jim Northrup, but catcher Bill Freehan dropped his throw from the outfield. (Alou went to third base on the play.) Oakland now led, 2–1. Next up was Ted Kubiak. His single scored Alou, increasing the visitors' advantage to 3–1. That is how the score stood when the side was retired.

With Detroit trailing by two runs in the bottom of the tenth inning, they were just three outs away from having their season come to a disappointing conclusion. Longtime A's announcer Monte Moore had moved to the Oakland clubhouse for the pennant celebration he thought was surely to come. "[The visitors] got none of those outs,"[23] Hal Bock wrote in his report.

Dick McAuliffe started the home team's comeback with a base hit into right field off Bob Locker, a 34-year-old righty, who started the inning on the mound for Oakland. The next Detroit batter, Al Kaline, singled to left field, advancing McAuliffe to second base. The game's momentum was clearly shifting again. Dick Williams summoned Joe Horlen, a 35-year-old righthander, from the visitors' bullpen to try to smother the Detroit rally. His wild pitch did not help matters for the reeling A's. Both runners moved up 90 feet. Pinch hitter Gates Brown drew a walk to load the bases with Tigers—with nobody out. Bock described what happened next:

> With the crowd of 37,615 roaring on every pitch, Bill Freehan grounded to third baseman Sal Bando. Bando was ready to concede the run to try for the double play. He threw to second [base]. Gene Tenace, ordinarily a catcher but playing the infield in manager Dick Williams' rotating procession of second baseman and shortstops, dropped the ball and everyone was safe.[24]

Oakland's lead had been whittled down to 3–2—and still no Tigers were out. Twenty-four-year-old lefthander Dave Hamilton then replaced Horlen on the mound. Hamilton was the 20th member of the A's to enter the game, equaling Tuesday's total. Norm Cash walked on a full count. (On the 2–2 pitch, the A's infielders thought Hamilton had struck out Cash, but plate umpire Don Denkinger called the pitch a ball. Sal Bando brazenly gave Denkinger the "choke" sign. Somehow, he was not ejected for his gesture.) Kaline trotted home to tie the score 3–3—and still there was no one out. Tiger Stadium was becoming a bedlam.

Thirty-two-year-old Jim Northrup came to bat for the Tigers. With the infield drawn in, Northrup, who was 0-for-4, walloped Hamilton's first pitch into the outfield. It could not be caught by right fielder Matty Alou. It sailed well over his head and landed near the base of the wall. Under baseball's scoring rules, Northrup was credited with a mere single for his mighty, game-deciding clout. The Detroit fans could hardly contain themselves. Wrote Bock,

> Northrup's dramatic hit set off a wild demonstration reminiscent of the scene here last week when the Tigers won the [AL's] East Division pennant. Fans streamed onto the field as the Tigers mobbed their veteran outfielder who drilled the winning hit ... to climax the rally.[25]

One UPI reporter was even more descriptive. He penned, "The fans, duplicating their performance when the Tigers a week ago won the AL East Division crown, tore up sod in numerous sections of the field, and were trying to make off with home plate until a security guard stood on it."[26]

With the A's possessing a two-run lead heading into the bottom of the tenth inning, Oakland's triumph looked to have been so certain it was later discovered that the Will Harridge Trophy, given annually to the AL pennant winners, had already been affixed with a small plaque saying that the 1972 champions were the Oakland A's. Of course, all evidence of it had to be hastily removed.

Mickey Lolich was pleasantly surprised by the dramatic turn of events. He candidly admitted he thought Detroit's season was about to come to an end. Lolich told a reporter from the *Windsor Star* that his mind had turned away from baseball after Oakland assumed the lead in the top of the tenth inning. Instead, he was pondering the mundane chores around his house that needed to be done. "I started thinking negatively, wondering what I'd do tomorrow. I thought 'I cut the back lawn today. I guess I'll cut the front lawn tomorrow.'"

Regarding his team's inability to put away the Tigers in the tenth inning, the A's manager was candid and pithy. "We didn't do the job," Dick Williams stated. "It's as simple as that."[27] Monte Moore sadly concurred. When he returned to the broadcast booth, he dejectedly noted to his partners, "This was the biggest inning the [Oakland] A's have ever played—and they blow the thing. I thought we had a better bullpen than that."[28]

Perhaps the most thankful Tiger in the home clubhouse was Chuck Seelbach. Had Detroit not mounted their comeback in the bottom of the tenth, he would have been the losing pitcher in Game Four. It would have been the fourth time in four relief appearances versus Oakland in 1972 that he had lost.

Another Tiger who was personally grateful for the stunning turn of events was Bill Freehan. The Detroit catcher had botched a suicide squeeze bunt while batting in the bottom of the eighth inning that killed a promising rally. He had also misplayed a throw at the plate in the top of the tenth that allowed Oakland to take the lead. "I just about sent [my teammates] to their winter vacations, but somehow I got out of the fire,"[29] he told an AP correspondent afterward.

With the home team having won all four ALCS games so far—and Detroit having captured the momentum—the 1972 AL pennant would come down to a fifth game at Tiger Stadium the very next day. The game truly was a tossup. Even bookmakers could not decide who the favorite was to win the clincher. Some had the A's listed at 6:5; others had the Tigers listed as the frontrunners at 11:10. Accordingly, savvy gamblers could guarantee themselves a profit if they could find two different bookies offering opposite odds.

To not disrupt NBC's evening television schedule too much, every LCS game in both leagues was slated to be an afternoon contest. Thus, Game Five of the ALCS would be contested in the daytime of Thursday, October 12. Despite the generally inconvenient 1:30 p.m. starting time, the best crowd of the ALCS by far, 50,276, turned out for the most important game of the season in Detroit. It was a memorable one. The paying customers saw plenty to talk about for years to come.

The same starting pitchers who had started Game Two faced each other again in Game Five: Woodie Fryman for Detroit and Blue Moon Odom for Oakland. The A's went down in order in the top of the first inning. The Tigers had a more productive half. Leadoff hitter Dick McAuliffe singled to right field. Al Kaline struck out, but Duke Sims drew a walk, pushing McAuliffe to second base. With Bill Freehan batting, catcher Gene Tenace allowed an Odom pitch to elude him. The passed ball moved the two runners up 90 feet. Freehan then hit a ground ball to shortstop Dal Maxvill. Maxvill had no play at home. Freehan was out at first base, but McAuliffe had scored the game's opening run. Detroit led, 1–0. "The run was greeted by a shower of paper by the happy Tiger Stadium crowd," noted AP reporter Hal Bock, "but it was the last time they had any real chance to be happy."[30]

The top of the second inning had implications that extended well beyond the ALCS. Reggie Jackson led it off by drawing a four-pitch walk from Woodie Fryman. Although Jackson was deceptively quick and had nine steals during the regular season, he surprised the Tigers by swiping second base to put himself in scoring position. Freehan's throw was way off the mark. Sal Bando lofted a fly ball to right field that allowed Jackson to tag up and advance to third base with one out. Mike Epstein was painfully hit on the hand by a Fryman pitch, putting him at first base. Trainer Joe Romo briefly entered the field to examine Epstein's hand. Epstein stayed in the game. Gene Tenace struck out swinging for out number two.

Dick Williams decided to roll the dice: He boldly ordered a double steal. With Dick Green batting, Epstein broke for second base. Freehan threw the ball toward second. It was caught by Detroit second baseman Tony Taylor well in front of the bag as Epstein slid into second base safely. Taylor fired the ball back to Freehan in an attempt to nail Jackson who was breaking for home. It was a close play, but Jackson's excellent slide got him across the plate just before Freehan could apply the tag. Umpire Nestor Chylak—working the plate for the second time in the ALCS—correctly signaled Jackson to be safe.

Jackson's daring baserunning had tied the score, but he could not enjoy the moment. Jackson immediately grimaced, pawing at his left leg in obvious agony. Again, Oakland trainer Joe Romo rushed onto the field, but there was little he could do. Jackson was severely injured. It was not a break, but a severe hamstring pull—an avulsion. (Jackson would later claim he felt something go wrong with his leg when he was about 20 feet from home plate.) Dick Williams would recall in his autobiography, "[Reggie] arrived [at the plate] just before the return throw from second, sliding so hard that something popped. It wasn't the ball into Freehan's glove, it was Reggie's hamstring.... Jackson had to be assisted off the field. Dick Green grounded out to Fryman to end the inning." The game was tied 1–1—and the A's were suddenly without Reggie Jackson. George Hendrick took over Jackson's spot in center field for Oakland. Hendrick had now appeared in all five ALCS games as a substitute. The lanky, part-time player would play an important role in how Game Five would unfold.

There was no further scoring until the top of the fourth inning. George Hendrick led off the frame by hitting a routine ground ball to Tiger shortstop Dick McAuliffe. McAuliffe made a low throw to first baseman Norm Cash who stretched to catch it. The ball clearly beat Hendrick to the base, but first-base umpire John Rice ruled that Cash's heel had come off the bag. Hendrick was safe—and the Tigers were furious at Rice. McAuliffe was given an error on the play. It was his fourth of the ALCS.

Cash turned around and kicked his spikes into the infield dirt, spraying loose soil at Rice, a 54-year-old Second World War veteran and longtime AL arbiter. Catcher Bill Freehan, who had moved down the line to cover the play, also joined in the lively dispute. Billy Martin entered the field to express his displeasure, too. Tiger first-base coach Frank Howard would continue the argument from the Detroit dugout so persistently that Rice ended up ejecting him before the Tigers batted in the bottom of the fourth. "The usually mild-mannered Frank Howard must have said something to Mr. Rice that was not too nice,"[31] said Detroit broadcaster Ray Lane when he noticed that Howard was no longer coaching at first base. Video replays of what turned out to be a critical play are inconclusive at best. NBC's Jim Simpson seemed to think Rice's call had been correct. Neither Lane nor his Tigers broadcasting partner Ernie Harwell proffered a strong opinion about Rice's call one way or another. *The Sporting News* only mentioned that the Tigers were displeased by the call. A United Press International story was more definite: It said that TV replays backed Rice's call as being accurate, and the Tigers' complaints were largely based on how seldom a first baseman is penalized on such a play when the ball clearly beats the runner to first base.

When play resumed, Sal Bando moved Hendrick to second base on a sacrifice bunt. Mike Epstein batted next and struck out. The Tigers looked to have escaped from danger, but Gene Tenace lined a single into left field. (It was both the first Oakland hit off Woodie Fryman in the game and the first hit for Tenace in the ALCS.) Hendrick had no intention of stopping at third base; he headed for home. Duke Sims, playing left field, unleashed a good throw to the plate, but Hendrick slid under Freehan's tag. Freehan also dropped the ball, making umpire Chylak's safe call a very easy one. Despite only having one hit in the game, Oakland now held a 2–1 lead.

For the rest of the game, scoring opportunities were limited for both teams. Odom was lifted after five innings and replaced by Vida Blue. (Actually, Odom removed himself from the game. He was so nervous that he became nauseous.) Over Game Five's remaining four innings, Blue faced 15 Tigers and retired 12 of them. Three Tigers managed to connect for singles, but no Detroit baserunner got to second base. Woodie Fryman was also having a solid game for the Tigers. He allowed just four hits over eight innings before being removed in the bottom of the eighth for a pinch hitter.

The bottom of the ninth inning was filled with tension. "You can hear the enormous crowd exhorting their heroes on,"[32] said Detroit radio announcer Ernie Harwell. The throng that filled Tiger Stadium, sensing that this was not to be their day, was becoming more and more volatile. Missiles of all sorts were being fired onto the field from the bleachers with regularity. Firecrackers, smoke bombs, and bottles by the dozen were aimed at the Oakland outfielders. "It's going to be amazing if someone doesn't get hurt with all that stuff,"[33] predicted A's broadcaster Monte Moore. Given the contentious way that Oakland had scored the go-ahead run in the fourth inning, there was a chance the ballpark could become the scene of a riot.

Bill Freehan led off the home half of the ninth by popping out in foul territory to Oakland first baseman Mike Epstein. Norm Cash followed with a single to center field to give the huge crowd one final glimmer of hope. Billy Martin made two managerial moves: He sent Joe Niekro to pinch run for the slow-footed Cash and sent Mickey Stanley to the plate to bat for Jim Northrup. Stanley hit a slow grounder to Dal Maxvill. The A's shortstop made sure of his throw to second base. Dick Green made the force out on Niekro. Stanley was safe at first base. The Tigers were down to their last out.

Tony Taylor, Detroit's second baseman, came to bat. He had no hits in three at-bats so far in the game. He had also struck out twice. He hit a solid line drive to center field that was casually caught by George Hendrick. A few more bottles were tossed from the bleachers at Hendrick as he ran to the infield with the ball. Gene Tenace would recall that there was hardly any celebration by the A's on the field; the players hustled to the visitors' clubhouse as quickly as possible because they were afraid of what the angry Detroit fans might do. For a moment, NBC's TV coverage focused on umpire John Rice exiting the field—presumably in case trouble ensued. He did so without incident.

The Oakland A's were the 1972 AL champions. It was the first pennant for the franchise since 1931 when it played home games at Shibe Park in Philadelphia, Connie Mack was the team's manager, and the star players were named Grove, Foxx and Simmons.

The major talking point in the Detroit clubhouse after Game Five was, of course, John Rice's contentious safe call in the top of the fourth inning. Billy Martin was mindful about what he chose to say to the media. "It's a lousy way to get beat, on a decision," he noted. "But I'm not going to second-guess anybody. We lost and that's it."[34]

Detroit's first baseman was not so veiled with his opinion, however. "I didn't come off the bag," Norm Cash would insist to reporters afterward. "That's the way the game is played. You catch the ball then you get off the bag. I made a special effort to stay on the bag!"[35]

Frank Howard was quite blunt about Rice's call. "If you want my honest opinion, Rice blew it," he said. "And I'll tell you something else:

I don't think umps always bear down. I don't think they always hustle and give 100 percent the way players are expected to do. In 15 years in organized baseball, this is only the fourth time I've been thrown out of a game."[36]

Upon hearing Howard's remarks, Cash continued with his own. "I've been in [professional] baseball for 15 years myself," he stressed, "and that's the first time I've ever had that called against me. The umpiring in this whole series was shaky, to put it mildly."[37]

Losing pitcher Woodie Fryman was more diplomatic in his assessment of the controversy. "We just got the wrong break at the wrong time," he said in his Kentucky drawl. "That's baseball, isn't it?"[38]

Not surprisingly, things were considerably more upbeat in the Oakland clubhouse, where the A's were unabashedly whooping it up. Red Smith wrote in his syndicated column, "The A's made the approved sounds of jubilation once the job was done, uttering animal cries upon arrival in their clubhouse, embracing like honeymoon couples, and dousing each other with champagne as protocol demands."[39] Owner Charlie Finley, celebrating his first AL pennant, was caught in the crossfire. He had champagne dripping down his face too. "These are tears of joy,"[40] he insisted.

Bert Campaneris was permitted to join the fun in the clubhouse for the postgame festivities, but he had been barred from the A's dugout during the game as part of his suspension. (Before Game Five, AL president Joe Cronin had rejected a plea from Charlie Finley to allow Campaneris to sit alongside his teammates for the deciding contest of the ALCS.) A UPI news photo of Finley embracing Campaneris in the A's clubhouse was widely circulated in the next day's newspapers.

Oakland manager Dick Williams declared his team's 2–1 win to be the "biggest game of all our careers." He explained, "Wednesday was the toughest loss we ever had, so we rebounded."[41] Williams doled out special praise to Vida Blue whose excellent four-inning relief stint shut down any hopes of another dramatic Detroit comeback. Blue himself was noticeably restrained in his postgame behavior, however. "It was just a ballgame," he calmly told a reporter. "We [potentially] still have seven more ballgames. I'm not really excited."[42]

In a strange interlude, Williams interrupted his celebrating and gleeful discussions with reporters to tend to a forlorn freckle-faced boy, about seven years old, who had somehow aimlessly wandered into the visitors' clubhouse. He was crying because he had become separated from an older brother—and because his hometown Tigers had lost the ALCS. "Root for your home team all the time," Williams told the distraught lad. "I know you're sorry the Tigers lost. Wait here and your brother will be along shortly."[43]

Oakland's Ken Holtzman, who was scheduled to pitch the first game of the World Series for the A's in two days' time, happily recalled a telephone call he had gotten about a year earlier. He told reporter Larry Paladino, "The day I got traded [from the Chicago Cubs], Dick Williams called me at my house and said, 'We're going to put you in the World Series.' And [I'll be] damned if he didn't!"[44]

# The NLCS

## *High Drama and History Made*

"They may regret it a couple of weeks from now, but citizens who now vote the straight National League ticket are saying the playoff between Pittsburgh and Cincinnati is going to decide who's best in baseball."[1]—William Leggett, *Sports Illustrated*

"They're either going to start celebrating again in Pittsburgh very shortly or all kind of something is going to break loose in Cincinnati."[2]—NBC's Curt Gowdy's comments as Johnny Bench led off the ninth inning for Cincinnati in Game Five of the NLCS

The Pittsburgh Pirates entered the NLCS as defending World Series champions but with a new manager at the helm. Citing health concerns, 54-year-old Danny Murtaugh, who had a history of heart problems, resigned as the team's manager about a month after Pittsburgh's 1971 World Series victory and moved into a less stressful job in the team's front office. Murtaugh hand-picked Bill Virdon to be his successor. Virdon had been a coach under Murtaugh. He had also been the center fielder on the 1960 Pirates—a team that famously upset the vaunted New York Yankees in the World Series in seven games that autumn.

Virdon, 41, had been gifted a team that was strong in both pitching and hitting. Roberto Clemente, Al Oliver and Richie Hebner all hit .300 or better in 1972. Both Manny Sanguillén and Willie Stargell's averages were just under that mark. Stargell was the team's most formidable power hitter, having belted 33 homers and driven in 112 runs. All five of Pittsburgh's starting pitchers had winning records. Steve Blass led the team in wins with 19. Three others were close behind: Dock Ellis had 15, Nelson Briles had 14, and Bob Moose had 13. None was an overwhelming strikeout pitcher, but none really needed to be. The Pirates were solid defensively from top to bottom. Even though he was 38, few runners dared to try to take extra bases on Roberto Clemente and his fabulous right arm. Catcher Manny Sanguillén was thought by many observers to be close to Johnny Bench's equal behind the plate.

Pittsburgh also had a new everyday shortstop. Gene Alley had supplanted Jackie Hernández, largely because Alley was perceived to be the better hitter of the two. Alley had been Pittsburgh's regular shortstop before breaking his hand in 1971. When Alley was healthy again in 1972, Hernández was reduced to a backup role on the team.

"Everybody knows about the Pirates," William Leggett wrote in his preview of the 1972 NLCS for *Sports Illustrated.* "They're the people with the bat rack that is constantly twitching and has to be chained down lest it become a UFO. At a time when the .275 hitter is supposedly a condemned species in the majors, the Pirates have stockpiled 10 of them."[3]

It was widely perceived in the baseball world that the NLCS would determine not only that league's championship team for 1972 but also the best team in MLB. The *Pittsburgh Post-Gazette* certainly thought so. A headline in that daily before Game One proclaimed, "Bucs, Reds— Two Best Teams in Land—Meet in Playoffs." William Leggett concurred. He opined that the Bucs-Reds NLCS contained the most promise of any LCS in either major league since the interleague playoff format was introduced by MLB in 1969.

When the Pirates clinched the NL East crown in New York on September 21, former manager Danny Murtaugh sent current manager Bill Virdon a telegram. According to the September 30 issue of *The Sporting News* it read, "Congratulations. You remembered the first lesson. Don't forget the other two." Virdon knew that Murtaugh was referring to the NLCS and the World Series titles. It was probably an unnecessary reminder. The Pirates only moderately celebrated the NL East crown at Shea Stadium, realizing it was just the first step toward their ultimate goal. Only when news photographers asked them to show some enthusiasm did they engage in dousing each other with champagne and beer. Pittsburgh would try to become the first National League club since the New York Giants of 1921 and 1922 to win successive World Series.

The 1972 NLCS opened at Three Rivers Stadium in Pittsburgh with Game One played on Saturday, October 7. A crowd of 50,241 turned out on a chilly and windy afternoon. The field's artificial turf was still damp in places from a recent downpour. Things began well for the visiting Reds. After Pete Rose flied out, Joe Morgan hit a home run over the right-field wall off a Steve Blass fastball to give Cincinnati a quick 1–0 advantage. (Morgan had been voted MVP of the 1972 MLB All-Star

Game in Atlanta.) Blass got the message and threw mainly off-speed pitches to the Reds for the rest of the game. Nearly 40 years later, in his autobiography, *A Pirate for Life*, Blass recalled,

> I went out to pitch Game #1, and the second batter I faced was Joe Morgan. I had two fastballs in my repertoire, a sinking fastball and a rising fastball. I threw Morgan a sinking fastball down and away, and he turned it back around and hit a home run to right-center. After he pulled my fastball like that, I said to myself, "Oh s**t. Is this what they're going to do with my fastball today?" So, for the next seven-plus innings, they probably saw about five fastballs.[4]

The visitors' lead was a short-lived one, however. It vanished in the bottom of the first inning. Pittsburgh scored three times courtesy of Rennie Stennett's single, Al Oliver's triple, Willie Stargell's double, and Richie Hebner's single as lefthander Don Gullett looked shaky on the mound for Cincinnati. (Reds outfielder Bobby Tolan fell on the wet artificial turf trying to field Oliver's hit, turning a single into a three-base hit. He would have similar misadventures 15 days later.) Gullett, to his credit, got over his early jitters and proceeded to retire 12 straight Pirates after his poor start.

The score remained 3–1 in favor of the home team until Al Oliver struck again. He blasted a two-run triple in the fifth inning. That was all the scoring the Pirates managed or needed. Pittsburgh won decisively, 5–1. Blass threw a complete game, but he had to deal with plenty of Cincinnati baserunners. Two Reds were on base with one out in the top of the ninth inning when Virdon removed Blass from the game. Relief pitcher Ramón Hernández came on and efficiently retired Joe Morgan on a fly ball and Bobby Tolan on a strikeout to end the game. The Reds had ample chances, stranding 11 men over the course of the swift-moving game. They had at least one man reach base in every inning. Despite the many baserunners, the game was over in just 117 minutes.

The most memorable part of Game One was umpire Ken Burkhart ejecting Cincinnati manager Sparky Anderson in the top of the fourth inning. With two Reds out and nobody on, César Gerónimo smacked a line drive down the outfield line beyond first base. The ball struck Burkhart who was straddling the foul line, as is customary for first-base and third-base umpires to do. Burkhart ruled the ball had hit a part of his body in *foul* ground. Thus, by rule, it was a foul ball. ("The weather was foul and the liner that Cincinnati's César Gerónimo ripped over first base was too,"[5] concurred Ron Fimrite of *Sports Illustrated*.) Anderson's objections to the call were so strong and persistent that Burkhart finally gave him the thumb. It was the first time the Cincinnati skipper had

**César Gerónimo is congratulated by third-base coach Alex Grammas for a regular-season home run. Not quite a regular for Cincinnati in 1972, the Reds center fielder of the future nevertheless played in all 12 of Cincinnati's postseason games (courtesy Cincinnati Reds Hall of Fame).**

been ejected from any game in 1972. Gerónimo popped out to shortstop Gene Alley shortly after the game—and his at-bat—resumed.

One local baseball scribe thought he had figured out why the Pirates had prevailed in Game One. Bob Smizik of the *Pittsburgh Press* wrote,

> Jack Billingham will pitch for Cincinnati today. That's the Jack Billingham who pitches with his right arm.
>
> Cincinnati found out by the rather hazardous means of trial and error yesterday that lefthanded pitching is not necessarily the best way to stop the Pirates. Don Gullett, who had only a 9–10 record in the regular season, started yesterday as the Reds worked with the belief that lefthanded pitching is the best way to stop the Pirates' big lefthanded hitters.
>
> The belief was proven absurdly incorrect. Al Oliver, Willie Stargell and Richie Hebner, each a lefthanded hitter, drove in all the runs and had four of the six hits as the Pirates defeated Cincinnati, 5–1, at Three Rivers Stadium in the first game of the best-of-five series to determine the National League champion.[6]

Perhaps Smizik was correct because Jack Billingham initially did quite well for the Reds in his Game Two starting assignment on Sunday. At least he fared considerably better than Pittsburgh starter Bob Moose.

The Pirate righthander who was one day shy of his 25th birthday gave up five consecutive hits to Cincinnati's first five batters in the top of the first inning as the Reds vaulted to a fast 4–0 lead. The key blows were two-run doubles by Bobby Tolan and Tony Pérez. Manager Bill Virdon mercifully pulled Moose from the game. He had not retired a single Red batter. Reliever Bob Johnson got the Pirates out of the first-inning mess without any further damage. He proceeded to throw five innings in which no more Cincinnati scoring occurred. He surrendered just one hit and one walk to the Reds to give the home team a fighting chance at a comeback.

Bobby Tolan's double off Moose was controversial—the second major fair/foul dispute of the NLCS—with the Pirates insisting it should have been called a foul ball. The ball landed down the left-field line. The home team thought it descended to the turf inches into foul territory. Umpire Harry Wendelstedt, stationed on the left-field line as part of the six-man crew, disagreed. Ruling that it clipped the line, Wendelstedt promptly gave the signal for a fair ball. One news service's report on Game Two said Pirate manager Bill Virdon came "roaring out of the dugout" to voice his displeasure with Wendelstedt's call. "Sure, I thought it was a foul ball," Virdon later told the press, "but the umpire said it clipped the line."[7]

Billingham shut down the Pirates for three innings, but he allowed a run in the home half of the fourth and fifth. He only went 4⅔ innings before Sparky Anderson replaced him with lefthander Tom Hall. Hall impressively pitched the remaining 4⅓ innings to finish what Billingham had started. He was credited with the win as the starter, Billingham, did not go the required five innings to qualify for it.

Hall, a 155-pound lefthander, had been a tremendous acquisition for the Cincinnati bullpen. Writer Charley Feeney interviewed Reds scout Ray Shore about Hall's emergence as a stalwart reliever. Shore was astonished at Hall's improvement. He said,

> I saw Hall pitch about five times with minor league clubs when he was with the Minnesota organization. He never impressed me. A couple of years ago I saw him, and I didn't believe he was the same pitcher. He developed an excellent fastball, something he didn't have when I saw him in the minors. He told me that his pitch got faster overnight. He can't explain it.[8]

The Pirates gallantly made a game of it. The Cincinnati lead had been reduced to just 4–3 after six innings as Milt May, Roberto Clemente and Dave Cash all drove in runs for Pittsburgh. However, with one out in the top of the eighth, Joe Morgan homered for the second straight afternoon to give Cincinnati an important insurance run. The final score was 5–3 in favor of the visiting Reds. The NLCS was tied after the two games in Pittsburgh. The rest of the series would be played at Cincinnati's Riverfront Stadium.

"We wanted this game badly," Bobby Tolan told reporters after the game. "Now we can go back to our home park and have the advantage." Tolan believed the Reds had underestimated the Pirates, despite the teams having almost identical regular-season records. "I think we may have been nonchalant," he suggested. "We had an easy time against them all year. I think losing [Game One] took us off the pedestal."[9] Indeed, the Reds had beaten the Pirates eight times in their 12 meetings during the 1972 regular season.

Winning pitcher Tom Hall credited Joe Morgan's home run for giving him some needed breathing space in the ninth inning. Hall said he was more relaxed with a two-run lead when Pittsburgh got a runner on base in the ninth inning than if he had just a one-run edge. "Morgan gave me working room."[10] Hall, who had spent the first four years in the AL as a member of the Minnesota Twins, graciously called the Pirates the best hitting club he had ever faced.

Morgan's torrid hitting versus the Pirates was a continuation of what he had done to the Pittsburgh crew during the 1972 season. In the 12 regular-season games Cincinnati played against the Bucs, he batted .370 with four home runs and nine RBIs. He also scored 12 runs and stole five bases.

Game Two featured a brave lineup change by the Pirates. Manager Bill Virdon benched Manny Sanguillén. Pittsburgh's star catcher had been in a month-long batting slump and failed to get a hit in Game One. Milt May caught and batted sixth for Pittsburgh in Game Two. He had a single and an RBI. Sanguillén's banishment was merely temporary. He did see action in Game Two as a pinch hitter, batting for May in the sixth inning, and stroking a double.

Oddly, Bob Moose did not feel too badly about his horrendous outing. Apparently serious, he told reporters, "Sure I gave up four runs, but I honestly thought I pitched well. A few breaks and [the outcome] might have been different." As an optimistic afterthought, Moose added, "I know this: I'll be ready to go from the bullpen for the rest of the series."[11] Sparky Anderson politely agreed with Moose's positive self-assessment. "Moose is one guy who comes to battle you," the Cincinnati skipper said. "We hit him, but he had some bad breaks."[12]

Roberto Clemente had uncharacteristically failed to get a hit in the first two NLCS games. "Sure, there's pressure," he admitted, "but I like to play under pressure. Now I know I have to do better."[13] Willie Stargell and Richie Hebner were struggling too. "We've got to get our big guys going," a frustrated Al Oliver said. "Sure, Stennett and I are hitting, but it is hard for us singles hitters to carry the team. We've found that when Stargell is hitting, it's a lot easier to win."[14]

Cincinnati manager Sparky Anderson was, of course, pleased with the series-leveling win, but he said that he still expected a long and hard-fought battle to decide the NL champions for 1972. "I said before it started that [the NLCS] would go five games. I still think it will,"[15] Anderson boldly predicted to the assembled media.

After Game Two, Nelson Briles was given the nod to start Game Three for Pittsburgh. In advance of his assignment, Briles said, "Both teams have ability and they can both produce. All I'm going to do tomorrow is go out and try to do my job. You've got to keep your feet on the ground."[16]

There was no scheduled day off in the NLCS. The two teams played Game Three on Monday in Cincinnati with a 3 p.m. start dictated by television, of course. One witty baseball scribe, Dan Donovan, made light of how alike the home ballparks for the two NLCS combatants were. He joked, "The Pittsburgh and Cincinnati stadiums are so similar that the architects put the same river beside them." The Pirates had been thoroughly beaten in their last visit they made to Cincinnati, from July 11 to July 13. The Reds won all three games by scores of 5–0, 6–3 and 2–0.

A huge crowd of 52,420 fans packed Riverfront Stadium beyond its official capacity for Game Three. They witnessed an excellent baseball game in which the hometown Reds started well. Run-scoring singles hit off Nelson Briles by Joe Morgan, Darrel Chaney and Bobby Tolan in the home half of the third inning put Cincinnati in front with a 2–0 lead.

The most spectacular defensive play of the game was turned in by Rennie Stennett in the bottom of the fourth inning. Johnny Bench began the frame with a triple off Briles. Tony Pérez failed to bring Bench home; he hit a tremendously high popup to the left side of the infield that Pittsburgh shortstop Gene Alley caught with his back to the plate in shallow left field. Bench held at third base. Next up was César Gerónimo who launched a fly ball to deep left field. Stennett made the catch. Bench tagged up and tried to score, but Stennett's throw was a beauty. It reached Manny Sanguillén on one hop. Sanguillén applied the tag to Bench for the third out. According to Cincinnati's scouts, the 21-year-old Stennett had a great throwing arm, but he was usually inaccurate with it. Contrary to those negative reports, his throw to the plate that nailed Bench could not have been better.

The home team sustained their 2–0 advantage until the top of the fifth inning when Manny Sanguillén—obviously back in manager

Virdon's good graces—cut the Cincinnati lead in half with a solo home run off Reds starter Gary Nolan.

Pedro Borbón relieved Nolan in the top of the seventh inning. He immediately got himself in a bind. Richie Hebner was hit by a pitch. Manny Sanguillén singled to center field, moving Hebner to second base. Gene Alley successfully laid down a sacrifice bunt. With one man out, the Pirates had runners occupying second and third base.

Sparky Anderson removed Borbón in favor of Clay Carroll. Pittsburgh skipper Bill Virdon chose to pinch hit for pitcher Briles with 10-year veteran Vic Davalillo who specialized in batting in such situations. He did not get a chance to shine. Anderson ordered Carroll to walk him, loading the bases. Panamanian-born Rennie Stennett leveled the game at 2–2 for Pittsburgh with a timely RBI single. It was a high bouncer beyond the reach of Cincinnati first baseman Tony Pérez. The bases were still filled with Pirates.

However, a potentially huge inning was eliminated on a strange play. Dave Cash lofted a fly ball to César Gerónimo in right field. The Cincinnati outfielder made the catch and fired to Johnny Bench at home plate. Bench faked a throw toward third base to dissuade Manny Sanguillén from trying to score. Bench then noticed that Davalillo had drifted far off second base. An accurate throw to Joe Morgan caught Davalillo napping for the third out. Despite Davalillo's careless baserunning gaffe, the momentum of the game had discernably shifted to the visitors.

In the bottom of the seventh, new pitcher Bruce Kison set the Reds down in order. In the top of the eighth, Pittsburgh took the lead for the first time since Game One. After Roberto Clemente grounded out to pitcher Clay Carroll, Willie Stargell reached first base on a walk. Gene Clines entered the game to run for Stargell. Al Oliver promptly doubled, sending Clines to third base. Richie Hebner was intentionally walked to load the bases.

Manny Sanguillén was up next. His sharply hit ground ball required a superb play by Cincinnati shortstop Darrel Chaney to prevent it from going into the outfield. Chaney could only get Hebner on a fielder's choice at second base—but not turn a double play—as Sanguillén barely beat Joe Morgan's throw to first base. Clines trotted home with the go-ahead run for the Pirates. The inning ended with Gene Alley hitting into another force play, but the visitors now led Game Three by a 3–2 score.

When Pete Rose hit a one-out double in the bottom of the inning, Kison was replaced on the mound by Pittsburgh's best closer, Dave Giusti. Rose got to third base on a Joe Morgan ground out, but he advanced no further. Rose was stranded there when the inning ended.

In the bottom of the ninth Cincinnati mounted one last rally. After Johnny Bench was called out on strikes, Tony Pérez knocked a single into right field. Sparky Anderson inserted Dave Concepción into the game to run for Pérez. Concepción remained on first base, however. Giusti got Denis Menke to pop up to second baseman Dave Cash for the second out of the frame. César Gerónimo was retired in a similar fashion for out number three. He popped out to shortstop Gene Alley. Alley made the catch in foul territory. Pittsburgh left Cincinnati's home field as happy 3–2 victors, one win away from a berth in the 1972 World Series and an opportunity to defend the title they had won the previous autumn. Kison got credit for the visitors' win. Dave Giusti picked up a well-earned save. The ineffective Clay Carroll, who had allowed two Pittsburgh hits and three walks in his 1⅔ innings of relief work, took the loss in Game Three for the Reds.

Bill Virdon took a page from Sparky Anderson's books and did not gloat following a big win. He too expressed concern that his opponent was still a dangerous foe who was not defeated yet. "It's no great feat for a good ball club like Cincinnati to win two straight games,"[17] Virdon cautioned the media.

Virdon confirmed that outspoken righthander Dock Ellis would pitch Game Four for Pittsburgh. Ellis had seen no action in more than a week. Rust was not a concern for either Virdon or Ellis. "The fact that he hasn't pitched [lately] doesn't affect Dock. His control is always good." Ellis, of course, concurred. "Right now, my arm feels good. I've got a lot of rest—and that was our plan."[18]

In the defeated Cincinnati clubhouse, Pete Rose steamed. "I hate to lose," he said, which was no great revelation to any serious fan. "And I hate it more when we lose after leading for six innings."[19]

Facing elimination, the Reds took the field for Game Four on Tuesday, October 10. Pete Rose seemed very loose before the do-or-die game for his team. He even took a few ground balls at the shortstop position. The former second baseman smiled as he told reporters he was preparing in case he might have to become an infielder again someday.

Before slightly fewer than 40,000 rooters, the Reds comfortably won the most one-sided game of the NLCS by a 7–1 score. Cincinnati starter Ross Grimsley only allowed two Pittsburgh hits and walked no one. His only blemish was surrendering a solo home run to Roberto Clemente in the top of the seventh inning. It was a terrible pitch for Clemente to hit as it was about six inches over his head. Grimsley later laughed at Clemente's awkward swing. "He just tomahawked it."[20] Despite Clemente's poor batting form, the ball fell into the right field seats. Cincinnati was up 5–0 at the time, so the damage was minimal.

The Reds rebounded to score two more runs in the bottom of the seventh to put the game effectively out of reach. The only other Pittsburgh hit in Game Four also belonged to Clemente, who hit a single in the fourth inning but was stranded on base.

The Reds managed 11 hits off four Pittsburgh hurlers. Grimsley himself got two of them—including a double! Starter Dock Ellis was victimized by some poor fielding. The Associated Press report of Game Four labeled the visitors "the fumbling Pirates"—with some justification. The Pirates made three errors—two by shortstop Gene Alley in the fourth inning—that led to three Cincinnati runs. Ellis allowed three runs in five innings of work. Because of the errors, none of them were earned runs. The game was completed in 118 minutes. Cincinnati had forced a fifth game, to be played the following day, and had recaptured the elusive momentum in this back-and-forth NLCS.

The most embarrassing moment in a game that featured plenty of misplays by the Pirates occurred in the bottom of the sixth inning. With a runner at third base, Darrel Chaney was intentionally walked. He did not stop at first, however. Noticing that second base was left completely unguarded, he made a beeline for the sack. Catcher Manny Sanguillén had to hold onto the ball when no teammate covered the bag. "The Pirates did not play like a good baseball team," wrote Pittsburgh scribe Charley Feeney. "They picked this sunny autumn afternoon to fall apart in places."[21]

Still most of the postgame focus was on Ross Grimsley's superb pitching. His dominance—he only threw 84 pitches—earned him three standing ovations from the fawning and supportive home crowd. "Today was the best game in Grimsley's career," said Sparky Anderson. "It might even make him the pitcher we thought he'd be two years from now. He showed a lot of heart."[22]

"He rose to the occasion," Johnny Bench said of his winning pitcher. "He kept the ball low and made no bad pitches."[23]

"I've never pitched a better game," the joyous Grimsley admitted. "The ovations? I couldn't believe it. It's unbelievable that they'd do that for me. Was I confident? No, I was scared—as scared as ever."[24]

Manny Sanguillén had a poor game defensively as the Reds stole three bases on him. (Two were thefts by Johnny Bench!) The normally reliable Pittsburgh catcher also made a throwing error in the first inning that allowed Bobby Tolan to score the first Cincinnati run of Game Four. "I embarrassed myself," Sanguillén candidly told the press. "I just lost my confidence. I have to get it back tomorrow."[25] Manager Virdon also acknowledged that his catcher was struggling. Virdon said Sanguillén had not been gunning many "strikes" to second base during the NLCS, but he figured the overall team speed of the Reds had forced Sanguillén to rush many of his throws.

The NL pennant for 1972 now rode on the outcome of Game Five scheduled for the following day, Wednesday, October 11.

The most anticipated NL game of 1972 was delayed by 88 minutes because of rain. The skies would be overcast and the field slightly damp for the rest of the epic battle. Except for a slight drizzle in the air when the first pitch was thrown, there would be no more serious precipitation. The pitching matchup was exactly the same as it had been for Game One: Don Gullett for Cincinnati and Steve Blass for Pittsburgh. Blass figured his high-pressure experience from pitching Game Seven of the 1971 World Series would help him win another big game. Gullett saw Game Five as a chance for personal redemption for his substandard outing in Game One. So did his manager. Sparky Anderson told the press he expected Gullett to pitch as he had in Game One—excluding the poor first inning. Gullett promised the Reds fans that he would be more relaxed on the mound than he had been for Saturday's NLCS opener.

Neither team scored in the first inning, although the Pirates got a two-out single from Roberto Clemente. In the bottom of the first, the Reds went down in order, but a well-hit ball by Joe Morgan gave Pittsburgh a scare. It was caught at the warning track in center field by Al Oliver.

Gullett had a difficult top of the second inning. Manny Sanguillén led off with a single. Richie Hebner doubled to right field. The Reds botched the relay back to the infield, and an error by shortstop Darrel Chaney allowed Sanguillén to score and Hebner to advance to third base. Dave Cash then singled home Hebner to give the Pirates a 2–0 lead. Shortstop Gene Alley—who had not gotten a hit in the NLCS—flied out to center field. Pitcher Steve Blass attempted a bunt, but a foul ball on the third strike retired him. Gullett threw a wild pitch that moved Cash to third base before he got Rennie Stennett to ground out to end the inning. It was the first time in the NLCS that the Pirates had opened the scoring in any of the five games.

The score remained 2–0 for the visitors until the bottom of the third inning. Darrel Chaney led off that frame with a single to right field. Gullett moved him to second base with an excellent sacrifice bunt. Pete Rose—having a terrific NLCS—got a lucky a double. His ground ball hit a seam in the artificial turf and bounced over first baseman's Willie Stargell's head into right field. It drove home Chaney and cut the Pittsburgh lead to just 2–1. Rose moved to third base on Joe Morgan's ground out, but there he stayed when Bobby Tolan grounded out to Steve Blass.

Rose would end the series with nine hits—a new NLCS record, surpassing Dave Cash's total of eight hits set the previous year in Pittsburgh's four-game victory over the San Francisco Giants.

Pittsburgh quickly got that run back in the top of the fourth inning. Manny Sanguillén and Richie Hebner both singled to center field. Cincinnati manager Sparky Anderson yanked the shaky Don Gullett from the game and replaced him with Pedro Borbón. Anderson had told the media that every pitcher on his staff would be available for Game Five except for Ross Grimsley and Gary Nolan. Despite the pitching change, Dave Cash got another single for Pittsburgh. It drove in Sanguillén as Pittsburgh assumed a 3–1 lead. No further damage occurred as the struggling Gene Alley flied out to right field and Steve Blass hit into a 4–6–3 double play.

The Reds whittled away at Pittsburgh's lead in the bottom of the fifth. Off a Steve Blass changeup, César Gerónimo led off with a home run that barely cleared the right-field wall. (It was just the fifth homer of 1972 for Gerónimo.) The Riverfront Stadium crowd became noticeably louder, but the Reds managed no further scoring in the inning. Pedro Borbón, who had pitched well in relief of Don Gullett, was lifted for pinch hitter Ted Uhlaender. The move paid no dividends; Uhlaender weakly grounded out to first baseman Willie Stargell. Tom Hall replaced Borbón on the mound for Cincinnati in the top of the sixth. The Reds still trailed the Pirates, 3–2, but the game was now a little bit closer.

Pittsburgh looked to have something brewing in the top of the eighth inning. Rennie Stennett singled to center field. Al Oliver moved him to second base with a sacrifice bunt. Roberto Clemente was intentionally walked by Hall. Willie Stargell, having a poor NLCS at the plate, was called out on strikes. (He finished the NLCS with just one hit in 16 at-bats for a miserable .063 batting average.) Manny Sanguillén grounded out to Joe Morgan on a close play at first base. The Pirate threat had vanished. Morgan was an excellent fielder. At one point during the 1972 season, he compiled a streak of 60 consecutive errorless games.

In the bottom of the eighth inning, Bill Virdon opted to make a defensive switch. He replaced Willie Stargell at first base with Bob Robertson, a better glove man. Sparky Anderson made a move too. Joe Hague batted for pitcher Tom Hall and drew a walk. Dave Concepción ran for Hague. Pete Rose came up and, somewhat surprisingly, bunted. The sacrifice moved Concepción to second base with one out. At this point, Virdon opted to pull Steve Blass from the mound. Ramón Hernández replaced Blass. The strategy worked. The pitcher, with his herky-jerky delivery, got Joe Morgan to ground out to second baseman

Dave Cash. Cash bobbled the ball and barely nipped the speedy Morgan with his throw to Robertson. Concepción moved to third base on the infield out, but he was stranded there when Bobby Tolan struck out swinging.

The new Cincinnati pitcher in the top of the ninth was Clay Carroll. Carroll had struggled in Game Three, but he had no trouble retiring the Pirates in order on this day. Pittsburgh still led 3–2 and only had to shut the Reds down in the home half of the ninth to make it two straight NL pennants. In the Cincinnati radio booth, Al Michaels said, "This place will go bananas now as the Reds come to bat."[26] Sparky Anderson was more fatalistic in his assessment. "We are about five minutes away from burial,"[27] he quietly said to his coaching staff, almost conceding defeat.

Bill Virdon made another pitching change. Dave Giusti replaced Ramón Hernández. Johnny Bench was the first batter of the inning. Bench would enjoy recalling that before the bottom of the ninth began, his mother, Katie, had somehow descended close to field level. Above the clamor of the crowd, she implored him to hit a home run. Bench answered her plea with a smile.

Bench swung and missed at the first Giusti offering. The next pitch was a ball. He swung and missed at the next pitch to fall behind 1–2 in the count. Bench hit a log foul ball on Giusti's fourth pitch. Bench straightened out the next pitch, however, belting a home run that sailed well over Roberto Clemente's head into the right field stands. Game Five was suddenly tied, 3–3. "I knew it was gone as soon as I hit it," Bench happily said later. "Pete Rose knew it too. He beat me to first base."[28] Al Michaels would later joke that his voice reached heretofore unknown high octaves on his most famous baseball call. After regaining some measure of calmness, Michaels noted that it was quite rare for the power-hitting Bench to homer to right field; he mostly pulled them to left field.

Bench was mobbed by his teammates and his manager upon crossing home plate. "Sparky Anderson tried to grab me," Bench said at the conclusion of the game, "but I was heading for momma."[29]

"I thought I had [Bench] all set up," Giusti later said. "I think he double-clutched to connect on that fourth pitch [sic]. I thought I fooled him."[30]

Tony Pérez was the next batter. He rapped a single to center field on the first pitch he saw. "The pennant is on first base!"[31] roared Al Michaels. George Foster entered the game to run for Pérez. With Riverfront Stadium going crazy, Denis Menke, batting with a full count, hit two foul balls before connecting for another base hit. It dropped into left field. Foster moved to second base. No Red had yet been retired

**Johnny Bench, perhaps the greatest catcher of all time, is shown heading home following his game-tying, ninth-inning home run in the fifth game of the 1972 NLCS. A true superstar, Bench appeared in 14 All-Star Games. He was a ten-time Gold Glove Award winner, the 1976 World Series MVP, and a first-ballot Hall of Famer (courtesy Cincinnati Reds Hall of Fame).**

in the bottom of the ninth. César Gerónimo was the next Cincinnati batter.

The first two Giusti pitches to Gerónimo were balls. Bill Virdon had seen enough of the strangely ineffective Giusti. He brought in Bob Moose to relieve him. Moose had been bombarded by Cincinnati in his Game Two start on Sunday, failing to get a single Red out in the five batters he faced. He hoped to redeem himself.

Gerónimo failed to get a bunt down. On a 2–2 pitch, Gerónimo hit a long fly ball to right field that was caught by Roberto Clemente—the last putout he would ever make. Foster advanced to third base on the out; Menke remained at first. Darrel Chaney was the next Cincinnati batter. He failed to bring home Foster. Chaney was retired on a popup to Pittsburgh shortstop Gene Alley in shallow left field. With two outs, Pittsburgh was close to escaping the jam, but there were still Cincinnati runners on the corners. Hal McRae was summoned by Sparky Anderson to pinch hit for Clay Carroll.

With Pete Rose waiting on deck, McRae swung and missed on the first pitch from Moose. His next offering was a ball. Here's how Al

Michaels called Moose's third pitch: *"In the dirt! It's a wild pitch! Here comes Foster! The Reds win the pennant!"*[32]

Indeed, Moose uncorked a pitch that touched down in the dirt. It eluded Manny Sanguillén and rolled to the backstop. Foster scored easily—he even had time to joyfully clap his hands as he approached home plate—and Riverfront Stadium naturally went berserk. "I can still see Hal McRae jumping 12 feet off the ground,"[33] Johnny Bench fondly recalled in an interview for MLB decades later. As for Moose's wild pitch, Floyd Johnson, who wrote Moose's SABR biography, declared with more than a smidgen of understatement, "This was a very tough end to what otherwise was a good season."[34]

The Cincinnati Reds had won one of the most dramatic games ever played in the 97 seasons of NL baseball. Only the classic at the Polo Grounds on October 3, 1951, featuring Bobby Thomson's pennant-winning home run for the New York Giants could rightfully be mentioned in the same breath as Game Five of the 1972 NLCS. The Reds, having finished the 1972 regular season with one fewer win than Pittsburgh had, became the first MLB team to qualify for a World Series without having the highest victory total in its league.

Manny Sanguillén told reporters that he thought Moose's final pitch struck something in the dirt to cause the fateful bad hop. "It looked like it hit something," the Pittsburgh catcher recalled. "I don't know what. I jumped toward the ball. The ball hit me on my hand and bounced on by. No, I didn't get my glove on it."[35]

Bill Virdon was questioned about his decision to bring in Dave Giusti to pitch the ninth inning. "When I have a chance to win, I go with my best," he explained honestly. "I think Giusti's my best."[36]

Pittsburgh starter Steve Blass thought Virdon's decision regarding the pitching change was logical too. "I'll still take my chances with Giusti every day," he opined. Then Blass saluted the victorious Reds. "You've got to give them credit. They came back."[37]

Virdon mercifully barred reporters from the Pirates' clubhouse for 20 minutes after Moose's fateful wild pitch. "I spoke to each player individually," he said. "I told them we had had a heck of a year and that we'd get 'em next season."[38] When asked if he had something special to say to Bob Moose, Virdon shook his head and said, "He's no kid. He knows how to handle something like this."[39]

When reporters were finally granted access to the defeated Pirates, they found Dave Giusti and Bob Moose to be crestfallen figures in the sullen clubhouse. Dock Ellis was doing his best to console Giusti. "It was a palm ball,"[40] Giusti sadly told Ellis, describing the home-run pitch he threw to Bench. Meanwhile Moose was trying to explain how his third

**Robert (Bob) Ralph Moose, Jr., is remembered by Pittsburgh fans for his infamous wild pitch (shown here) that allowed George Foster to score the winning run in the deciding game of the 1972 NLCS. Often a victim of bad luck, Moose underwent surgery in 1974 to remove a blood clot under the shoulder of his pitching arm as well as one of his ribs. In 1976, on his 29th birthday, Moose was tragically killed in a car accident while traveling to a Pirates alumni golf event (courtesy Cincinnati Reds Hall of Fame).**

pitch to Hal McRae went awry. "I didn't want to throw him a strike. It just took a bounce and bounced over his head, that's all."[41] The usually reliable Giusti was saddled with the loss; it was his first defeat in any game since May 27.

Bob Broeg sympathetically wrote in *The Sporting News,*

> For Moose, who became a goat, the physical misplay was most unfortunate because the 25-year-old righthander had pitched quite well after taking over with two men on base and none down. Moose, just one out away from extra innings and perhaps spotlighted stardom, will be remembered, sadly, more for his part in the pennant that was decided on a wild pitch than for his contributions....[42]

Although he was not statistically responsible for any of the runs the Reds scored in Game Five, Bob Moose's ERA for the 1972 NLCS was a godawful 54.00. The infamous wild pitch he threw to Hal McRae was the last pitch Moose ever threw in postseason play.

In the victorious home clubhouse, Joe Morgan pondered how much things had changed in his baseball life in less than a year. "I think of all those years I wasted in Houston. This is something." He felt the need to emphasize it, so he repeated himself. "This is something."[43]

A beaming Bobby Tolan chimed in, "This is my fourth pennant winner—and it's tops! We were behind and we beat the world champions." Tolan, who had won two NL crowns with St. Louis and now his second with Cincinnati, felt compelled to add praise to the man who hit the fifth-inning home run for the Reds and moved George Foster to third base in the climactic inning with his long fly ball. "They called César Gerónimo the 'sleeper' in the trade with Houston. They won't be calling him a 'sleeper' anymore."[44]

Not everyone was jumping for joy in the home team's clubhouse. Cincinnati's 46-year-old third-base coach, Alex Grammas, was too exhausted to celebrate. He sat quietly in his cubicle after the emotionally draining victory. "I'm so weak I can't stand up," he claimed. "I've never been so weak in my life."[45]

"I claim this game represented the world championship," Pete Rose boldly said. "I don't want to get anyone in the American League mad, but these were the two best teams [in the major leagues]. The Pirates have nothing to be ashamed of."[46]

Sparky Anderson went a little bit further in his praise of the vanquished. "This series proves that neither team is better than the other. There are two National League champions,"[47] he noted.

The man who scored the game-winning run said he had been prepared if a pitch happened to get by Sanguillén. "When you get to third base, you have to think about a wild pitch or a passed ball," George Foster noted. "Grammas said to be alive for a wild pitch. The coach doesn't tell you to go. You just watch the play and instinct tells you to go. When I saw the ball go over [Sanguillén], I knew there was no way that I wasn't going to score."[48]

Apparently, the Reds—or at least some of their associates—were prescient. Bobby Tolan's wife, Cheryl, an astrology buff, told her husband long before the game began that it would be decided on a wild pitch. While eating breakfast at a local restaurant, George Foster was informed by his waitress that Cincinnati would win Game Five by a single run. "Good," Foster replied. "I'll score that run."[49]

Waite Hoyt, the former Reds broadcaster who had pitched for the 1927 New York Yankees, experienced a touch of déjà vu in seeing Moose's wild pitch. When the Yankees swept the Pirates in that year's World Series, the winning run scored on a wild pitch committed by Pittsburgh relief pitcher Johnny Miljus. Hoyt was asked to compare MLB's two most famous wild pitches. Hoyt told a Pittsburgh columnist that he and his New York teammates thought Miljus had gotten a raw deal 45 years before. They collectively figured the blame should have been put on Pirate catcher Johnny Gooch and the miscue should have been scored as a passed ball. Both Johnnies were still alive in 1972 to witness history repeat itself.

The day after their loss in Game Five, the Pirates returned to Three Rivers Stadium to clean out their cubicles and to say goodbye to each other until spring training 1973. None of them seemed especially interested in watching the deciding game of the Detroit-Oakland ALCS which was being shown on the clubhouse TV without sound. As the Pirates packed their belongings, the groundskeepers were busily changing the baseball diamond into a football field for the next Pittsburgh Steelers home game three days hence. The baseball diamond had been left in place in anticipation of the World Series opening in Pittsburgh on Saturday afternoon. Had the Pirates won the NLCS, the October 15 NFL game between the Steelers and Houston Oilers would have been shifted from Pittsburgh to Houston. When Dan Rooney, the owner of the Steelers, was asked if he were happy the Pirates had lost so his team could play at the scheduled venue, he diplomatically withheld his opinion. Rooney stated his only interest was football.

None of the Pirates was especially bitter about how the NLCS and a second consecutive trip to the World Series had slipped from their grasp with just three outs to go.

"We had our chances, but it just didn't work out," said Pittsburgh manager Bill Virdon. "We wish it could have been different, but it wasn't."[50]

Bob Smizik of the *Pittsburgh Press* summed up the Pirates' failure to win the NLCS this way: The team that lived by its bats had died by its bats. He wrote,

> There were many particular instances on the field that could have turned the National League playoffs around, but there was one overriding reason why the Pirates didn't win: They failed to hit in five games versus Cincinnati.
> The Pirates were the best hitting team in baseball going into the playoffs, but such skills never surfaced at they fought for the pennant.[51]

The Pirates were generally philosophical about their shattering defeat. Most realized that such dramatic turnarounds were part of MLB. Pitcher Nelson Briles was part of two World Series championship teams, but he was also a member of the 1968 St. Louis Cardinals who allowed a three-games-to-one lead in the 1968 World Series slip away. Briles spoke from experience. "I've been on both sides before," he noted. "Sure, there is disappointment, but there is certainly nothing to be ashamed of."[52] Pittsburgh trainer Tony Bartirome was not surprised by how gracefully his charges were accepting their defeat. "This is the most professional team in baseball," he declared. "They won't go around crying about this."[53]

The Pittsburgh players were heartened by the vast volume of mail and telegrams arriving at the stadium from their loyal fans—and baseball fans in general. A lot of it was addressed to pitchers Dave Giusti and Bob Moose. They had been two of the heroes in the postseason for the 1971 Pirates, but they were each on the mound when the ninth inning unraveled in Cincinnati, and together they now wore the goat's horns. Most of the correspondence was of the encouraging variety. One cliché-filled telegram, sent by "Pittsburgh fans," was placed on a table for every player to read. It said, "Thanks for a great season. Remember today is the first day of the rest of your lives. Behind every cloud is a silver lining. Smile. Smile. Smile. Smile."[54]

Pat Livingston, the sports editor of the *Pittsburgh Press* summed up the general gloom pervading the NL team he covered. He wrote,

> For the first time this year, the inky gloom of defeat hung over the Pirate clubhouse. The Pirates had lost before—in April they dropped six in a row—but not once did this ball club concede anything. There was always tomorrow.
>
> But now, with Bob Moose's uncontrolled pitch bouncing into the dirt, there was no tomorrow.[55]

Al Abrams, the sports editor of the *Pittsburgh Post-Gazette*, took a broader view of what was happening in baseball and saw a very bright side to it, despite the heartbreaking loss Pittsburgh's baseball fans were experiencing. He wrote,

> Those 4–3, almost identical finishes in Detroit and Cincinnati on Wednesday had baseball officials and lovers of the game crowing almost as loudly as the cheering Reds fans. And being human, they needled pro football fans with, "Let them try to match what millions saw on television today!"
>
> Arguments aside, there is no denying the excitement generated by the two contests. The clinical experts will point out that the action in the Detroit-Oakland game that day was sloppy in parts. It was.
>
> And the wild pitch which crushed the Pirates' hopes wasn't the ideal way to decide a pennant. But who can take away from baseball what could be its biggest day in history?
>
> Fans the country over were emotionally drained by the series of events leading to the thrilling endings.[56]

Meanwhile in Cincinnati, the locals celebrated the hometown team's comeback victory in Game Five by assembling at Fountain Square Plaza. Police estimated there were 10,000 revelers who gathered for an impromptu party that lasted well past midnight. "It was loud, but it wasn't bad,"[57] said Cincinnati police chief John McLaughlin who had seen much worse behavior when the Reds captured the NL pennant 11 years before in 1961.

The suds were flowing freely, and the crowd was predictably boisterous, but only five arrests were made: three for drunkenness, one for disorderly conduct and one for ticket-scalping World Series ducats. A local singing group, clad in red jackets, warbled "Take Me Out to the Ballgame" several times as teenage girls and boys kicked empty beer cans across the pavement. Most of the beer being consumed was sold by the nearby eateries. Their profits were substantial. "Those fancy restaurants were getting 80 cents to a dollar per can,"[58] marveled one officer of the law.

Whatever might happen to the Reds in the subsequent World Series, Cincinnati's baseball fans would always have Game Five of the 1972 NLCS to fondly recall. Kipp Martin, who was in a nosebleed seat at Riverfront Stadium that fateful Wednesday, penned the following reminiscence in a 2020 blog:

> To say that utter pandemonium broke out [after Bench's homer] is an understatement. No one sat down after the home run. No one! Not only did everyone stand and scream, but everyone was jumping up and down. Riverfront Stadium was literally shaking like we were having an earthquake. I honestly thought it might collapse. I have never witnessed anything like this.[59]

# 1972 MLB Esoterica

## *The Good, Bad, Ugly, and Quirky*

"Some people could do without the games as long as they got the box scores."—*New York Times*, July 13, 1976

Each MLB season has its share of thrilling highs, soul-crushing lows, and record-setting performances—sometimes amazing and often times forgettable. The 1972 season was no exception. The following is a compilation of some of the more noteworthy events that transpired over the course of this memorable MLB season.

On Friday, May 12, the Milwaukee Brewers and Minnesota Twins began a marathon game at Metropolitan Stadium that would span two days. The game was tied 3–3 after seven innings—and would remain that way through 21 innings. According to AL rules, no new inning could start after 1 a.m. local time, so the game was suspended at 1:05 a.m. when the Twins failed to break the deadlock in the bottom of the 21st inning. The game resumed about 12 hours later. It ended in the 22nd inning with Milwaukee manufacturing a run with two singles and a sacrifice bunt to earn a 4–3 victory. After a 15-minute respite, the two teams began their game scheduled for Saturday afternoon. It lasted 15 innings. Minnesota won it, 5–4.

That same day, May 12, brought the end of an era for the Giants franchise when 41-year-old Willie Mays was traded from San Francisco to the New York Mets for pitcher Charlie Williams and $50,000. Mays had joined the New York Giants in 1951. Said Giants manager Charlie Fox, "Look, [for] the past 20 years he's been the greatest player to ever walk on a ball field. He could do it all. Naturally that type of player is going to be missed."[1]

On Sunday, May 14, the Cincinnati Reds swept a doubleheader from the St. Louis Cardinals, 4–3 and 2–0. Tony Pérez drove in all six Cincinnati runs. He was 4-for-8 over the two games, with a double and a home run.

On Friday, July 14, AL umpire Bill Haller worked behind the plate for a Kansas City-Detroit game at Tiger Stadium. His brother, Tom Haller, was the Detroit catcher that night. The playing Haller, age 35, got one hit in four at-bats in his team's 1–0 loss to the Royals. Fortunately for the sake of family bliss, the 37-year-old umpiring Haller did not have to call out his younger sibling on strikes at any time.

On Monday, July 31, Dick Allen became the seventh player in modern MLB history to hit a pair of inside-the-park home runs in a game. Both were surrendered by Minnesota's Bert Blyleven in an 8–1 Chicago White Sox victory over the Twins at Metropolitan Stadium. The first was a line drive to center field with two men on base that got past outfielder Bobby Darwin and found its way to the warning track. The second home run, a two-run shot, also was helped by Darwin considerably who tried to make a shoestring catch on a towering blast. He mistimed it—and the ball eluded him.

Nate Colbert of the San Diego Padres had quite the productive doubleheader on August 1 at Atlanta Stadium. Over the two games versus the Braves, he smacked a record five home runs to tie the MLB record for circuit clouts in a twin bill. He also drove in 13 runs to set an outright record for a doubleheader. The only other man in MLB history to hit five home runs in a doubleheader was the fabulous Stan Musial who achieved the feat 18 years earlier, on May 2, 1954. Remarkably, Colbert was in the crowd at Sportsman's Park in St. Louis that Sunday to see Musial's awesome batting display. Colbert, who still holds the career home run record for San Diego with 163, had the distinction (for lack of a better term) of playing for nine consecutive last-place teams from 1968 to 1976. Of course, the 1972 San Diego Padres were one of them.

On Saturday, September 2, Milt Pappas of the Chicago Cubs retired the first 26 San Diego Padres he faced at Wrigley Field. With two out in the top of the ninth inning, and holding an 8–0 lead, the 33-year-old righthander faced pinch hitter Larry Stahl. With the count at 2–2, Pappas fired two straight pitches that he believed were strikes. Plate umpire Bruce Froemming, in his second year as an NL arbiter, called both pitches balls, giving Stahl a walk and squelching the rare perfect game. (Pappas retired the next Padre, Garry Jestadt, to earn a no-hitter, however.) Pappas, who died in 2016, would always maintain that three of the four balls that he threw to Stahl should have been called strikes. "I went crazy," Pappas remembered. "I called Bruce Froemming every name you can think of. I knew he didn't have the guts to throw me out, because I still had the no-hitter."[2] (Pappas was also irked that Froemming smirked after calling the fourth ball on Stahl. Froemming denied that accusation, but a 92-second clip available on YouTube shows Pappas was correct.) About 25 years later, Pappas was being interviewed on a Chicago radio station. The host managed to get Froemming on the phone, too—and the ex-pitcher and recently retired umpire shouted at each other for several minutes. Regarding the unfortunate and long-running acrimony between the two men, Froemming once commented, "It's gotten ugly now. Right after the game, he [Pappas] said the 3–2 pitch had missed, but as time has gone on, that pitch has gotten better and better."[3] In 1972 Pappas became the first pitcher in MLB history to attain 200 career wins without ever winning 20 games in a single season.

At Cleveland Stadium on Tuesday, October 3, Roric Harrison, a 6'3", righthanded, Baltimore Oriole rookie pitcher, hit a leadoff, solo home run in the sixth inning of the second game of a doubleheader off Ray Lamb of the Indians. To purists who oppose the designated-hitter rule, Harrison's blast was quite noteworthy. With the advent of the DH in 1973, Harrison became the last AL pitcher to homer in a regular-season game until the advent of interleague play in 1997. The 1972 season was the only one that Harrison played in the AL—and his home run on October 3 was his only round-tripper in the junior circuit. (He hit five home runs in three NL seasons.) Harrison was also the winning pitcher in that game as Baltimore prevailed 4–3 over Cleveland.

Similarly, on that same October 3 night, 20-year-old Terry Forster, in his second season with the Chicago White Sox, stole second base versus the Minnesota Twins. That made him the last AL pitcher to swipe a bag before the inception of interleague play 25 years later. It was the only base Forster ever stole in his 16 MLB seasons. [Authors' note: To be totally accurate, Forster, who was 6–5 as a reliever with 29 saves in 1972, stole the aforementioned base in a *pinch running* assignment. So does that *really* make Forster the last AL pitcher to steal a base in the pre–DH and pre-interleague eras? The co-authors of this book hold contrary opinions on the issue.]

Historically, Frank Robinson, the only man to win MVP awards in both major leagues, had always been an offensive force. In 1972, however, he was a bust. After leading Baltimore to four AL pennants in six seasons, Robinson was surprisingly dealt to the Los Angeles Dodgers (along with his pricey $130,000 salary) at the end of the 1971 season because youthful Don Baylor was his heir apparent in the Baltimore outfield. In 1972, Robinson struggled mightily in his return to the NL, hitting just .251 with 19 home runs. After just one disappointing year in Los Angeles, the 37-year-old Robinson was traded again, this time just down the road to the California Angels.

Rod Carew of the Minnesota Twins achieved a quirky first in 1972: He became the first American League player to win his circuit's batting title without hitting a home run. (Brooklyn's Zack Wheat had gone homerless in winning the NL batting title in 1918.) Carew, who turned 27 on the last weekend of the regular season, hit .318 (170 hits in 535 at-bats). Curiously, in the 19 MLB seasons Carew played, he hit 92 career home runs—twice he belted 14 in a single year—but the 1972 season was the only one in which Carew failed to homer at least once.

The indefatigable Wilbur Wood, a lefthanded knuckleball hurler, started the remarkable total of 49 games for the Chicago White Sox! It was the greatest number of starts in a single season for any MLB hurler since 1908. (Three MLB pitchers had more than 50 starts that season. Ed Walsh had 66!) The 30-year-old Wood, who frequently pitched on two days' rest, led the AL in wins with 24. In 1972, Wood pitched the astonishing total of 376⅔ innings—a figure unmatched in the MLB's live-ball era.

Steve Carlton, the mercurial lefthanded ace of the Philadelphia Phillies, won 15 consecutive games during the 1972 season—and 27 games overall. Under normal circumstances these would be terrific stats. For the 1972 Phillies they were almost unbelievable. Philadelphia finished dead last in the NL East, winning just 59 games. Thus, Carlton alone accounted for 45.8 percent of his team's victories—a sizable chunk unmatched by any other MLB hurler since the modern pitching distance of 60'6" was established in 1893. Carlton had 30 complete games (out of 41 starts) and 310 strikeouts in 346 innings pitched. He won the NL Cy Young Award. Carlton had been traded prior to the 1972 season, on February 25, from the St. Louis Cardinals in exchange for Rick Wise. (The trade was made because each man was embroiled in contentious contract negotiations with his club.) Wise went 16–16 for St. Louis in 1972. Carlton's 27 wins in 1972 marked the last time in the 20th century that an MLB pitcher won at least 25 games in a single season.

Dick Allen was named the AL's Most Valuable Player for 1972. The 30-year-old had a terrific season for the Chicago White Sox, a team that finished second in the AL West. Allen batted .308 with 37 home runs and had 113 RBIs. Oakland's Joe Rudi was runner-up to Allen in the MVP voting. He modestly and graciously commented, "I think it would have been unjust if anyone but Dick had won it after the year he had."[4]

During Game Two of the 1972 World Series, Al Michaels said that Cincinnati's Johnny Bench had a good chance to be named the NL MVP. Michaels was correct. Although many fans thought Steve Carlton's one-man show in Philadelphia should have gotten him the nod, Bench was certainly a worthy winner. Bench, not quite 25 years old when the season ended, batted .270 while hitting 40 home runs and driving in 125 runs. He walked 100 times in 1972—23 of them were intentional passes. He also won the Gold Glove for NL catchers.

Hank Aaron reputedly became the first MLB player to earn $200,000 a season when he signed a three-year deal on February 29 with the Atlanta Braves. Aaron was rewarded for his remarkable 1971 season which saw him, at age 37, hit 47 home runs and notch 118 RBI, while maintaining a solid .327 batting average. During the 1972 season Aaron drove in his 2,000th career run and broke Stan Musial's NL record for total bases (6,134) that had stood since 1963.

To no one's surprise, Boston's young and talented catcher, Carlton Fisk, won the AL Rookie of the Year Award unanimously. The 24-year-old batted .293, hit 22 home runs, played in the All-Star Game, won a Gold Glove, and finished fourth in AL MVP voting. Fisk also tied for the AL lead in triples, with nine, becoming the only catcher from the junior circuit to ever finish atop that offensive category.

Jon Matlack of the Mets won the NL Rookie of the Year honors. The New York lefty won 15 games, threw four shutouts, and had an impressive 2.32 ERA. It was probably the highlight of his 13-year MLB career. He finished with an overall 125–126 won-lost record.

The first ever MLB no-hitter pitched beyond American borders occurred on Monday, October 2. It was tossed by Bill Stoneman of the Expos at Montreal's Jarry Park. His club beat the New York Mets that night, 7–0. Stoneman, a 28-year-old righthander, had nine strikeouts and seven walks in the game. It was the last complete game that Stoneman ever pitched.

Nolan Ryan led the AL in both strikeouts (329) and shutouts (nine) in 1972 while playing for the fifth-place California Angels.

Emphasizing the new emphasis now placed on relief pitching in MLB, righthander Clay Carroll of the Cincinnati Reds set a new seasonal MLB record for saves with 37. A lefthander, Sparky Lyle of the New York Yankees, led the AL with 35 saves.

# Oakland vs. Cincinnati

## *The Hairs vs. the Squares*

"The National League plays its games in zillion-dollar concrete palaces with wall-to-wall carpeting, upholstered furniture and sweeping views of rivers and lakes and bays and oceans. The American league performs in tenement buildings slapped together at the time of the Roosevelt Administration—Teddy's not Franklin's—and on fields of common grass and dirt. The National League has all the superstars, the batting averages, the stolen bases, the home runs and the crowds. American League stars—such as they are—are merely recycled National Leaguers."[1]—Ron Fimrite, *Sports Illustrated*

"It was a matchup of two soon-to-be dynasties that created one of the most exciting World Series in history. The 1972 World Series was a clash of styles, affectionately dubbed 'The Hairs vs. The Squares.'"[2]—Matt Kelly, National Baseball Hall of Fame

Not long after the final out of the ALCS was made by George Hendrick at Tiger Stadium, oddsmakers in Nevada listed the Cincinnati Reds as 7:5 favorites to win the 1972 World Series. The betting odds had shifted slightly more towards Cincinnati, 3:2, by Saturday morning. Although the two franchises had absolutely zero postseason history with each other, this perceived edge given to the Reds was expected.

Entering the 1972 Fall Classic, the American League was suffering from an inferiority complex. The generally held perception of the sport's serious followers was that the higher quality of baseball and MLB player could be found in the senior circuit. "People ask me every year if I'll get my 200 hits," Cincinnati's Pete Rose said in the October 23, 1972, issue of *Sports Illustrated*. "How many players get asked that in the American League?"[3] In that same article, Oakland's Sal Bando conceded that the style of play in the NL—with its aggressive baserunning and go-for-broke batting strategies—was likely more appealing to average baseball fans. "Maybe we're just too buddy-buddy in our league."[4] Recent World Series results did not show any sort of National League dominance, however. In fact, a pattern of parity was quite evident. A quick glimpse of World Series results since 1965 showed the two leagues had quaintly exchanged championships every year, with the NL winning in the odd years and the AL triumphing in the even years. With the Pittsburgh Pirates taking all the marbles in 1971, if the trend continued, it was the AL champions' turn to win the Fall Classic in 1972.

Nevertheless, Cincinnati manager Sparky Anderson was more than happy to promote the idea of the NL being the superior loop in MLB. He told the media, "I'm not saying Oakland can't beat us. But I am saying you can't compare our league to theirs. Our league is tougher from top to bottom. In [the NL] you can go from first to fifth just like that. The Giants did it this year. It could happen to us next year."[5]

In a post–NLCS interview that ran in the *Pittsburgh Post-Gazette* on October 13, Anderson continued to proclaim the NL was the superior circuit. He stated,

> Frank Robinson spent several seasons in both leagues. He said that when he was with the Orioles, he tried to convince himself that the leagues were equal. A few months ago, he came out and said there was no comparison. Our league is much better. We play a much more aggressive-type game.

When informed of Anderson's assessment of the two leagues, A's Manager Dick Williams replied, "Oh, I don't know. I've seen some pretty bad National League teams on television. If we get 27 outs, we may have them. Which team is best remains to be seen."[6]

Some savvy baseball reporters posed questions to recent Oakland acquisitions, Dal Maxvill and Matty Alou. Each man had recently come to the A's after spending his entire MLB career in the NL. Not only were they quite familiar with the Reds' lineup, but they also had plenty of experience playing on artificial turf—a surface that was still a bit of a novelty to AL teams. (Chicago's Comiskey Park featured an artificial turf infield; all other AL parks had entirely real grass.) After answering a battery of questions from reporters, Maxvill and Alou spent several minutes bouncing balls on Riverfront Stadium's ersatz grass and making mental notes of what they observed.

When asked what the biggest adjustment he had had to make since arriving in Oakland was, Maxvill said, half-seriously, it was trying to remember which uniform combination to wear—a sartorial issue that only the A's had in MLB. Maxvill noted in the October 7 issue of *The Sporting News*, "We wear white pants every day, but one day we wear a green jersey with a yellow undershirt, and the next day a yellow jersey with a green undershirt. Then on Sundays we wear all white with green undershirts."

The opposing World Series managers had a few things in common. Both Sparky Anderson and Dick Williams were managing in the Fall Classic for the second time; each man had lost in his first attempt to win MLB's biggest prize. On their respective ascensions to the majors, both had managed the Toronto Maple Leafs of the International League. Both men had deserved reputations as tough taskmasters who got positive results through their methods.

Dick Williams will be forever remembered in Boston as the man who, as a first-year manager, led the Red Sox to their "Impossible Dream" pennant in 1967. The Red Sox were 100–1 longshots to attain that feat when the season began. Promising only that Boston would merely win more games than they lost that year, Williams guided an unfashionable team that had finished ninth in the AL in 1966 to the top of the standings in 1967. Williams showed more than an average amount of moxie in 1967. At one point that summer he stripped Carl Yastrzemski of his captaincy in order to foster equality among the entire team. (It worked. Yaz responded with one of the greatest seasons ever. His wins above replacement stat for 1967 was the fourth best attained in the 20th century. The top three were compiled by Babe Ruth.) Williams also restored the Red Sox to local prominence. On Opening Day 1967, fewer than 9,000 fans showed up at Fenway Park. By the final weekend of the season, however, Red Sox tickets were almost unattainable. Boston lost a seven-game World Series that October to the St. Louis Cardinals and the nearly invincible Bob Gibson. Williams' Red Sox were defeated but hardly disgraced. Williams' playing career in MLB was certainly far more substantial than Sparky Anderson's. He once possessed a strong throwing arm, but he injured his shoulder trying to make a diving catch in 1952 while a member of the Brooklyn Dodgers. His arm strength never did fully return. To stay in MLB, Williams had to become more versatile. He did. Williams eventually played in 1,023 games for seven clubs over 13 seasons, first as an outfielder, then as a first baseman and then as a third baseman. One team he played for was the Athletics—the Kansas City version—in 1959 and 1960.

Sparky Anderson was mostly a minor leaguer with a good glove. At 5'9" and 170 pounds, Anderson possessed little power at the plate. (Nevertheless, while playing for a Double-A team in Fort Worth, Texas, Anderson's fiery enthusiasm for the game earned him the nickname "Sparky." It was bestowed on him by a local radio broadcaster who thought the adjective was quite fitting. It was. Anderson did not like the moniker very much at first, thinking it sounded cartoonish. He grew to accept it, though.) Anderson's hustle and smarts caught the attention of scouts when he was a high school player. Professional baseball beckoned. Teammate and lifelong friend Billy Consolo (who would play 10 MLB seasons and later serve as one of Anderson's coaches in Detroit) said of Sparky,

> He had some talent. He could run and he had great hands. But the best thing about him is that he always wanted to play. He never wanted to quit. He understood the game more than any of us did. He knew all the little things. He couldn't stand to lose. Nobody played harder. He was a feisty little pepper pot.[7]

In his best minor league season, Anderson batted .296 with zero home runs. He had just a single season as an MLB player. In 1959, Anderson played in 152 of 154 games for the Philadelphia Phillies as their second baseman. He batted leadoff in his very first MLB game; it was a home contest versus Cincinnati on April 10. His lone hit in four trips to the plate drove in the game-winning run off Don Newcombe. However, by the end of the season, Anderson was batting just .218 with just 34 RBIs and zero home runs for a last-place club. Ninety-two of his 104 hits that year were singles. Anderson was demoted to the minors for the 1960 season and never again returned to the big leagues—as a player. Anderson holds this quirky distinction in baseball history. Of the hundreds of players who have appeared in just one MLB season, Anderson played the most games of any of them.

Dick Williams and Sparky Anderson were both old-school types, but they were employed by teams that had distinctly opposite personas. Williams knew who signed his paycheck, so he went along with the mustaches and long hair of Charlie O. Finley's Swingin' Oakland A's. He himself even grew facial hair to fit in. Sal Bando later recalled, "I think a lot of things are mislabeled on Dick, I mean, he was a strong disciplinarian, in terms of fundamental baseball and what he expected.... [But] as far as being a disciplinarian in terms of your curfew, your dress, your hair, Dick was very flexible there."[8] Such liberties were verboten with Cincinnati Reds. (It was reported that on more than one occasion during the 1972 season someone from upper management phoned down to the Reds' bullpen to remind the pitchers, who were leisurely slouched in their chairs, to sit up straight and look respectable.) At a time when the national pastime was still such a conservative entity that American Legion Baseball had no qualms about barring individuals and entire teams from its tournaments for sporting long hair or mustaches, some media folks amusingly dubbed the 1972 Fall Classic "The Hairs vs. The

Squares." Other writers took the comparison to a greater degree, referring to the World Series as "The Bikers vs. The Boy Scouts."

Decades later, Pete Rose chuckled at the "squares" label bestowed on his team in 1972. "We weren't squares," he said with a grin in a 2017 interview. "Tony Pérez, Johnny Bench, Joe Morgan, Davy Concepción … they're not long-haired guys. It isn't in their DNA."[9]

Like Dick Williams, Sparky Anderson had managed in a previous World Series in an underdog role and lost. Anderson was hoping for a better outcome in 1972, of course. "The last time I was in a World Series I was naive," the Reds manager told Charley Feeney of the *Pittsburgh Post-Gazette*. Anderson continued,

> I was just happy to be out there, and I think many of our players felt the same way. I almost didn't mind losing to the Orioles [in 1970]. Being there seemed to be the big thing. This time will be different. I'm going to be very mad if we lose. I want to prove that the National League is the best. You can't prove it if we lose.[10]

Anderson figured his 1972 team was a better club overall than his 1970 squad. He said his current pitchers were markedly better than those who had been roughed up by the Baltimore Orioles two Octobers before. Anderson also believed the 1972 Reds were superior in team defense, too.

Pete Rose, who had an excellent NLCS at the plate, exuded confidence going into the World Series. "I expected to hit pretty well against Pittsburgh," he said. "I wasn't hitting against them early in the year, but in the long run I started coming along." When it was pointed out to Rose that he had gotten nine hits in the NLCS but had scored just a single run, Rose explained, "That's just baseball; you can't really blame anyone for it. All you can do is try your best. I'll just try to get my knocks [in the World Series] and score more runs than I did in the playoffs."[11]

When the ALCS was still deadlocked at two games apiece, Rose was asked which AL team he preferred to play in Saturday's World Series opener. Without hesitation, Rose replied, "We don't care who we play; we're ready for anyone."[12]

Joe Morgan was seen soaking his right foot in a whirlpool in the Reds' clubhouse. He told reporters he had injured his ankle during the fourth game of the NLCS, but he assured baseball fans everywhere that he expected to be completely healthy for the World Series opener.

The Oakland A's continued to battle amongst themselves even in the aftermath of victory. It was reported that Vida Blue and John (Blue Moon) Odom nearly got into a fistfight after the team's Game Five win in the ALCS. Apparently Blue mildly teased Odom about having to come into the game as a reliever to "rescue" him—and things began to escalate from there. Tempers flared, but things calmed down quickly, Blue assured a gathering of sports writers. "It was just one of those things that happen," he said with a smile. "John and I have no hard feelings toward each other."[13]

The city of Cincinnati was excited to be hosting the 1972 World Series. Fountain Square was where the peripheral fun was to be had by baseball fans. Bands were playing continually before "dancing and shouting thousands," according to one impressed visiting scribe from Canada. "The occupants of every downtown building," he noted, "had agreed to turn on their lights as a salute to the Reds."[14] Another writer was also impressed by Cincinnatians' enthusiasm for the Series. Ed Levitt of the *Oakland Tribune* reported, "In this noisy, happy town, there isn't a hotel, restaurant, bar, cafeteria or hot dog stand not covered with signs and slogans. Redlegs are painted on the sidewalks and street corners."[15]

Columnist Jim McKay predicted wonderful things from Oakland's Matty Alou. Alou, age 33, had batted .281 since being acquired from St. Louis. He wielded even hotter lumber in the ALCS, batting .381 in the five games versus Detroit. McKay figured Alou would strive to put on a show versus his old NL adversaries. "Watch him closely in the World Series," McKay wrote. "He's going against the National League for the first time, and that will give him a little extra desire. He just may slap and slice the Reds to death. Even if he doesn't, he'll entertain you anyway."[16]

MLB announced its selection of the six-man umpiring crew, comprised of three men in blue from each league. Chosen from the NL were Mel Steiner, Bob Engel and Chris Pelekoudas. The AL umpires were Bill Haller, Frank Umont and Jim Honochick. Engel was uniquely making his first World Series appearance. Honochick was the veteran arbiter of the bunch; he was making his sixth appearance in a Fall Classic. His first was 20 years before when the Brooklyn Dodgers faced the New York Yankees in 1952.

Commissioner Bowie Kuhn also announced the committee of official scorers for the World Series, one scribe from each team's local media and a neutral third party: Earl Lawson of the *Cincinnati Post*, Ron Bergman of the *Oakland Tribune*, and Max Nichols of the *Minneapolis Star*. Nichols was currently serving as the president of the Baseball Writers' Association of America.

NBC proudly announced its radio and television broadcasting crews for the 1972 World Series: To no one's surprise, the familiar and popular Curt Gowdy would be the lead announcer on TV. Tony Kubek, an excellent *Game of the Week* analyst whose talents had been wasted largely doing superfluous fluff interviews in the stands at previous Fall Classics, was elevated to the television booth too.

The 53-year-old Gowdy, who was once a state tennis champion in Wyoming, was the versatile dean of NBC's television broadcasters. Joe Falls was full of praise when he described the very popular Gowdy in *The Sporting News*. Falls wrote,

> I've always had the feeling that [television's premier sports announcer] is Curt Gowdy.
>
> I probably feel this way since he seems to do the most important assignments—the Super Bowl and the World Series, plus all the Saturday baseball and Sunday football.
>
> The thing about Gowdy is that he wears so well. He may not have "ups," but he doesn't have many "downs." When you are on TV as much as he is, the danger of overexposure is almost critical.
>
> It just doesn't happen with Gowdy. His approach is smooth but knowledgeable. He may not excite you with a flamboyant phrase, but neither will he bore you. He is not a middle-of-the-roader, either, because he does have his own distinctive style. He seems to like his job, and he seems to know what it is about, and both those things come through, at least to me. And he makes few errors too, and usually corrects the boo-boo as soon as it is pointed out.[17]

Falls had kind words for Tony Kubek, too:

> I find his boyish, almost-too-eager approach very refreshing. It is a pleasant departure from the rehearsed goody-goody, handsome-faced style that is so irritating on TV. Kubek can get away with his lack of TV polish because he knows what he's talking about. While it may take him a little while to get there, you come away with a feeling that you've just listened to someone who knows his subject.[18]

As was customary, one announcer from each team's local coverage was also selected by NBC to give valuable in-the-know insights of his club for MLB's annual showcase. Monte Moore and Al Michaels were the chosen twosome.

The folksy 42-year-old Monte Moore was an Oklahoman who had been calling A's games since the team's Kansas City days in 1962. He had been hired on the spot by Charlie Finley after the A's owner heard Moore call a basketball game. Initially he was saddled with describing loss after loss. "Those weren't exactly glory years in Kansas City," Moore remembered in a 1993 interview. "I went through a growth period with a lot of those guys."[19] Moore was hugely popular with his listeners. In a 1977 newspaper poll, Moore was voted the most popular sports announcer in the Bay Area. One complimentary fan wrote, "[Moore] is completely knowledgeable about his subject, he speaks clearly, has a good sense of humor and projects an image of a good, sound, down-to-earth person; someone you'd like to know personally. Above all, though, is his professional ability as [an] announcer."[20] The upwardly mobile A's winning the AL pennant now gave Moore the wonderful opportunity to call World Series games across the vast NBC network. It was, of course, Moore's greatest thrill in his broadcasting career.

For the 28-year-old Al Michaels it was his first extended exposure to a national television audience. Blessed with a superb and engaging voice, the already excellent Michaels was in just his second season with the Reds. Remarkably, the World Series marked the second time in 1972 that Michaels was a short-term hire by NBC. In February, he had covered the Winter Olympic hockey tournament in Sapporo, Japan for the network—mostly in small segments of highlights. Michaels' voice had already been heard nationally (and internationally) by baseball fans for five straight days: The Cincinnati Reds' radio broadcasts of the NLCS had been simulcast by both NBC Radio and American Forces Radio. Near the dramatic conclusion of Game Five, Michaels quaintly apologized to his suddenly wide-ranging audience if his understandable bias for the Reds may have come across in any of his descriptions of those games.

Moore and Michaels would individually work alongside Gowdy and Kubek for his team's home games—and then do radio work with the very capable Jim Simpson for the other games for NBC radio. Baseball fans were getting quality announcers for their sport's premier event.

# Game One

## *Tenace, Anyone?*

**Date:** Saturday, October 14, 1972
**Site:** Riverfront Stadium, Cincinnati, Ohio

> "It's a pleasure to play Oakland. In fact, it's a pleasure to play anyone in the World Series. I won't have any trouble getting up for this one. I know how important it is. I know what's at stake."[1]—Gary Nolan, Cincinnati's Game One starter's pregame comments

> "Any time a batter hits a home run, he hits a pitcher's mistake—and I see a lot of that behind the plate. Tenace hit a curveball that hung and a couple of sliders that didn't slide. But Gene knew what to do when he got those mistakes, and that's what counts."[2]—Cincinnati catcher Johnny Bench discussing Gene Tenace's home run heroics in Game One

The day before Game One began, the Oakland A's received some good news and some bad news regarding the availability of two of their most important players.

The bad news, not entirely unexpected, was that Reggie Jackson would miss the whole World Series regardless of its length. He had arrived in Cincinnati hopeful that he might get into the Series at some time, but he received the medical news that this would be impossible. (When asked if he would play in the first game, Jackson humorously responded he'd be in the lineup only if snow fell in his Arizona hometown.)

Jackson was laboring in the visitors' clubhouse at Riverfront Stadium, moving about on crutches. His injured leg was noticeably swollen. Doctors had already scolded Jackson for trying to be mobile so soon; he should not have even tested the leg for at least a week. "If this is a pulled hamstring," the 26-year-old Jackson complained, "it's as serious as a heart attack. I'm in considerable pain. I couldn't sleep last night—and there's no way I can play here."[3] Jackson used a graphic comparison when he told Ron Fimrite of *Sports Illustrated* what his leg felt like the moment he injured it. "Imagine someone reaching inside your leg," he said, "and pulling everything apart."[4] Years later Jackson would write in his autobiography, "If somebody had told me that night ... that I'd be known as Mr. October someday—that I'd set all sorts of World Series records and have the greatest night the Series had ever seen, I wouldn't have known whether to laugh or cry."[5]

During the teams' workouts the day before Game One, Johnny Bench graciously sought out Jackson to tell him that he and the other Reds wanted to play the best team the A's could field—which was now plainly impossible with Jackson sidelined. But with Jackson out of action, Cincinnati was even more confident of winning the World Series. Commissioner Kuhn gave the A's permission to activate a player to take Jackson's place in the club's 25-man lineup for the Fall Classic. They chose Allan Lewis, a speedy, pinch-running specialist.

When asked about his injury being of the heroic variety because it scored a hugely important run in the deciding game of the ALCS, the bearded Jackson replied, "I feel I helped with the run I scored." Jackson then thoughtfully considered the bigger picture: "[Playing in the World Series] means a lot of extra money for a lot of our guys. But I tell you this: I'd trade all my share for a chance to play. You dream about the World Series as a child. It's a strange feeling. This is the World Series. I'm here—but I'm not in it."[6] Jackson's absence meant that promising rookie George Hendrick would take Jackson's place in the Oakland lineup in center field. Jackson, hobbling on his crutches, entered the field with his teammates for the pregame player introductions.

Ian MacDonald of the *Montreal Gazette* opined, "There can be no minimizing Jackson's hitting and running abilities, but George Hendrick, who replaces him in center field, is a better, consistent defensive ballplayer."[7]

Almost overlooked because of Jackson's injury was a similarly catastrophic injury to the A's best relief pitcher, 30-year-old Darold Knowles, a capable lefty who had a 5–1 record in 1972 in 43 appearances and a very impressive 1.37 ERA. Knowles' unfortunate mishap occurred while he was batting on a slick field in the tenth inning of an Oakland home game versus the Minnesota Twins on Wednesday, September 27. Years later Knowles recalled,

> It had rained the night before, which was a rarity in Oakland, and the field was not in great shape. Anyway, I hit the ball. I thought when I hit it that it

had a chance to be a double. I rushed out of the [batter's] box and slipped. I jammed my thumb into the ground and broke it. [Minnesota outfielder César Tovar] caught the ball anyway. That was a low point in my life because if you play this game you want to get in the World Series; you want to perform in the World Series. But I missed it all. I was there, but I didn't have an opportunity to pitch.[8]

Oakland eventually won the game, 1–0, in 11 innings. It was a key win, putting the team 5½ games in front of the second-place Chicago White Sox with just a week remaining in the regular season. However, the loss of Knowles for the rest of 1972 had the potential to be devastating to the A's chances of doing well in the upcoming postseason.

The good news the A's received before Game One was both surprising and controversial. It was decided that shortstop Bert (Campy) Campaneris would be suspended without pay for the first week of the 1973 season for the bat-throwing incident in the ALCS, but he would be allowed to play in the 1972 World Series. Campaneris' loss of salary in 1973 was estimated to be about $3,000. Campaneris first learned about Bowie Kuhn's decision from reporters who showed him a written news release they had gotten from the Commissioner's Office. Although Kuhn noted that the ugly incident with Lerrin LaGrow was "an extremely serious and intolerable act which requires a further penalty," Kuhn decided *not* to suspend the Oakland shortstop for the premier event on the 1972 MLB calendar. Kuhn stated, "I have decided that suspending him during the World Series would unfairly penalize his innocent teammates and impair the ability of the Oakland club to perform at its best in the Series."[9]

Campaneris read the Commissioner's statement carefully, showed visible relief, and then predictably commented to reporters, "I was worried I would not be able to play in the [World] Series. I am very happy. I think it is fair."[10] Interestingly, Cincinnati's Pete Rose agreed with Kuhn's ruling; he welcomed Campaneris' inclusion in the World Series. "That's good," Rose said. "We think we can beat them—and we want to beat them with their best."[11] (Of course, Oakland truly being at "their best" would have also included both the injured Reggie Jackson and Darold Knowles in their lineup.) According to an anecdote published in *Baseball Digest* after the World Series, Rose injected some levity into the situation. When Rose managed to speak to Campaneris before Game One, he politely informed him that bats did not carry as well in Riverfront Stadium as they did in Oakland!

Campaneris did prompt a laugh shortly thereafter. When a news photographer asked him to hold a bat while posing for photos, the Oakland shortstop initially agreed and picked up the first bat he saw—and then he dropped it as if it were a red-hot coal. "Oh, no—not with a bat!"[12] he blurted.

There were 12 Reds from the 1970 lineup on their 1972 World Series roster. One was starting pitcher Gary Nolan. Starting the first game of a World Series was nothing new for Nolan. He had done the honors two years before versus Baltimore in the 1970 World Series. (That game was also contested in Cincinnati.) Nolan pitched 6⅔ innings, but he was a 4–3 loser to the Orioles that day, allowing all four Baltimore runs. When reminded of his loss to the eventual-champion Orioles, Nolan shook it off. "Our guys were a little young then," he explained, "but we know what we missed by not winning in 1970."[13] Despite having the benefit of Fall Classic experience, Nolan was not at 100 percent for Game One in 1972. He was battling a neck ailment that had been bothering him for weeks.

As always, a World Series could not open without some sort of pregame ceremony. Before Game One, the American Legion championship team from Ballwin, Missouri (a St. Louis suburb) was honored. The national anthem was played by the Roger Bacon High School marching band and sung by the recently crowned Miss America, Anne Meeuwsen. She hailed from DePere, Wisconsin (part of metropolitan Green Bay) and would assume her duties on New Year's Day 1973. MLB Com-

Despite being suspended during the ALCS for throwing his bat at Lerrin LaGrow, Oakland shortstop Bert Campaneris' controversial reinstatement for the 1972 World Series was done to not unfairly punish the rest of the A's who were already missing the injured Reggie Jackson and Darold Knowles. Campaneris' presence turned out to be insignificant. He batted just .179 in the World Series with no RBI while committing one error (Doug McWilliams/National Baseball Hall of Fame and Museum).

missioner Bowie Kuhn threw out the traditional first ball from his box seat.

Bert Campaneris was the first man to bat in the 1972 World Series. He was roundly booed, of course. The first pitch was a strike at the knees called by plate umpire Chris Pelekoudas, but the Oakland shortstop eventually singled into center field. Joe Rudi, the next batter, connected well with the first pitch he saw, but Bobby Tolan chased it down in center field for the first out. Matty Alou then looped a ball that appeared to have a chance to fall into shallow right field for a base hit. Campaneris certainly thought so. He ran on contact—only to discover that Joe Morgan, playing deep at second base, had retreated a few steps and made the simple catch. He easily doubled off Campaneris. The foolish baserunning gaffe was an inauspicious start for the visitors.

A World Series veteran, Gary Nolan was given the starting assignment for the Reds in the opener of the 1972 Fall Classic. Similar to his result versus Baltimore in 1970, Nolan lost Game One to Oakland (courtesy Cincinnati Reds Hall of Fame).

Ken Holtzman was Oakland's starting pitcher. A lefthander, Holtzman won 19 games and lost 11 in 1972. Holtzman and Gary Nolan faced each other previously: It was on June 3, 1971, when Holtzman was pitching for the Chicago Cubs. He threw a 1–0 no-hitter that day—the first one ever tossed at Riverfront Stadium. Overall, Holtzman possessed an 8–3 record versus Cincinnati from years in the NL from 1965 to 1971. Holtzman was aware of his fine record versus the Reds, but he also knew his no-hitter was the only complete game he had ever pitched versus Cincinnati.

Greeted by an enthusiastic cheer, Pete Rose led off the bottom of the first inning for the hometown Reds. He grounded out to Sal Bando at third base. Next up was Joe Morgan who was also applauded loudly. Morgan smacked a ground ball to first baseman Mike Epstein who made an unassisted putout. Bobby Tolan then grounded out to Bert Campaneris who made a long throw to narrowly nip the swift Tolan at first base. The first inning of the 1972 World Series had produced no runs.

Mike Epstein led off the second inning for Oakland. He drove a Gary Nolan fastball about 370 feet to right field, causing the hometown fans to gasp, but César Gerónimo chased it down and made the catch in front of the wall. Sal Bando—frequently called "Captain Sal" by broadcaster Monte Moore—also flied out to Gerónimo. George Hendrick patiently worked Nolan for a walk. Next up for Oakland was Gene Tenace. Tenace had struggled in the ALCS, going a dismal 0-for-15, before connecting for the winning hit in Game Five in Detroit. His batting heroics continued. When Nolan served him a fastball over the heart of the plate, Tenace smashed a two-run homer. It sailed far over Pete Rose's head and well over the left field wall just under the outfield seating area. Tenace had hit just five home runs in the regular season. A native of Lucasville, Ohio, Tenace had about 15 friends and family in the ballpark for Game One to cheer him on. Dick Green quickly lined to Denis Menke at third base for the third out, but the damage was done. Oakland was in front, 2–0.

Johnny Bench, a 40-home-run man in 1972, led off the bottom of the second inning. He thought he had drawn a walk on a 3–1 pitch from Ken Holtzman and started for first base. However, plate umpire Chris Pelekoudas called the borderline pitch a strike. Displeased but undeterred, Bench fouled off the next pitch, and then drilled a single into left field. The next Cincinnati batter, Tony Pérez, also connected for a single to left field. Bench stopped at second base. Suddenly the Reds had two men on base with nobody out. Denis Menke was the next Red to face Holtzman. He drew a walk to load the bases. With no one out, a big inning for the Reds was a distinct possibility.

César Gerónimo was the next Cincinnati batter. On a 1–0 pitch, Gerónimo lofted a pop up that was easily playable by Bert Campaneris. The infield fly rule was invoked, but the Oakland shortstop made the routine catch for the first out. No runners advanced. Dave Concepción came to bat next for Cincinnati. On a 2–2 pitch he hit a ground ball to Campaneris. Playing deep, Campaneris had to charge at the ball to make the play at second base to retire Menke, but the hustling Concepción spoiled the potential double play by beating Dick Green's relay throw to first base—and earning an RBI for his efforts. Bench scored on the fielder's choice and narrowed Oakland's lead to 2–1. It wasn't exactly what the Reds' supporters had wished for, but they still applauded their team getting on the scoreboard. Tony Pérez moved to third base on the play. The home team's rally ended when pitcher Gary Nolan came to bat and promptly struck out swinging. Oakland had survived a big scare; only minimal damage had been inflicted upon the AL champions.

Ken Holtzman, who pitched with his left hand but was a righthanded hitter, led off the top of the third inning. He made good contact, but he flied out to Pete Rose in left field. Bert Campaneris was the next Oakland batter. He got his second hit of Game One, lining a single past Denis Menke into left field. Including Game Two of the ALCS, it was Campaneris' fifth consecutive postseason hit. With Joe Rudi batting, Campaneris attempted to steal second base when Gary Nolan threw an off-speed pitch. The A's discovered the stories about Johnny Bench's arm strength were all true. Bench nailed Campaneris with a perfect throw to Joe Morgan. "I want to tell you, that takes some kind of arm," declared NBC Radio's Jim Simpson, "when you throw a changeup-curve to have a man gun down Campaneris at second base."[14] Shortly thereafter, Rudi grounded to Denis Menke at third base to end the visitors' half of the third inning. The score remained 2–1 in favor of Oakland.

Before the Reds batted in the bottom of the third inning, the sell-out crowd at Riverfront Stadium was entertained by The Swingers—the Oakland A's Dixieland band colorfully decked out in Kelly green and gold. They got a rousing, appreciative cheer from the Cincinnati fans when they completed their number. Pete Rose, who had 198 hits in the regular season and batted .450 in the NLCS, made Oakland third baseman Sal Bando work for the first out of the inning. He hit a ground ball that took a high bounce on the artificial turf. Bando had to wait for the ball to descend, but his quick throw still managed to beat Rose to first base. Next up was Joe Morgan. He hit a tricky, sinking line drive to Joe Rudi in left field. It was caught for the second out. Bobby Tolan got Cincinnati's third hit of the game by driving a ball over shortstop Bert Campaneris' head. Shortly thereafter, Tolan was erased from the bases by a fine pickoff throw by Ken Holtzman. Tolan was caught in a rundown and was eventually tagged out at second base by Dick Green for the inning's third out. A smattering of boos rained down on Tolan as he exited the field after the 1–3–4 putout.

Matty Alou led off the top of the fourth inning for Oakland. Alou was not known as a power hitter. In fact, just eight of his 161 hits in 1972 went for extra bases. He grounded out to pitcher Gary Nolan. Mike Epstein hit a check-swing ground ball to third baseman Denis Menke who made the easy play to first base for the second out. Sal Bando made it three quick outs for Oakland with a fly ball to Joe Morgan who caught it in shallow right-center field.

Johnny Bench, who scored the lone Cincinnati run in the second inning, was the first batter to face Ken Holtzman in the bottom of the fourth. Both teams had squabbles with plate umpire Chris Pelekoudas during Bench's plate appearance. As had happened earlier, Bench believed he had drawn a walk on a 3–1 pitch, but it was called a strike. Holtzman then thought his following pitch to Bench was strike three, but Pelekoudas ruled it to be ball four. With the free pass, Bench was aboard for the second time in the game. Tony Pérez gave the Cincinnati fans hope by slapping a single just under second baseman Dick Green's glove. Bench moved to third base on the hit, giving the Reds runners on the corners with nobody out. Riverfront Stadium came to life again. Denis Menke hit a ground ball to Bert Campaneris. The throw to second base retired Pérez, but Menke was safe at first as Bench scored another run for the home team. The game was tied, 2–2. Both Cincinnati runs had been scored by Johnny Bench—and both had come via unspectacular infield outs.

César Gerónimo batted next. His ground ball to the right side of the infield was a bit of a challenge for Oakland second baseman Dick Green. Denis Menke, the Cincinnati runner on first base, was on the move when Holtzman pitched to Gerónimo. Green initially moved toward second base but had to abruptly reverse his course to field the ball. Nevertheless, Green skillfully corralled the bouncing ball and threw to first baseman Mike Epstein to retire Gerónimo for the second out as Menke advanced to second base. With first base open and two outs, the A's opted to intentionally walk Dave Concepción and pitch to Cincinnati pitcher Gary Nolan. Oakland's strategy was booed by the record home crowd of 52,918, of course, but it was sound baseball. The plan worked. Nolan struck out swinging on a breaking ball. After four full innings, Game One of the 1972 World Series was level.

George Hendrick faced Gary Nolan to start the top of the fifth inning. His ground ball to second baseman Joe Morgan resulted in an extremely close play at first base. The Reds got the benefit of the doubt as AL umpire Jim Honochick called Hendrick out. Oakland's Dick Williams did not like Honochick's call at all and came onto the field briefly to let him know it. Television replays were inconclusive, prompting Monte Moore on NBC Radio to comment to his partner Jim Simpson, "Which proves, Jim, that even if the umpires had videotape replays, they couldn't always tell."[15]

Gene Tenace began the 1972 season as the backup catcher for Oakland, but he was given the opportunity to shine in the postseason. He did not disappoint. Tenace's four home runs and nine RBI in the World Series dwarfed his regular-season numbers (five homers and 32 RBI in 82 games) and paved the way to his winning the coveted MVP award (courtesy Cincinnati Reds Hall of Fame).

The dispute over Honochick's decision was quickly forgotten after Gene Tenace's at-bat. He achieved a World Series first: He solidly hit a hanging curveball from Nolan. It sailed down the left-field line just inside the foul pole. It was Tenace's second home run of the game. Thus, he became the first player in nearly seven decades of modern World Series history to swat homers in his first two Fall Classic at-bats. It was also the first time Tenace had homered twice in a game in 1972. The last man before Tenace to homer twice in a World Series game was Rico Petrocelli of the Boston Red Sox who did it in Game Six of the 1967 Fall Classic. Oakland's Dick Williams had a splendid view of Petrocelli's pair of clouts; he was Boston's manager in that World Series.

Dick Green flied out to Bobby Tolan in center field for out number two. Ken Holtzman, who had a decent batting average for a pitcher (.178), drove a fly ball to deep left field that was caught by Pete Rose for the final out of the frame. Thanks entirely to Gene Tenace's two home runs, Oakland had retaken the lead in Game One, 3–2.

Pete Rose started the bottom of the fifth inning by driving a Holtzman 0–1 offering 400 feet to deep center field. The crowd let out a hopeful cheer, but the ball was casually grabbed by George Hendrick. Joe Morgan struck out, although it took a throw from Tenace to Mike Epstein at first base to retire him on a dropped third strike. Bobby Tolan also failed to get a hit off Holtzman. He flied out to Joe Rudi in left field.

The top of the Oakland batting order confronted Gary Nolan in the top of the sixth inning. Bert Campaneris ripped a line drive at Reds third baseman Denis Menke. The 6'2" Menke had to leap adroitly to make the catch, pleasing the Reds' faithful. Joe Rudi was the next man up for Oakland. He hit a 3–1 pitch that was hauled in by César Gerónimo in right field. Matty Alou walked. The fourth ball got by Bench, but Alou wisely stopped at first base. Mike Epstein, who had once played football at the University of California, followed Alou to the plate. He grounded out to Joe Morgan at second base to conclude the inning.

Johnny Bench strode to the plate to begin the Cincinnati half of the sixth inning. It was the third time in the game he had led off an inning—and for the third time he reached base. This time he connected with a standup double that rattled off the right-field fence. Bench was the last batter Ken Holtzman faced. Dick Williams opted to replace him with Rollie Fingers. (The graphic on NBC's television coverage formally called him "Roland Fingers.") Fingers was born in Steubenville, Ohio, but his family had moved to California before Fingers' tenth birthday. Still, the 26-year-old Fingers had extended family members in the ballpark rooting for him.

The first Red that Fingers faced was Tony Pérez. Fingers struck him out. Denis Menke was the next Cincinnati batter. He also went down on strikes. César Gerónimo fared slightly better than Pérez and Menke, but he was retired, too. Gerónimo hit a line drive that was caught by left fielder Joe Rudi. The inning concluded with Bench still stationed at second base, his double wasted. Oakland still retained its 3–2 lead after six innings. The visitors' confidence was growing.

Gary Nolan was removed from the game by Sparky Anderson after six innings of decent work. He had given up just four Oakland hits— but two of them were Gene Tenace's home runs that had accounted for all the visitors' scoring. Pedro Borbón replaced Nolan on the mound for Cincinnati. Displaying an excellent sinking fastball that consistently produced a bevy of ground balls throughout 1972, Borbón had a very efficient top of the seventh inning. Sal Bando grounded out to second baseman Joe Morgan. George Hendrick grounded out to Borbón. The third man to face Borbón was Gene Tenace. He did not homer this time. The hot Oakland catcher was finally cooled down, grounding out to Dave Concepción at shortstop on a check swing. Oakland's lead in Game One remained 3–2.

Dave Concepción faced Rollie Fingers to start the home half of the seventh inning. He lined a 3–2 pitch into left field for a base hit. Ted Uhlaender batted for Pedro Borbón. Uhlaender had a poor batting average but he was an excellent bunter. With one strike on Uhlaender, Dave Concepción tried to steal second base. The A's anticipated the move and called for a pitchout. On a close play at second base, Concepción was called out by NL umpire Mel Steiner and briefly argued the point. (Television replays showed Steiner's call to be wrong; Concepción had slid under Bert Campaneris' high tag.) Uhlaender struck out, but Pete Rose drew a four-pitch walk. With Joe Morgan coming to bat, Dick Williams decided to bring in Vida Blue to replace Fingers.

Vida Blue was an unhappy member of the A's pitching staff. After making a paltry $14,750 in 1971 when he was named the AL MVP, the 22-year-old Blue wanted a $75,000 salary for 1972—a sizable amount that he figured he deserved. Blue's agent, a lawyer named Bob Gerst, had an even loftier figure in mind: $115,000. Charlie Finley countered with an offer of $45,000 or $50,000, depending on which newspaper one read. Blue was so miffed over the impasse that he considered retirement rather than playing in 1972. He held out through spring training and into the first week of May—threatening to quit baseball altogether. Blue claimed he had another job lined up and was fully prepared to embark on a new career far from the limelight of professional sports. (Apparently, Blue had been offered the vice-presidency of a company that manufactured toilets!) With Blue ready to go, Commissioner Bowie Kuhn, fearing that MLB might witness one of its brightest new stars and gate attractions go down the drain, got personally involved in the pitcher's salary negotiations with Finley. A compromise was reached: Blue signed for $63,000 to play for the A's in 1972. Flushed with success, Blue left the toilet business ... behind. Despite the hefty raise in pay from 1971, the squabble created a negative aura for the AL's reigning MVP. "Charlie Finley has soured my stomach on baseball,"[16] he gruffly told the media on May 6. Joe Falls of *The Sporting News* was unimpressed by Blue's demeanor at the press conference. He wrote, "[Blue] seemed to be laughing at all of us and he seemed to take every tack he could think of—smirking, sneering, yawning—to show his contempt for the whole affair."[17]

Blue had fared poorly in the tail end of the regular season in 1972, winning just one of his final eight starts. Accordingly, Dick Williams had chosen not to have Blue start in any of the five ALCS games—although he did fine work in an unfamiliar role as a reliever. Still, Blue was rumored to be the starting pitcher in Game Four in Oakland, so his appearance in Game One as a reliever was somewhat surprising. It did not start especially well. The second pitch Blue threw to Morgan went through catcher Gene Tenace's legs. It was scored a wild pitch and it put Pete Rose on second base with two out. Morgan drew a walk. Bobby Tolan came to bat for Cincinnati. Blue—who stylishly sported a blue baseball glove—got his team out of a major jam by coaxing Tolan to pop up to Tenace.

Clay Carroll, who had accrued an MLB record 37 saves for Cincinnati in 1972, was the new Cincinnati pitcher in the top of the eighth inning. (Carroll had easily been the best pitcher for the Reds during the 1970 World Series versus Baltimore. He did not allow a run in the nine innings he pitched in four games versus the Orioles.) The first A's batter he faced was a pinch hitter, Gonzalo Márquez. On the first pitch Márquez saw, he flied out to shortstop Dave Concepción in short left field. Vida Blue stayed in the game and batted. Blue had just two hits in 45 at-bats in 1972, but he drew a walk off Carroll. Bert Campaneris bunted Blue to second base. There he stayed because Joe Rudi flied out to Pete Rose in left field for the third out.

Vida Blue faced Johnny Bench to start the bottom of the eighth inning. On the first pitch, Bench jolted a ball to right field—but not far enough. It was caught by Matty Alou for a quick out. Tony Pérez was the next Red to bat. He made solid contact, but he too flied out. George Hendrick made the catch in center field. Blue completed a perfect inning as Denis Menke struck out. With an inning to play, Oakland was still clinging to its tenuous one-run lead.

In the top of the ninth inning, Matty Alou hit the first pitch he saw from Clay Carroll on the ground to Joe Morgan at second base. Alou was retired easily for the first out. Mike Epstein was the next Oakland batter. He drew a four-pitch walk. Epstein was replaced by Allan Lewis—a pinch-running specialist who had been elevated to the A's from the minors late in the 1972 season. With Sal Bando batting, Lewis broke for second base on Carroll's first pitch. He was thrown out by Johnny Bench for the second out. Sal Bando struck out swinging to end the top of the ninth.

Cincinnati had three outs left to try to salvage Game One. The Reds had the bottom of their order scheduled to face Vida Blue. Mike Hegan, a good defensive player, was now stationed at first base for Oakland. Sparky Anderson sent up Hal McRae, a righthanded pinch hitter with a fine .278 batting average in 1972, to bat for César Gerónimo. Blue got ahead of McRae in the count 0–2, but the pinch hitter knocked a single into left field on a hanging curveball. Anderson made another move: George Foster, who scored the winning run for the Reds in the NLCS against Pittsburgh, was sent in to run for McRae. The next batter, Dave Concepción, successfully dropped a sacrifice bunt between third base and the pitcher's mound. Sal Bando threw to new second baseman Ted Kubiak (another defensive replacement), who was covering first base, for the putout. Sparky Anderson made yet another move: Julián Javier, who had excellent World Series for the St. Louis Cardinals in both 1967 and 1968, batted in the pitcher's spot. "This has been a well-played, very exciting first game of the 1972 World Series,"[18] said Monte Moore just before Javier grounded out to Kubiak. George Foster moved to third base on the fielder's choice.

With two out and George Foster at third base, the game's outcome now rode on Pete Rose's at-bat. Rose, batting right, tried to bunt the first pitch, but it went foul. On the next pitch he hit a high bouncer to Kubiak. The second baseman's throw nipped Rose at first base to end the game. Kubiak had figured in every out in the bottom of the ninth inning with two assists and a putout. Oakland, the visiting team, had defied the oddsmakers and had taken the first game of the 1972 World Series in a 3–2 nail-biter.

History was now on the side of the Oakland A's. Statistics showed that in the previous 68 World Series of the modern era, the team that won Game One had won the Fall Classic 40 times—nearly 59 percent of the time. Recently, however, initial success did not mean very much: the teams that had dropped the World Series opener in 1968, 1969 and 1971 had all triumphed in the end.

Prior to the 1972 World Series, there had been eight players who had homered in their first at-bat in MLB's grandest showcase: Dusty Rhodes, Elston Howard, Roger Maris, Don Mincher (who was on the 1972 A's roster), Brooks Robinson, José Santiago (a pitcher!), Mickey Lolich (another pitcher!), and Don Buford. None of those men homered in his second World Series at-bat. Gene Tenace did. Gary Nolan was an unlikely target for Tenace's home run prowess. Not one opposing batter in 1972 had hit two homers off him in the whole season, much less in a single game. In compiling a fine 15–5 record that year, Nolan had only allowed multiple home runs in a game twice.

Some writers thought Tenace appeared cocky after belting his second home run. He lingered at the plate, transfixed, as he watched the ball sail into the stands. "I wasn't showing off," Tenace insisted. "I just wasn't sure the ball would stay fair—and I wanted to help it all I could."[19] As Tenace was answering reporters' questions, happy owner Charlie O. Finley approached him and whispered something into his catcher's ear that brought a broad smile to his face. Finley apparently told Tenace his record-setting performance had just earned him a $5,000 bonus.

Pete Rose, who was retired for the last out of the game, bemoaned his team's lost opportunities in Game One. "The A's pitchers kept me, Morgan and Tolan from hitting, with the exception of Tolan's single," he stated. "As a result, Johnny Bench led off an inning four times. His single, double and walk did not move anybody around. When Bench and Pérez get two hits apiece, we should score some runs, but only if Bobby, Joe and I get on base. That's how we won all year."[20]

Ken Holtzman agreed with Rose. "That was the big thing today," Holtzman noted, "keeping those first three guys off base. That meant we could afford to challenge Johnny [Bench] with no one on base. If he hit it out, it would be just one run."[21]

The Oakland players had no trouble adjusting to playing on Riverfront Stadium's artificial turf, according to Dal Maxvill, who, as a reserve player, did not figure to see too much playing time in the World Series. "Fellows like Campy Campaneris and Sal Bando like it because of the true bounces and because the ball gets to them faster,"[22] Maxvill said.

Although Cincinnati's much-heralded Johnny Bench had two hits in Game One, the generally unknown Gene Tenace had clearly been the star performer. Accordingly, the *Montreal Gazette* ran an amusing headline over its World Series coverage: "The 'Other Catcher' Leads A's." Bench himself said, "If there was going to be a catcher hitting two home runs, I was kind of hoping it would be me."[23]

Sparky Anderson was asked if the Reds' scouting reports had erred regarding how to pitch to Gene Tenace. Anderson said, "The first homer came off a fastball out over the plate. The second was a hanging curve. No scouting report is going to help with either of those pitches."[24]

All acrimony had subsided between Vida Blue and Charlie Finley—at least according to the A's omnipresent owner. "We couldn't ask anything more of Blue," Finley told reporters after the 1971 MVP recorded the save in Game One. "Vida Blue has done one great job in the playoffs and World Series. Here's a pitcher who has never been anything but a starter and becomes a reliever almost overnight. You don't make relievers that way. Blue has contributed immeasurably to this club."[25]

Blue himself had told the media before Game One that he was only pitching for himself—not for the team or its manager. He softened his stance somewhat after Oakland's victory. "This game is a business and pitching is my job," he said. "[The game] starts when I have the ball. We won this one for Oakland."[26]

# Box Score: Game #1
## Oakland Athletics 3, Cincinnati Reds 2
Game played on Saturday, October 14, 1972, at Riverfront Stadium

| Oakland Athletics | ab | r | h | rbi | Cincinnati Reds | ab | r | h | rbi |
|---|---|---|---|---|---|---|---|---|---|
| Campaneris ss | 3 | 0 | 2 | 0 | Rose lf | 4 | 0 | 0 | 0 |
| Rudi lf | 4 | 0 | 0 | 0 | Morgan 2b | 3 | 0 | 0 | 0 |
| Alou rf | 3 | 0 | 0 | 0 | Tolan cf | 4 | 0 | 1 | 0 |
| Epstein 1b | 3 | 0 | 0 | 0 | Bench c | 3 | 2 | 2 | 0 |
| Lewis pr | 0 | 0 | 0 | 0 | Pérez 1b | 4 | 0 | 2 | 0 |
| Hegan 1b | 0 | 0 | 0 | 0 | Menke 3b | 3 | 0 | 0 | 1 |
| Bando 3b | 4 | 0 | 0 | 0 | Gerónimo rf | 3 | 0 | 0 | 0 |
| Hendrick cf | 2 | 1 | 0 | 0 | McRae ph | 1 | 0 | 1 | 0 |
| Tenace c | 3 | 2 | 2 | 3 | Foster pr | 0 | 0 | 0 | 0 |
| Green 2b | 2 | 0 | 0 | 0 | Concepción ss | 2 | 0 | 1 | 1 |
| Marquez ph | 1 | 0 | 0 | 0 | Nolan p | 2 | 0 | 0 | 0 |
| Kubiak 2b | 0 | 0 | 0 | 0 | Borbón p | 0 | 0 | 0 | 0 |
| Holtzman p | 2 | 0 | 0 | 0 | Uhlaender ph | 1 | 0 | 0 | 0 |
| Fingers p | 0 | 0 | 0 | 0 | Carroll p | 0 | 0 | 0 | 0 |
| Blue p | 0 | 0 | 0 | 0 | Javier ph | 1 | 0 | 0 | 0 |
| **Totals** | 27 | 3 | 4 | 3 | **Totals** | 31 | 2 | 7 | 2 |

| | | | | | | | | | | | | | |
|---|---|---|---|---|---|---|---|---|---|---|---|---|---|
| Oakland | 0 | 2 | 0 | 0 | 1 | 0 | 0 | 0 | 0 | — | 3 | 4 | 0 |
| Cincinnati | 0 | 1 | 0 | 1 | 0 | 0 | 0 | 0 | 0 | — | 2 | 7 | 0 |

| Oakland Athletics | IP | H | R | ER | BB | SO |
|---|---|---|---|---|---|---|
| Holtzman W (1–0) | 5.0 | 5 | 2 | 2 | 3 | 3 |
| Fingers | 1.2 | 1 | 0 | 0 | 1 | 3 |
| Blue SV (1) | 2.1 | 1 | 0 | 0 | 1 | 1 |
| **Totals** | 9.0 | 7 | 2 | 2 | 5 | 7 |
| Cincinnati Reds | IP | H | R | ER | BB | SO |
| Nolan L (0–1) | 6.0 | 4 | 3 | 3 | 2 | 0 |
| Borbón | 1.0 | 0 | 0 | 0 | 0 | 0 |
| Carroll | 2.0 | 0 | 0 | 0 | 2 | 1 |
| **Totals** | 9.0 | 4 | 3 | 3 | 4 | 1 |

E—None. DP—Cincinnati 1. 2B—Cincinnati Bench (1, off Holtzman). HR—Oakland Tenace 2 (2, 2nd inning off Nolan 1 on, 2 out, 5th inning off Nolan 0 on, 1 out). SH—Campaneris (1, off Carroll); Concepción (1, off Blue). IBB—Concepción (1, by Holtzman). CS—Campaneris (1, 2nd base by Nolan/Bench); Lewis (1, 2nd base by Carroll/Bench); Concepción (1, 2nd base by Fingers/Tenace). WP—Blue (1). IBB—Holtzman (1,Concepción). U—Chris Pelekoudas (NL), Jim Honochick (AL), Mel Steiner (NL), Frank Umont (AL), Bill Haller (AL), Bob Engel (NL). T—2:18. A—52,918.

# Game Two

## *Rudi to the Rescue*

**Date:** Sunday, October 15, 1972
**Site:** Riverfront Stadium, Cincinnati, Ohio

> "Oh, what a catch Joe Rudi made! And since it came in the setting of a World Series, it will never be forgotten. It shouldn't."[1]—Bob Smizik, *Pittsburgh Press*

> "The Big Red Machine has stalled. It may have run out of gas in the emotion-drenched [NLCS]. More likely it is simply a case of superb Oakland Athletic pitchers jamming the gears."[2]—Ian MacDonald, *Montreal Gazette*

Jim Simpson of NBC radio called it "topcoat and turtleneck weather."[3] On a sun-splashed but chilly Sunday afternoon at Riverfront Stadium, Cincinnati's young lefthander, Ross Grimsley, was handed the ball for Game Two by manager Sparky Anderson. He had been brilliant in the fourth game of the NLCS, utterly stifling the Pittsburgh Pirates. (Grimsley had admitted to the press that he was irked that he had not been given the pitching assignment in the second game versus Pittsburgh.) For a 22-year-old rookie, Grimsley had an unusual allotment of spunk. Perhaps he was entitled to be on the cocky side. Reds pitching coach Larry Shepard informed NBC's Tony Kubek that, in his opinion, Grimsley had the best all-around stuff of any pitcher on the Cincinnati staff.

A special pregame ceremony was held to recognize the 25th anniversary of Jackie Robinson's historic 1947 season in which he became the first black man to play major league baseball since Moses Fleetwood Walker in 1884. As a nice touch, ex–Dodger broadcaster Red Barber served as the on-field emcee. The 53-year-old Robinson, in a clear voice despite declining health, spoke for only about a minute. He thanked Commissioner Bowie Kuhn for the honor and expressed sadness that

Branch Rickey—the late baseball executive whose behind-the-scenes work largely made his MLB career possible—was not alive to witness the festivities. He modestly called himself a minor spoke in the success the Brooklyn Dodgers experienced 25 years previously. Robinson concluded his speech by saying it was his sincerest hope to one day see a black man in the third-base coach's box at a major league game. [Authors' note: For many years it was typical for a baseball team's manager to also serve as its third-base coach. That custom was slowly dying out by 1972.] Robinson was then escorted to the Commissioner's box where he threw out the ceremonial first pitch to Johnny Bench. Two of Robinson's old Dodger teammates—Pee Wee Reese and Joe Black—were present to witness the ceremony. So was Larry Doby, the first black ballplayer in the AL. Because of diabetes, Robinson's eyesight was severely failing. He sadly told an Associated Press reporter, "It's difficult for me to watch a game now. I don't know where the ball is. I don't react at all."[4] It was Robinson's last public appearance.

In the stands to watch his son pitch for the Reds was Ross Grimsley, Sr. The elder Grimsley, also a left hander, had been a big-league pitcher too, albeit briefly, 21 years before. As a reliever he appeared in seven games for the 1951 Chicago White Sox. (He compiled a 0–0 record with a 3.86 ERA in his lone MLB season.) The elder Ross Grimsley had been

**Ross Grimsley was given the starting assignment for the Reds in Game Two. He had never lost an MLB game when his father, a former White Sox pitcher, was present in the stands (courtesy Cincinnati Reds Hall of Fame).**

present on five previous occasions to watch his son pitch for the Reds. Cincinnati had won each of those games.

Oakland's starting pitcher was the very efficient and underrated Jim (Catfish) Hunter. The 26-year-old acquired his terrific nickname once he signed a $75,000 major league contract with the Athletics. Perhaps "acquired" is not quite an accurate verb. Team owner Charles O. Finley independently decided his hurler from North Carolina (who enjoyed hunting and fishing) needed a countrified nickname because Jim Hunter was simply too bland for a marquee baseball player. It lacked pizzazz. Thus, Finley bestowed the moniker "Catfish" on his gifted righthander. Finley conveniently provided Hunter with all the fictitious background details in case reporters asked about it: As a small boy of five or six, little Jim Hunter had run away from home one morning. When he returned that night, he had a string of catfish that he had caught while fishing all day. There was zero truth to the story whatsoever, but Hunter, as ordered by Finley, repeated it for years when asked to explain how he came to be called Catfish. Although he remained plain old Jim Hunter to his family, friends and neighbors in Hertford, North Carolina, Finley's memorable concocted nickname stuck with him until the day Jim Hunter died.

The large Ohio State University marching band played the national anthem. Tony Martin, bedecked in a pink suit, sang the lyrics. As it was departing the field, the band struck up "Buckeye Battle Cry"—the familiar and catchy OSU fight song.

Bert Campaneris led off Game Two for Oakland against Ross Grimsley. He was greeted with a noticeable round of boos from the Riverfront Stadium crowd—but not as many catcalls as had been the case in Game One. With the nasty incident involving Lerrin LaGrow from the ALCS lingering long in fans' minds, NBC's Curt Gowdy duly noted, "Campaneris expected to be booed yesterday. He was. He hopes they'll die out."[5] Al Michaels chimed in, "He'll be suspended the first week of the regular season in 1973." Stating the obvious with Campaneris standing in the righthanded batter's box, Michaels added, "But he is eligible for the World Series."[6]

Grimsley's first toss was a strike called by umpire Jim Honochick. The 55-year-old arbiter had been an AL umpire since 1949. The partisan crowd roared its approval. On the fifth Grimsley offering, Campaneris hit an easy hopper to second baseman Joe Morgan. Morgan casually made the routine throw to first baseman Tony Pérez for the game's first out.

Matty Alou batted second for Oakland. A newcomer to the AL, Alou had broken into the majors with the San Francisco Giants in 1960.

Acquired by the Pirates in 1966, Alou won the league batting championship that same year with a solid .342 average. He hit a slow chopper to third baseman Denis Menke who fielded the ball near the pitcher's mound. Menke's accurate throw to Pérez retired Alou.

Joe Rudi was the third member of the A's to face Grimsley. On the first pitch he saw, Rudi found a hole in the Cincinnati infield, slapping a single into left field. Pete Rose retrieved the ball and swiftly fired it back into the infield. The hit snapped an 0-for-13 slump for Rudi. It was a harbinger of positive things to come from Oakland's left fielder.

James (Catfish) Hunter dominated in the 1972 World Series with two wins, 16 innings pitched, 11 strikeouts, and a respectable ERA of 2.81. He would become a familiar face in the World Series, appearing in six of the seven Fall Classics between 1972 and 1978 for Oakland and the New York Yankees (Doug McWilliams/ National Baseball Hall of Fame and Museum).

Clean-up hitter Mike Epstein came up next. The A's power-hitting first baseman had batted .188 in the ALCS. He got a reprieve when Denis Menke failed to catch his high pop-up on a 2–2 pitch in foul territory. Menke seemed a trifle hesitant in pursuing the ball that landed near the visitors' on-field bullpen area, pulling up several feet before reaching the unpadded fence separating the fans from the playing field. The ball harmlessly fell to earth within inches of his extended glove. Epstein did not take advantage of his second life, however. He struck out swinging on an off-speed pitch with the count full. Joe Rudi was stranded at first base.

Pete Rose, batted left against righthanded Oakland pitcher Jim (Catfish) Hunter to lead off the home half of the first inning. As Hunter prepared to face Rose, Curt Gowdy said of the A's superb starter, "[He's] very underrated nationally. A 20-game winner the last two seasons, he really battles you. Hunter doesn't look overpowering from the stands or from your TV, but he moves the ball up and down, in and out, different speeds, around the plate. And when he gets two strikes on you, he doesn't mess around."[7] Hunter's 2.04 ERA during the 1972 regular season was a testament to Gowdy's praise. His 21–7 record gave him the best winning percentage (.750) among all AL starting pitchers.

Rose was looking for his first hit of the 1972 World series having gone 0-for-4 in Saturday's opener. He was 0-for-5 after lofting a fly ball into the outfield on Hunter's first offering to him. Oakland shortstop Bert Campaneris backpedaled furiously into shallow left field. He was sensibly called off by Joe Rudi who made an easy catch for the first out.

Second baseman Joe Morgan was the next Red to face Hunter. Oakland third baseman Sal Bando, realizing that Morgan was an excellent bunter, positioned himself in front of the bag. Morgan did not put the ball into play, however. He struck out swinging.

Bobby Tolan batted third for Cincinnati. The tall, lefthanded hitter possessed a quirky batting technique, as NBC's Al Michaels acknowledged in his commentary. "A lot of people think [Tolan] has a hitch in his swing," said Michaels, "but with his average, I guess you call it style, don't you?"[8] Tolan, who had missed the entire 1971 season with an Achilles tendon tear he suffered in an offseason charity basketball game, rebounded to bat .282 for Cincinnati in 1972—despite reinjuring his foot in May. Tolan did not look especially threatening in his first at-bat of Game Two. He missed the ball completely on a bunt attempt, and then, with two strikes on him, Tolan was called out on half swing. Tolan clearly offered at Hunter's pitch in the dirt, but apparently hoped that umpire Honochick did not see it that way. The ball squirted away from Oakland catcher Gene Tenace for a moment, but Tolan did not budge, remaining in the batter's box. Honochick checked with third-base umpire Bob Engel who affirmed that Tolan had indeed swung at Hunter's extremely low pitch. Tenace retrieved the ball and was pleased to find that Tolan had not moved. Tolan was tagged out by Tenace to complete the delayed putout and end the bottom of the first. There was no score after one inning of play.

Sal Bando was the first man up for Oakland in the top of the second inning. Al Michaels noted that Bando, a native of Cleveland, was one of several MLB players who were products of Arizona State University's baseball program. (Reggie Jackson was another.) Bando's bat had gone cold in the postseason—he was 4-for-20 in the ALCS; all four hits were singles. Bando was hoping to get back on track in Game Two. Something clicked. Bando rapped a base hit into center field.

Righthanded George Hendrick followed Bando to the plate to face Ross Grimsley. Despite having a meagre .182 batting average from only 58 MLB games in 1972, Curt Gowdy lauded the promising 22-year-old. "There isn't a club in baseball that wouldn't take him. He has all the physical tools."[9] On the first pitch he saw, Hendrick hit a bounding ball that deflected off Grimsley's glove toward second baseman Joe Morgan. Morgan was close enough to second base to make an underhand toss to shortstop Darrel Chaney who was covering the bag. Bando was out easily. Chaney's throw to first baseman Tony Pérez, however, was a little bit late to catch the swift Hendrick who was properly called safe by NL umpire Mel Steiner. Typical of the times, Bando had veered well off the basepath in an attempt to upend Chaney and disrupt his throw to first base. "It's really illegal," Gowdy said of Sando's mildly malicious baserunning, "but you see it all the time around second base."[10] However, it was Grimsley deflection more than Bando's baserunning that was responsible for the Reds not turning a double play. Hendrick turned out to be a significant baserunner in the top of the second inning.

Gene Tenace, the surprise hitting star of Game One, was the next batter. Like Hendrick, Tenace connected on the first pitch he saw from Grimsley. He lofted a fly ball to shallow left field. Both left fielder Pete Rose and center fielder Bobby Tolan moved in pursuit of the ball. Rose made the catch. Two A's were now out.

Oakland's 31-year-old second baseman, Dick Green, was up next. He had played in just 26 games in 1972 due to surgery on a herniated disc in his back. Green hit an 0–1 delivery past Grimsley that skipped into center field. Bobby Tolan quickly fielded the hit, forcing Hendrick to halt at second base. The A's were mounting a two-out rally but their number-nine hitter, pitcher Catfish Hunter, was coming to bat. Hunter was no slouch with the lumber, however. In fact, he was one of baseball's best hitting pitchers. Hunter batted a respectable .219 in 1972 with five RBI and had gotten hits in 10 of the previous 12 games he had started. He had managed 11 hits in his last 31 plate appearances—a heady .355 clip. Clearly, Hunter was not an automatic out.

Hunter delivered some timely offense, smacking Grimsley's second pitch—a curveball—into left field. It was well out of reach of Reds shortstop Darrel Chaney who was playing very close to second base. The fleet Hendrick had no intention of stopping at third base. Making a sharp turn, he rumbled toward home plate. Pete Rose's throw from the outfield was accurate but it was not in time to get Hendrick. (Johnny Bench also bobbled Rose's throw as he attempted to apply a quick tag before he truly had possession of the ball.) Hendrick slid home with the game's first run. Green moved to second base. Catfish Hunter, standing on first base with a grin on his face, had his first World Series hit and RBI. Oakland led Game Two, 1–0. Grimsley had already surrendered four hits to the A's in just 1⅔ innings. That was twice the total he had allowed to Pittsburgh in the entire game during his one hugely successful start in the NLCS five days earlier. Alarmed, Sparky Anderson ordered his Dominican-born righthanded reliever, Pedro Borbón, to warm up in the Cincinnati bullpen.

Bert Campaneris, batting for the second time in the game, got the fifth Oakland hit off Grimsley. Pete Rose played the ball well in shallow left field and came up gunning when Dick Green tried to score from second base. Green, unlike Hendrick, made a broad turn at third base. It was costly to him. Rose's throw to Johnny Bench was on the mark and well ahead of Green. Bench had the ball securely in his possession when Green was still about 15 feet from home plate. Cincinnati's catcher advanced up the baseline to apply the tag. Umpire Jim Honochick made the easy out call. The two-out Oakland threat had been squelched, but the Reds still left the field trailing by just a run. They were fortunate the deficit was not greater.

The man who made the final putout of the previous inning, Johnny Bench, was the first Cincinnati man to face Catfish Hunter in the bottom of the second inning for the hometown Reds. It was the fifth time at the plate in the 1972 World Series for the popular Reds catcher. Remarkably it was also the fifth time that Bench had led off an inning! The Oakland infielders were all playing Bench especially deep. This strategy backfired when Bench reached first base on an infield single. By the time Oakland shortstop Bert Campaneris had fielded the ball and thrown it to first baseman Mike Epstein, Bench was safe by half a step.

Tony Pérez followed Bench. Hunter lost his fine control momentarily as Pérez drew a walk, pushing Bench to second base. Trouble was brewing for Oakland. With Reds third baseman Denis Menke batting, Hunter dug himself into a bigger hole when his low pickoff throw to second base skipped into center field off the slick artificial turf. Bench advanced to third on the error (charged to Hunter). Pérez advanced to second base with no one out. It was apparently Cincinnati's turn to mount a second-inning rally.

Unfazed by the series of setbacks, Hunter proceeded to retire Menke on a swinging strikeout. (Early in the count, before Hunter's throwing error, Menke had tried to bunt, but fouled off Hunter's pitch.) Oakland manager Dick Williams strolled to the mound to ask Hunter if he wanted to intentionally walk the next Red scheduled to bat, right fielder César Gerónimo. Hunter told his skipper he preferred to pitch to Gerónimo with the intent of striking him out. That was exactly what happened. Gerónimo, like Menke, went down swinging, but it was a prolonged battle. It took Hunter 11 pitches to retire him.

Switch-hitting shortstop Darrel Chaney, batting eighth for the Reds, was next up. He had batted .250 in 82 games in 1972. Amidst a chorus of boos from the hometown crowd, Dick Williams came to the mound once again to discuss strategy with Hunter. (Williams exploited a very liberalized World Series rule to the fullest, common to the era, that generously allowed managers and coaches unlimited trips to the mound during the Fall Classic. At the end of the 1972 Fall Classic, Williams had made 38 such trips.) Manager and hurler jointly agreed to walk Chaney, thus loading the bases, and take their chances with Cincinnati pitcher Ross Grimsley. "If Hunter gets out of this," NBC's Curt Gowdy noted, "it will be some kind of pitching job."[11]

Grimsley was generally not considered much of an offensive threat. In fact, his lack of hitting prowess was a source of amusement among the regulars in the Cincinnati clubhouse. (During the 1972 regular season, Grimsley had managed just eight hits in 66 at-bats. All eight hits were singles.) Somehow Grimsley had remarkably managed a single and a double in his NLCS victory over Pittsburgh. However, Grimsley reverted to the norm by striking out swinging on four pitches against Hunter. Excluding Chaney, who was intentionally passed, Hunter had whiffed three straight Reds to extricate himself form a potential disaster. Oakland kept its 1–0 advantage. The Oakland starter had struck out five Reds in just two innings.

Matty Alou led off the top of the third inning for the A's. He punched a ground ball directly at Cincinnati third baseman Denis Menke. Menke's accurate throw to Tony Pérez at first base made Alou an easy out. Joe Rudi was the next Oakland man to face Ross Grimsley. A very capable batsman, Rudi's .305 batting average was good enough for fifth place in the AL in 1972. He had led his league in hits with 181. He also swatted 19 home runs. This at-bat produced number 20. Rudi belted a 1–0 Grimsley curveball deep to left field. There was no doubt it was a home run. Pete Rose retreated only a couple of steps toward the wall as he watched the ball sail high into Riverfront Stadium's second-deck outfield seats. Rudi circled the bases to give his A's a 2–0 lead in Game Two. Oakland surprisingly had managed six hits off Grimsley already.

Mike Epstein followed Rudi to bat but he was retired quickly on a two-hopper to Tony Pérez just inside first base. Pérez efficiently made the unassisted putout. Sal Bando grounded out to shortstop Darrel Chaney to end the top of the third inning.

Pete Rose led off the bottom of the third inning by lining a single into center field off Catfish Hunter. It was Rose's first hit of the 1972 World Series. He had hit safely nine times versus Pittsburgh to set an NLCS record. The enthusiastic Rose clapped his hands several times, igniting the crowd who tried to get their favored Reds back into Game Two.

The next batter, Joe Morgan, who was enduring the pain of a sore heel, popped up the first pitch he saw from Hunter. Catcher Gene Tenace made the catch in foul territory for the first out of the inning. Morgan had yet to get a hit in the 1972 World Series. Bobby Tolan fared no better. He popped out as well. Shortstop Bert Campaneris caught Tolan's fly ball in shallow left field.

Johnny Bench, the hottest of the Cincinnati hitters through 11 World Series innings, strode to the plate with two outs and Rose still stationed at first base. (For the first time in the Fall Classic, he was not leading off an inning.) Bench, the 1970 NL MVP, launched a fly ball to fairly deep center field, but George Hendrick was positioned well to make the catch for the third out. After three full innings, Oakland retained its 2–0 advantage.

The man who scored the first Oakland run of the game, George Hendrick, led off the top of the fourth inning for the A's. NBC's Al Michaels commented that both teams' center fielders—Hendrick and Bobby Tolan—had attended Fremont High School in Los Angeles. Hendrick hit a slow chopper back to Ross Grimsley in front of the mound. The Cincinnati pitcher had to hustle on the play, but his throw to Tony Pérez still managed to beat Hendrick to first base by a comfortable margin. Gene Tenace grounded to shortstop Darrel Chaney for the second out.

Before Dick Green came to bat, NBC's TV cameras focused on the injured Reggie Jackson in the A's dugout. Dressed in civvies, Jackson was using a bat as a cane as he aimlessly paced nervously but very slowly. Curt Gowdy commented, "[Jackson] has a cast on the back of his leg from the middle of the thigh to the middle of his calf to immobilize the hamstring portion. He's out of the World Series all the way."[12] Green lofted the first pitch he saw from Grimsley to right fielder César Gerónimo. It was the first time the A's had been retired in order in Game Two.

Cincinnati had another promising start in the bottom of the fourth inning. Tony Pérez led off and knocked a single into center field. However, Pérez was quickly erased from the basepath when Denis Menke grounded into a 6–4–3 double play. César Gerónimo was the next Red batter. He grounded out to first baseman Mike Epstein. The unassisted putout ended the bottom of the fourth. Oakland still led Game Two, 2–0.

Ross Grimsley had another strong inning in the top of the fifth as the A's once again were unable to get any baserunners. Catfish Hunter grounded out to second baseman Joe Morgan. Bert Campaneris flied out to right fielder César Gerónimo. Matty Alou grounded out to shortstop Darrel Chaney. Reds first baseman Tony Pérez dug Chaney's throw out of the dirt for the out. Alou was the last man Grimsley would face in the game. His father's alleged aura as a good-luck charm had paid no dividends on this day.

Darrel Chaney led off for Cincinnati in the bottom of the fifth. He scorched a line drive to center field that was chased down by George Hendrick for the first out. Sparky Anderson sent up pinch hitter Ted Uhlaender to bat for Grimsley. The move paid dividends as Uhlaender connected for a double that skipped by Joe Rudi in left field. Pete Rose, batting lefthanded, came up next with one out and Uhlaender standing on second base. On the first pitch he saw, Rose flied out to Matty Alou. Uhlaender, a 6'2" 190-pound man who surprisingly had 52 career stolen bases, did not advance on Rose's out. Joe Morgan got a break when A's first baseman Mike Epstein misplayed his easy grounder. Epstein lost his grip on the ball on what should have been a simple unassisted putout. Uhlaender advanced to third base while Morgan was safe at first. While Bobby Tolan batted, Joe Morgan stole second base uncontested. However, Tolan weakly popped up to shortstop Bert Campaneris to end the rally. A noticeable number of edgy hometown fans booed the Reds' sudden inability to drive in baserunners.

Pedro Borbón, who had a strong Game One in relief for the Reds, faced Oakland's Joe Rudi to start the top of the sixth inning. There was a minor controversy immediately. On an attempted bunt, Rudi made contact—and the ball then struck him. Catcher Johnny Bench maintained that the ball had hit Rudi's body in fair territory outside of the batter's box, so he should have been declared out for interference. The Reds did not get the call from Umpire Jim Honochick. It mattered little as Rudi eventually struck out. Mike Epstein followed by drawing a walk. Allan Lewis—a Panamanian who once stole 102 bases one season in the minors—was sent in to run for Epstein. As had happened in Game One, Lewis was thrown out by Bench on an attempted steal. Sal Bando struck out on the same pitch to end the inning.

For the bottom of the sixth inning, 30-year-old Mike Hegan entered the game to play first base for Oakland. (Hegan's father, Jim, had twice played in the World Series for the Cleveland Indians, in 1948 and 1954.) As was becoming a habit, Johnny Bench again led off for Cincinnati. He drew a base on balls and the noticeably subdued crowd at Riverfront Stadium became livelier. Tony Pérez batted next. He grounded to Sal Bando at third base. Bench was retired at second base by Dick Green on a force play, but Pérez was safe at first base. Denis Menke was the next Red batter. The righthanded Menke made contact on a check swing and nearly benefited by it. The slow bouncer between the mound and third base was adroitly fielded barehanded by Hunter, however, who nipped Menke at first base with a strong and accurate throw. It was an above-average defensive play; Monte Moore told his NBC Radio audience he doubted whether third baseman Sal Bando would have made the play in time. Pérez advanced to second base on the fielder's choice. He was stranded there, however, when César Gerónimo hit a fly ball to center field. George Hendrick made the simple catch to retire the Reds.

Hendrick led off the top of the seventh inning for Oakland with Pedro Borbón still pitching for Cincinnati. Borbón did well. On the second pitch he saw, Hendrick flied out to César Gerónimo in right field. Gene Tenace struck out as did Dick Green as the A's went down quickly. Borbón's work was over. He had done his job well again, striking out four of the six Oakland men he had faced. The A's had now gone four innings without a hit since Rudi's home run in the top of the third.

Darrel Chaney led off the bottom of the seventh inning against Catfish Hunter. Chaney flied out to Joe Rudi in shallow left field. Joe Hague was summoned by Sparky Anderson to pinch hit for Borbón, but he flied out to Matty Alou in right field for the second out. Pete Rose went down on strikes to end the swift inning. Hunter was cruising along—and the vaunted NL champions had now surprisingly gone 12 consecutive innings without scoring.

The next Cincinnati pitcher was Tom Hall, an odd physical specimen at six feet tall and just 150 pounds. A former Minnesota Twin, his trim figure earned him the nickname "The Blade." In 1972, Hall, a righty, had compiled an eye-catching 10–1 record with eight saves and 134 strikeouts in 124⅓ innings pitched. Catfish Hunter was the first Oakland batter in the top of the eighth. He popped out to Tony Pérez at first base. Bert Campaneris followed Hunter. He lined out to Bobby Tolan. Matty Alou had a seven-pitch at-bat and singled to right field. With Joe Rudi batting, Alou stole second base largely because Hall appeared to forget about him being on base. Johnny Bench had no chance to throw him out. Rudi drew a walk. No harm was done to the Reds, however, as Mike Hegan went down swinging on three pitches.

With his Reds still trailing 2–0, Joe Morgan led off the bottom of the eighth inning. Catfish Hunter coaxed Morgan to pop out harmlessly to left fielder Joe Rudi. Bobby Tolan flied out to Matty Alou as the sellout crowd moaned. Johnny Bench drove a long fly ball to right field, exciting the Riverfront Stadium patrons momentarily, but Alou caught it at the warning track. The Reds failed to score again. So far, Hunter had held the NL champs to just four hits over eight innings.

Sal Bando led off the top of the ninth by grounding out to shortstop Darrel Chaney. With Tom Hall still on the mound, George Hendrick reached base safely when Joe Morgan, playing deep, made a bad throw to first base. The generous scoring decision—a base hit for Hendrick rather than an error on second baseman Morgan—was greeted by hoots from the crowd. Gene Tenace hit a fly ball to short left field that was caught easily by Pete Rose for the second out of the inning. Dick Green, Oakland's second baseman, came to the plate next. He connected for a base hit to center field. Hendrick stopped at second base. A's pitcher Catfish Hunter came to bat. The sportsmanlike Cincinnati fans applauded him for his fine pitching through eight innings. Surprisingly Hunter drew a four-pitch walk. The crowd booed Hall. After falling behind the next batter Bert Campaneris, 2–0, the anxious crowd booed some more. Hall regained his control and struck out Campaneris to end the threat. The fickle fans cheered.

The Cincinnati Reds had only been shut out four times at home in 1972, but they were three outs away from having that indignity thrust upon them in Game Two of the World Series. Catfish Hunter, who had pitched 16 complete games in 1972, was still on the mound for Oakland to try for another. On the first pitch he saw, Tony Pérez lined a base hit into left field that sailed over the outstretched glove hand of shortstop Bert Campaneris. It was only the fifth hit Hunter had surrendered to the Reds.

With nobody out, Reds third baseman Denis Menke came to bat next representing the tying run. His plate appearance resulted in the most memorable defensive play of the 1972 Fall Classic. Menke connected solidly on the first pitch he saw, too. He hit a terrific line drive to deep left field that sent Joe Rudi scurrying in retreat to the base of the high wall. Afterward, Menke told reporters he was certain he had belted a two-run homer to tie the game. Here is how Jim Simpson called it for NBC Radio:

> The pitch.... Lined to left field! Back goes Rudi.... Looking up.... He's got it! Against the wall! And now retreating to first base goes Pérez—and there's the fielding gem of the 1972 World Series! Hendrick is all the way over in left field slapping Rudi on the back! He went four or five or six feet in the air! When he came down it's what they call an ice cream cone—a lot of the white was showing. But Joe Rudi catches the line drive of Denis Menke....[13]

It was a tremendous, game-saving play. Rudi leaped and extended his body to make an acrobatic backhanded snag of Menke's drive with no room to spare. A photo of Rudi's catch would appear in numerous newspapers the next day. It was front-page material for many dailies—and rightfully so.

Oakland manager Dick Williams, while pleased with the magnificent catch, would later criticize Rudi for wasting valuable moments showing the ball to the umpire. He figured if Rudi had hurried the ball back into the infield, Pérez, who was running on contact, may have been doubled up before he could get back to first base. Instead, Pérez was able to scamper back to the bag safely.

Monte Moore interjected that Rudi had been the most consistent overall player—offensively and defensively—on the A's roster throughout 1972. Moore also made a very safe assumption: "When they make the World Series highlight film this year, that [catch] will be one of the opening shots."[14]

The spotlight was on Oakland's Joe Rudi in Game Two of the 1972 World Series. After belting a solo home run in the third inning, he made an amazing game-saving catch in the ninth inning to preserve a 2–1 victory for the Athletics. His prowess with the bat was limited to Game Two, however. He would not record another RBI in the remainder of the Fall Classic (Doug McWilliams/National Baseball Hall of Fame and Museum).

Remarkably, the A's fielding gems did not stop with Rudi's fabulous catch. The very next batter was César Gerónimo. On an 0–1 pitch, first baseman Mike Hegan—an Oakland player without a mustache—saved an extra base hit by sprawling to knock down a line drive that appeared to be headed into right field. Hegan had the ball in his glove momentarily, but it squirted out. (Pérez, again running on contact, would have been doubled off easily had Hegan completed the catch.) Hegan picked up the loose ball and lunged toward first base, touching the bag with his hand, in plenty of time to retire Gerónimo. Pérez moved up to second base on the fielder's choice.

"That ball was hit so hard, it was just a blur going toward first base," declared Curt Gowdy. "That was a cinch double, at least."[15] Monte Moore credited Dick Williams for sagely inserting Hegan into the game defensively for the chance to shine with his glove at such a crucial junction.

Hal McRae was sent up to bat in the number-eight spot for Darrel Chaney by Sparky Anderson. He promptly singled to left field, driving in Pérez. The Oakland lead was reduced to 2–1—and Hunter's shutout was gone. Hunter himself was gone too. With the Reds having hit four balls solidly off him in the bottom of the ninth, Dick Williams had seen enough. Righthanded reliever Rollie Fingers entered the game to try to get the final out for the visitors.

Dave Concepción ran for McRae and Julián Javier batted for pitcher Tom Hall. Finishing his MLB career, the 35-year-old Javier had just 100 plate appearances in 1972. Fingers efficiently disposed of him on four pitches. Javier popped up the last one to Hegan who easily caught the ball in the first base coach's box. It had been a struggle to get the final three outs, but Oakland was heading home holding a surprising 2–0 lead in the World Series.

Cincinnati now faced the daunting prospect of trying to win a World Series after dropping the first two games at home. No team had ever managed to accomplish that difficult task. It was also pointed out that Cincinnati had now lost seven straight World Series games at home—dating back to when Crosley Field was where they plied their trade. The Reds' most recent home World Series win occurred in Game Seven of the 1940 Fall Classic.

The Bay Area's baseball writers were happily reporting the unexpected results. George Ross of the *Oakland Tribune* merrily wrote in his report,

> The Oakland Athletics are out in front of the Cincinnati Reds, 2–0.
>
> At least 90 percent of the country's experts of these fun and games said the real World Series was played in Cincinnati and Pittsburgh last week by baseball's two best teams.
>
> But shortly after Commissioner Bowie Kuhn threw in the first ball For Saturday's Game One and Jackie Robinson threw in the first ball for Game Two, an eye-popping truth dawned like a new sun over Ohio: The A's are as good as the best—or better.

At the game's conclusion, the main subject of discussion among the players and media in the winners' camp was Joe Rudi's terrific catch against the high outfield wall in the game's final inning. Rudi himself expressed surprise. "I didn't think I had a chance; I thought it was gone,"[16] he admitted to reporters. In a postgame television interview with NBC's Tony Kubek, Catfish Hunter said he thought Menke had hit a home run to tie the game. Rudi also informed Kubek that he had trouble flipping his sunglasses into position. He had to do it twice—and almost lost track of the ball in the interim.

Oakland manager Dick Williams was pressed by reporters to rank Rudi's grab among the best in World Series history. Williams was forced to admit that he was not the most qualified person to handle such a query, but he did state a strong opinion about his left fielder's sensational snag. "It was better than two catches I've heard and read about. It was better than Willie Mays' catch on Vic Wertz in the 1954 World Series. And it was better than Al Gionfriddo's catch on Joe DiMaggio in the 1947 World Series. Rudi's catch today was better than both [of those]. What makes Rudi's catch so great was that he had to challenge the wall."[17] Williams told UPI writer Gene Caddes with a smile that Rudi's catch was the greatest because "it was made for me."

Roger Angell, the superb baseball scribe for *The New Yorker*, provided this wonderfully vivid description of Game Two's most important play: "Rudi, in pursuit of a very long drive hit by Denis Menke, plastered himself belly-first against the left-field wall like a pinned butterfly, and somehow plucked down the ball."[18]

Afterwards, Rudi gave credit for his catch to.... Joe DiMaggio! The great Yankee Clipper had been an A's coach in 1968 and 1969. Rudi said DiMaggio had taught him the proper technique for going back on fly balls when approaching outfield walls. He apparently was a top-notch pupil.

Years later Rudi reflected on his famous World Series catch and provided these insights:

> I was playing Menke straightaway at the time. He was a line-drive hitter, not known as a big power hitter. Not like Bench and those other guys. When he first hit the ball, I thought it was out [of the ballpark]. But, as it turned out, it was exactly the type of hit [the coaches] had worked on with me for two years: a ball straight over my head, and, on this one, a little to my left. I broke on the ball, ran like hell until I got to the wall, flipping my glasses down. Then I turned back in. I put my hand out, concentrating on the ball and just feeling where the wall was. I haven't talked much about it, but the ball was right on the edge of the sun when I spotted it; there was no sky between the sun and the ball. If the ball had been a few more inches to the left, there's no way I'd have caught it.
>
> I remember catching it, trying to turn my glove so the ball wouldn't pop out when I hit the wall. All those things happened in slow motion. But I do know one thing: I never would have made that catch without all the practice. Never would have gotten near it.[19]

After the game, Rudi was asked which was his greater thrill in Game Two: his home run or his game-saving catch. Rudi pondered the question for a moment before saying said he could not decide, so he would take both.

Lowell Reidenbaugh of *The Sporting News* placed the blame for Cincinnati's second straight setback on the lack of offense from their usually reliable sources. He wrote,

> As in the opener, Cincinnati's first three batters were held rigidly in check. Pete Rose, Joe Morgan and Bobby Tolan, who as a trio delivered only one hit in the first game, totaled only one hit among them [in Game Two], a third-inning single by Rose.
>
> During the regular season, Morgan reached base 282 times, Rose 278 and Tolan 221. But then they weren't facing Catfish Hunter.[20]

Al Abrams of the *Pittsburgh Post-Gazette* reported a poignant interaction between a fan and 53-year-old Jackie Robinson. The former Brooklyn standout was lingering at Riverfront Stadium after Game Two had concluded: The scribe wrote, "His head is held high and his voice is as firm as it ever was, but Jackie Robinson is near blindness. Diabetes has taken its toll. A fan with a baseball in his hand asked the former Dodger great before yesterday's game if he would autograph it for him. 'Surely,' replied the Hall of Famer, groping for a pen. 'Please show me where I can sign. I can't see too well anymore.'"[21]

Abrams also described an amusing anecdote centering on Casey Stengel, whom Abrams described as "83 years young and still bouncing around." [Authors' note: Abrams misreported Stengel's age by a year. Casey was born in 1890, so he had celebrated his 82nd birthday—not his 83rd—on July 30.] The esteemed ex-manager eagerly addressed the contingent of baseball media from Pittsburgh with the following apology: "Tell that fella it isn't my fault I had to cancel my hotel reservation in your town. Those Pirates didn't do what I expected 'em to."[22] When pressed for further details, the aging but thoroughly lovable Stengel could neither recall the fella's name—nor the Pittsburgh hotel where he had canceled his room. Remembering names was never a strong point for one of baseball's greatest characters.

Abrams concluded his miscellany from Game Two by lauding the victorious visitors' highly successful trip to Ohio. "If Oakland wins this World Series, it will demand #1 recognition," he wrote. "Only the Reds can take it away from them by bouncing back in Oakland and winning here next weekend. The A's have no immediate plans to return to Cincinnati, however."[23]

Charley Feeney of the *Pittsburgh Post-Gazette* wrote, "The jubilant

A's became believers. They believe they can whip the Reds. They believe they can beat anybody. They have silenced the Reds' bats and silenced the talk that the Reds and Pirates are the best two clubs in baseball."[24]

An article in the October 7 edition *The Sporting News* about Catfish Hunter said the pitcher who won Game Two of the World series would be seeking a substantial pay raise in 1973. If the A's didn't give it to him, he'd prefer to be traded. "I feel I'm the best pitcher on the staff," he said to *TSN* reporter Ron Bergman, "and I want to be the best paid."[25] Hunter was paid $50,000 for the 1972 season. Two other pitchers on the team were higher paid than the 26-year-old hurler. Hunter, who had never played an inning in the minor leagues and did not miss a starting assignment in seven of his eight years with the A's, was the first pitcher to post consecutive 20-win seasons for the Athletics since Lefty Grove in the early 1930s. Hunter told Bergman he figured he was worth $80,000 per season. Dick Williams had nothing but praise for Hunter. After the game the Oakland manager said,

> Catfish Hunter is the Robin Roberts of this generation. He's a grinder, he's got a tremendous ERA, he's consistent, and he's great to play behind because he gets rid of the ball. I think he should be the Cy Young winner.[26]

Dropping the first two games of the World Series was unfortunately a familiar scenario to Sparky Anderson. In fact, his Reds lost the first three games to Baltimore in the 1970 Fall Classic. A late, desperate rally gave Cincinnati a clutch 6–5 win in Game Four, but the Reds lost Game Five badly, 9–3, the next day. History and personal experience told Anderson that digging out of an 0–3 hole in a World Series was almost an impossible task.

"I'm not going to panic yet. I'm close to it, but not yet," said Anderson following Game Two of the 1972 World Series. "I know we're against the wall, but I know we'll be back at Riverfront Stadium this weekend. I know the National League is stronger than the American League—and I'll say that again even if we should lose four straight."[27]

Anderson conceded that Oakland's pitching in the first two games of the World Series had been tremendous, but the feisty Cincinnati field pilot claimed, "I'll tell you one thing: I'm glad I don't have to face a Seaver or a Carlton now."[28]

"This was another day for the mustaches,"[29] joked Catfish Hunter in the victorious Oakland clubhouse. Mike Hegan, who made two fine defensive plays at first base for the A's, disagreed. He said he was dedicating his fielding gems "to the few of us who are clean-shaven."[30]

With Gene Tenace becoming a baseball celebrity, his hotel roommate on road trips, Sal Bando, was suddenly being asked questions about the slugging catcher—especially about their common Italian ancestry. The jovial, quick-witted Oakland third baseman was happy to oblige when asked if Tenace was bilingual. "Gene doesn't speak Italian at all," quipped Bando. "Hell, he hardly speaks English."[31]

With his team down a pair of games in the Series, Cincinnati center fielder Bobby Tolan could not help but be impressed by the AL champs. "I give the A's credit; they're two games up."[32] Sparky Anderson agreed too, "They're as good as the reports," he noted. "We thought maybe they were overrated, but not from what we've seen so far."[33] The oddsmakers were now convinced. Oakland was listed as 7:5 favorites to win Game Three.

Dick Williams was, of course, happy to be ahead 2–0 in the World Series, but he was not counting his chickens yet. "We've had some outstanding pitching, sure," he admitted. "But heck they've hit some balls really hard and we've had to come up with some good fielding plays to stop the Reds. Believe me, this is not over. This is going to be some Series."[34]

Williams did admit his outlook on the World Series had been altered after Game One. He told reporters that entering the World Series he would have been satisfied with splitting the first two games in Cincinnati. This changed after Williams' club took the first game. A mere split was no longer satisfactory. He also knew his managerial tactics were being highly scrutinized—and he had a ready answer for his critics. "I know I've been accused of overmanaging. Well, I've overmanaged two games in a row now."[35]

Sparky Anderson was keeping up a cheerful façade despite being two games in arrears in the Series. He and Dick Williams were playful with each other in the postgame press conference. When Williams preceded Anderson to the huddle with reporters, the Reds manager joked, "How come I'm always second—on the field and at the mike?" Anderson cracked a smile and told the assembled scribes, "Dick and I are friends. We're not mad at anyone. It's the National League versus the American League."[36] Anderson cited an interesting statistic that gave him cause for optimism. His Reds had compiled a considerably better road record (53–25) in 1972 than they had at Riverfront Stadium (42–34). Thus, Anderson believed, playing three games in Oakland ought not to trouble his team.

The wordy sports editor of the *Youngstown Vindicator* showered the A's with stilted, flowery praise in the following day's newspaper. Lawrence M. Stolle declared, "The all-conquering Oakland Athletics, boasting a 2–0 cushion, bolstered by tradition, and all strategy jelling, are enjoying the jubilant stratosphere as they rest today, intent on applying more embarrassment to the embattled Cincinnati Reds."[37]

During the NBC Radio's broadcast, Jim Simpson mentioned an obscure factoid provided to him by statistician Alan Roth: Game Two of the 1972 Fall Classic was the 400th game in the history of the modern version of World Series to have been played to a decision—meaning one team ended up as the victor. It was actually the 403rd World Series game as there had been a tie game in each of the 1907, 1912 and 1922 Fall Classics. Apparently, there was no bit of esoterica too trivial for the hardcore baseball fan.

## Box Score: Game #2
### Oakland Athletics 2, Cincinnati Reds 1
Game played on Sunday, October 15, 1972, at Riverfront Stadium

| Oakland Athletics | ab | r | h | rbi | Cincinnati Reds | ab | r | h | rbi |
|---|---|---|---|---|---|---|---|---|---|
| Campaneris ss | 5 | 0 | 1 | 0 | Rose lf | 4 | 0 | 1 | 0 |
| Alou rf | 4 | 0 | 1 | 0 | Morgan 2b | 4 | 0 | 0 | 0 |
| Rudi lf | 3 | 1 | 2 | 1 | Tolan cf | 4 | 0 | 0 | 0 |
| Epstein 1b | 2 | 0 | 0 | 0 | Bench c | 3 | 0 | 1 | 0 |
| Lewis pr | 0 | 0 | 0 | 0 | Pérez 1b | 3 | 1 | 2 | 0 |
| Hegan 1b | 1 | 0 | 0 | 0 | Menke 3b | 4 | 0 | 0 | 0 |
| Bando 3b | 4 | 0 | 1 | 0 | Gerónimo rf | 4 | 0 | 0 | 0 |
| Hendrick cf | 4 | 1 | 1 | 0 | Chaney ss | 2 | 0 | 0 | 0 |
| Tenace c | 4 | 0 | 0 | 0 | McRae ph | 1 | 0 | 1 | 1 |
| Green 2b | 4 | 0 | 2 | 0 | Concepción pr | 0 | 0 | 0 | 0 |
| Hunter p | 3 | 0 | 1 | 1 | Grimsley p | 1 | 0 | 0 | 0 |
| Fingers p | 0 | 0 | 0 | 0 | Uhlaender ph | 1 | 0 | 1 | 0 |
| **Totals** | 34 | 2 | 9 | 2 | Borbón p | 0 | 0 | 0 | 0 |
| | | | | | Hague ph | 1 | 0 | 0 | 0 |
| | | | | | Hall p | 0 | 0 | 0 | 0 |
| | | | | | Javier ph | 1 | 0 | 0 | 0 |
| | | | | | **Totals** | 33 | 1 | 6 | 1 |

| | | | | | | | | | |
|---|---|---|---|---|---|---|---|---|---|
| Oakland | 0 | 1 | 1 | 0 | 0 | 0 | 0 | 0 | 0 |
| Cincinnati | 0 | 0 | 0 | 0 | 0 | 0 | 0 | 0 | 1 |

| Oakland Athletics | IP | H | R | ER | BB | SO |
|---|---|---|---|---|---|---|
| Hunter W (1–0) | 8.2 | 6 | 1 | 1 | 3 | 6 |
| Fingers SV (1) | 0.1 | 0 | 0 | 0 | 0 | 0 |
| **Totals** | 9.0 | 6 | 1 | 1 | 3 | 6 |
| Cincinnati Reds | IP | H | R | ER | BB | SO |
| Grimsley L (0–1) | 5.0 | 6 | 2 | 2 | 0 | 1 |
| Borbón | 2.0 | 0 | 0 | 0 | 1 | 4 |
| Hall | 2.0 | 3 | 0 | 0 | 2 | 2 |
| **Totals** | 9.0 | 9 | 2 | 2 | 3 | 7 |

E—Epstein (1), Hunter (1). DP—Oakland 1, Cincinnati 1. **2B**—Cincinnati Uhlaender (1, off Hunter). HR—Oakland Rudi (1, 3rd inning off Grimsley 0 on, 1 out). IBB—Chaney (1, by Hunter). SB—Alou (1, 2nd base off Hall/Bench); Morgan (1, 2nd base off Hunter/Tenace). CS—Lewis (2, 2nd base by Borbón/Bench). IBB—Hunter (1, Chaney). U—Jim Honochick (AL), Mel Steiner (NL), Frank Umont (AL), Bob Engel (NL), Chris Pelekoudas (NL), Bill Haller (AL). T—2:26. A—53,224

# Game Three

*Slipups*

**Date:** Wednesday, October 18, 1972
**Site:** Oakland-Alameda County Coliseum, Oakland, California

> "Oakland nights can be punishing at this season, but today's baseball hierarchy is totally subservient to television, and the sport's electronic masters want to broadcast their shaving cream commercials at prime time in the eastern markets."[1]—Red Smith, *New York Times* syndicated sports columnist, on the coming of World Series weeknight games in 1972

> "Those who saw the third game will never forget what happened to Johnny Bench. Neither will Johnny."[2]—Harold Friend, *Bleacher Report*

An unexpected, large welcoming committee greeted the A's when they returned from their highly successful first two World Series games in Cincinnati. Years later Catfish Hunter wrote in his autobiography, "What's this? A mob of 10,000 screaming A's fans waiting for us at the Oakland airport. It had to be a mirage."[3] Sal Bando, unused to the sudden adulation, concurred, telling Hunter he too had never witnessed such a sight in Oakland. Dick Williams thought the huge gathering of supporters was a tremendous sight, an indication that his team was finally being embraced by the locals. Demand for World Series ducats in Oakland seemed to indicate Williams was correct. "Our telephones have been going bananas," said an overworked A's office employee prior to Game Three. "This is bigger than we expected. Everyone wants a ticket."[4]

Nobody was present in large numbers to greet the NL champions when their plane touched down in the Bay Area. In fact, the Reds and most of the NL dignitaries learned that their longstanding reservations at the Jack Tar Hotel in San Francisco had been cancelled. (Apparently, the hotel's owners thought the A's would not be in the World Series when Detroit leveled the ALCS, so they cancelled their baseball bookings in order to accommodate a convention!) Fortunately for the Reds, they were able to use reservations at another hotel that had been made by the Pittsburgh Pirates in anticipation of the Bucs being in the Fall Classic.

With the World Series coming to Oakland for the very first time, it was going to be an extremely busy few days of sports for the small city that was often overshadowed by its neighbor, the larger and more glamorous San Francisco. Traffic problems along the Admiral Nimitz Freeway leading into the Oakland-Alameda County Coliseum would be a certainty.

For the benefit of east-coast television viewers, the three World Series games on the west coast were all scheduled for 8:15 p.m. Eastern time on Tuesday, Wednesday and Thursday—which is 5:15 p.m. in Oakland. Basketball's Golden State Warriors and hockey's California Golden Seals had their home openers scheduled for Tuesday and Wednesday night respectively. (The Golden Seals were also owned by Charles O. Finley.) Both those teams played their home games in the same arena adjacent to the baseball park. That meant, quite probably, that 50,000 baseball fans would be trying to exit the area as thousands of fans of the other sports would be trying to enter it.

Further complicating matters were the iffy weather forecasts for the Bay Area. Decidedly nasty and rainy weather had been striking Oakland while the first two games of the 1972 World Series were being contested half a continent away in Cincinnati. The first pitch of Game Three was scheduled for Tuesday, October 17 at 5:15 p.m. local time, but the conditions simply did not allow for it.

That day—the tenth consecutive one to feature foul weather in the Bay Area—the already damp field at the Oakland-Alameda County Coliseum was hit with another heavy downpour plus a shower of hailstones just minutes before the game was supposed to begin. Hal Bock, a veteran baseball scribe covering the World Series for the Associated Press, described the unexpected arrival of the storm: "The storm hit with such suddenness that the formally dressed orchestra assembled in center field for pregame entertainment was caught right in the middle of it. The musicians scurried off the field as the groundskeepers started to cover it. Thunder roared in the background and soon the hailstones hit."[5] Both teams' dugouts flooded rapidly. It was par for the course that October. Meteorological records showed it was the wettest October in Oakland since 1890.

Even before the latest surge of bad weather, a helicopter had been enlisted earlier in the day to help dry the accumulation of moisture on the field—on which the outline of a football field was quite visible. (The NFL's Oakland Raiders played their home games at the Coliseum too.) Now, after the rain and hail, there was no way that Game Three could possibly start on Tuesday night. Bock readily agreed. He wrote that the diamond "was in totally unplayable condition."[6] Commissioner Bowie Kuhn officially but ruefully announced a one-day postponement at 5:41 p.m.—some 26 minutes after Game Three was scheduled to start and about 43 minutes after the skies had opened again.

Kuhn, appropriately dressed in a raincoat, had walked across the field to personally assess the grim situation. He told reporters, "In some places the water is up over your shoe tops. It's the only decision that could be made, probably one of the easiest I've had to make. The outfield was in rotten shape, totally unplayable. It would have taken three hours to get the water off there. We would not have been able to stage a proper World Series game."[7]

As sensible as Kuhn's call to postpone Game Three was, the disappointed sellout crowd still loudly booed it when the announcement was made. Dick Williams was mildly irked that he was not notified about the rainout in advance of the paying customers. He told Lawrence M. Stolle of the *Youngstown Vindicator*, "All Mr. Finley and Commission Kuhn said to me was 'Hello.' I learned about the postponement over the loudspeaker."

Oakland's groundskeepers received some negative reviews from baseball writers about how leisurely they acted in covering the field with a tarpaulin once the rainfall struck. Given the large amount of moisture that fell in such a short time, it may not have mattered much. Clearly, the crew had not had much practice recently. Local scribes reported that only one A's home game had been postponed due to rain in the past two seasons while one other was terminated in the sixth inning.

It was very much a local storm. Richard Paloma, who pens a baseball blog for A's fans, recalled the peculiar weather he had witnessed on October 17, 1972, as a 13-year-old living in San Leandro, California, just seven miles away from the ballpark. "I couldn't believe what I was seeing on television—dark skies and a downpour—when just outside [my home] it was a sunny fall afternoon. When the NBC cameras pulled back, viewers could see a funnel cloud located only above the Coliseum, causing fans to wonder if some divine intervention was keeping a World Series game from ever being played in Oakland."[8] Similarly, two days earlier the crowd at a San Francisco 49ers NFL home game endured a heavy rainstorm while, not too far away, the folks watching the Raiders at the Oakland Coliseum enjoyed lovely weather.

The injured Reggie Jackson, still moving about with the aid of crutches, welcomed the inclement weather. He jokingly said of the persistent rain that he hoped it kept up for a month so that he could play in the World Series. Dick Williams said the rainout gave the Reds another 24 hours to consider their unfavorable position, adding to their psychological woes. In contrast, however, Pete Rose was predictably champing at the bit. "I didn't come to Oakland to sit around a hotel,"[9] he noted. Rose also took the opposite view of Dick Williams, saying the extra day off was killing any momentum the A's had acquired after winning the first two games in Cincinnati.

Reds starter Jack Billingham was eager to pitch, so the postponement was a huge letdown for him, too. "You get yourself up for a game like this, so I'm disappointed." Billingham added, "Don't forget I pitched in the [Houston] Astrodome for three years, so I'm not used to rain."[10] Billingham was reputedly a distant cousin of Christy Mathewson, the late great pitching star of the New York Giants in the early years of the 20th century and one of the first five players voted into the Hall of Fame in 1936.

Jack Billingham was the best starting pitcher for the Reds during the 1972 World Series, falling just short of a complete-game shutout in Game Three (courtesy Cincinnati Reds Hall of Fame).

A rainy World Series in the Bay Area was a familiar sight to Oakland right fielder Matty Alou. The last time the Fall Classic had been played in northern California was in 1962 when the San Francisco Giants and New York Yankees clashed. That World Series was delayed for three days because of successive rainouts at San Francisco's Candlestick Park. Alou was a member of the 1962 Giants. Alou sagely told reporters there was little anyone could do but wait.

Having a full house for a home game in Oakland was a novelty for A's owner Charlie Finley. (He proudly had the marquee in front of his ballpark state that all three World Series games slated for Oakland were sold out.) The residents of the Bay Area were finally recognizing the obvious: They had a superb MLB team to support—if they chose to do so. Now they chose to do so.

Finley reveled in his long-awaited role as the AL's host of this World Series once the games moved to Oakland. Not surprisingly, Finley gave the festivities his own personal touch. A's historian Ron Hertzel wrote in a 2010 piece,

> The media got to feast on Finley's favorite foods—fried chicken and oatmeal cookies. It was wise not to leave anything over, for walking through the media tent would be Finley, Charley-O in hand, the mule willing to gobble up whatever leftovers he could get to. It was a three-ring circus that became as entertaining and suspenseful in a baseball sense as the best lion tamer Barnum and Bailey ever employed.[11]

Given the unprecedented excitement the A's were generating since the franchise's relocation from Kansas City to Oakland, Finley was especially irked to have to send the Tuesday night assemblage of nearly 50,000 people home unhappy. Finley briefly and unsuccessfully tried to persuade Kuhn and the umpires to reconsider the postponement. Bock noted that the two ALCS games played in Oakland earlier in the month had been contested under threatening leaden skies, but no rain had actually fallen during either of them. Over the next three days the field would remain wet in spots. As it turned out, its lingering slickness would impact several key plays.

UPI baseball writer Milton Richman reported that Johnny Bench and Reggie Jackson were becoming regular dinner companions, despite MLB supposedly having a strict "no-fraternization rule" for players of the opposing World Series teams. Although he had only met Jackson briefly at All-Star Games, on the Friday before Game One, Bench had approached the injured AL star at Riverfront Stadium to inquire about his health. He also invited Jackson to dine with him that evening at a local eatery. Jackson readily accepted. The two men amiably chatted for about five hours over Italian food. "Maybe he felt sorry for me. I don't know," Jackson told Richman. "He's a good person. He cares about other people."[12] Jackson returned the favor in Oakland, taking Bench to one of his favorite restaurants after Tuesday's game was rained out.

The postponement meant that Game Three was moved from Tuesday night to Wednesday night, Game Four was shifted from Wednesday night to Thursday night, and, if necessary, Game Five would be moved from Thursday night to Friday afternoon. Friday was supposed to have been set aside as a travel day if the World Series returned to Cincinnati. That luxury was now gone. Of course, Oakland hoped no such eastward trip would have to be arranged.

The rainy spells were causing havoc with other routines for the two clubs. The wet field had prevented the Reds and A's from taking batting practice for three days. In fact, the Reds were considering taking cuts at San Francisco's Candlestick Park if Game Three happened to be rained out again.

There were more threatening skies, but Bay Area's fickle weather cooperated sufficiently on Wednesday; Game Three could finally be played. The Serendipity Singers performed the national anthem. Their irregular, creative, harmonic version earned them a boisterous cheer from the anxious crowd. California governor Ronald Reagan threw out the ceremonial first ball. He put too much pepper on his toss. It sailed over the head of Oakland catcher Gene Tenace, eliciting a large laugh.

**Although they entered the postseason as rivals, Johnny Bench and Reggie Jackson developed a cordial relationship during the 1972 World Series. (Jackson has called Bench one of his most respected friends.) The pair dined together at least three times during the Fall Classic. Although Jackson was sidelined due to an injured leg, Bench sought him out after Game Seven to offer his congratulations (courtesy Cincinnati Reds Hall of Fame).**

Oakland's starting pitcher was 27-year-old John (Blue Moon) Odom. Odom's colorful nickname was not another fanciful creation of A's owner Charles O. Finley; it dated back to Odom's elementary school days in Macon, Georgia. A fifth-grade classmate said Odom's round face resembled the moon—and began referring to him as "Moon Head." Odom recalled, "A few days later, he started calling me 'Blue Moon.' He said he could not call me 'Yellow Moon' because of my complexion; and 'Black Moon' would not sound right. So, he decided to call me 'Blue Moon.' I used to hate that name, but now I love it."[13]

Odom's best pitch was a sinking fastball that he sometimes struggled to master. "I don't know where it's going," Odom admitted in a 1969 interview. "It's kind of hard for me to be a control pitcher because my ball moves so much. Some games it just moves a lot. Other times it doesn't move as much. It takes me about the first or second inning to see how it's going. I'll either have a good sinker or I'll have to pitch to spots."[14]

Jack Billingham, a 29-year-old sinkerball pitcher with good control, was the starter for the Reds. Born in Florida, Billingham had begun his pro baseball career with the Dodgers' organization, primarily as a relief pitcher. He was traded to Houston after the 1968 season and spent three years with the Astros before being dealt to Cincinnati. Billingham led the Reds with 31 starts in 1972. His record was 12–12 with a 3.18 ERA. He had not pitched in 10 days, so he was well rested. That was normally the case for Billingham who was well known among his teammates for his love of naps and his unrivaled ability to fall sleep anywhere, anytime. He answered to the nickname "Rip." It was short for Rip Van Winkle.

Pete Rose, who had just one hit in eight at-bats so far in the World Series, led off Game Three against Blue Moon Odom. He was caught looking at an Odom fastball on a full count that sailed across the heart of the plate, taking him by surprise. NL umpire Mel Steiner signaled the strikeout. Joe Morgan went down swinging, too, also on a full count. On NBC Radio, Al Michaels declared the number of times in 1972 that Rose and Morgan had struck out back-to-back could likely be counted on the fingers of one hand. Bobby Tolan only fared slightly better: He tapped a grounder back to Odom for an easy third out.

Bert Campaneris led off for Oakland against Jack Billingham. Billingham struck him out on three pitches. Matty Alou, a lefthanded batter, was the second Oakland batter of the game. He grounded to shortstop Darrel Chaney and was out by a considerable margin at first base. Joe Rudi was called out on strikes. It was a harbinger of an impending pitchers' duel. "With two strikeouts each, both pitchers have been impressive so far,"[15] noted Al Michaels.

As was becoming the habit, Johnny Bench led off another inning—the top of the second—for the Cincinnati Reds. So far in the 1972 World Series, only twice Bench had come to bat with a runner on base. He grounded out to Sal Bando at third base. Righthanded batter Tony Pérez, who was 4-for-7 in the Series, was the next Red to face Odom. He hit a 3–2 pitch to Joe Rudi who hauled it down in left field. The dampness in the air was turning well hit balls into very catchable fly outs. Denis Menke became the game's first base runner. His hit fell into the soggy right field grass. César Gerónimo followed Menke in the Cincinnati batting order. He grounded out to second baseman Dick Green to end the visitors' half of the inning.

Mike Epstein led off the bottom of the second inning for Oakland. He was hitless in five World Series at-bats thus far. Newspaper reports had Epstein unhappy with his manager, Dick Williams, for being lifted in Game Two. Epstein drew a four-pitch walk from Billingham. Oakland captain Sal Bando was the next A's batter. The slumping Bando attempted to bunt. Billingham fielded the ball quickly and had time to retire Epstein at second base. Bando was safe at first base on the fielder's choice. George Hendrick, who was celebrating his 23rd birthday, was up next for the home team. Hendrick hit a ball to shallow right field that was caught by second baseman Joe Morgan who was playing deep in the infield. Gene Tenace came to the plate and hit a grounder to shortstop Darrel Chaney. Bando was retired on a force play at second base to end the inning. Game Two had yet to produce a run after two complete innings.

Switch-hitting Darrel Chaney, batting lefthanded against the righty Odom, led off the top of the third for the Reds. Odom's changeup on a full count baffled Chaney; he went down swinging. Pitcher Jack Billingham, who possessed a lifetime batting average of .096, lasted just one pitch against Odom. He hit an easy ground ball to the Oakland pitcher. Pete Rose came to bat next for Cincinnati accompanied by a chorus of boos. He walked on four pitches. Joe Morgan, who had gone 12 at-bats without a hit, followed Rose. With Morgan batting, Rose, who had stolen 10 bases in 1972, broke for second base. Had catcher Gene Tenace made an accurate throw, Rose would have likely been tagged out. However, the catcher's peg was far too high. The ball sailed into center field. Rose easily took third base on Tenace's error. He was stranded there as Morgan's batting slump continued. Oakland second baseman Dick Green had to make a fine defensive play—it included making a throw from his knees—to retire Morgan at first base. Morgan limped noticeably as he headed back to the visitors' dugout.

The defensive hero from the previous inning, Dick Green, led off the bottom of the third inning for Oakland. He tried to bunt for a base hit, but the ball died in the damp grass just in front of home plate. Johnny Bench easily threw out Green at first base. Blue Moon Odom was the next man to face Billingham. He struck out swinging on a curveball. Shortstop Bert Campaneris grounded out to his Cincinnati counterpart Darrel Chaney. Chaney comfortably threw out Campaneris to set down the A's in order. Game Three was a scoreless tie after three innings.

Bobby Tolan was the first Red to bat in the top of the fourth. He had just one hit in nine at-bats in the World Series. He grounded out to Dick Green. Next up was Johnny Bench. He again came to bat with no runners on base. Bench was caught looking for Blue Moon Odom's fourth strikeout of the game. Tony Pérez was whiff number five. He struck out on a full count. Odom had now impressively pitched 23 consecutive innings without allowing an earned run.

Matty Alou started the bottom of the fourth inning for the hometown A's. Center fielder Bobby Tolan had to run a long way, but he caught Alou's fly ball not far behind second base. Joe Rudi got the first Oakland hit of the game by surprising Jack Billingham with a bunt single. Al Michaels made this observation:

> Credit the A's scouting for that. Billingham has one major problem: He does not follow through correctly. He is never in position to field anything hit back toward the mound. The Reds have been working with Jack all season long, but it just seems to be a thing he can't do anything about at this point. I guess somebody with the A's scouting noticed it. It paid off for Rudi.[16]

Mike Epstein came up next. His ground ball to Joe Morgan resulted in Rudi being forced out at second base, but Epstein beat the return throw to first base to keep the inning alive. There were now two outs with Sal Bando coming to bat. He was retired on a called third strike. Billingham now had four strikeouts. Game Three was still scoreless.

Denis Menke, the only Red with a hit so far in Game Three, led off the top of the fifth inning. Menke walked on four pitches. It was the second base on balls that Blue Moon Odom had permitted. César Gerónimo batted next and got a huge break thanks to an ugly Oakland defensive miscue. Mike Epstein, playing deep, fielded Gerónimo's routine ground ball behind first base. Epstein first looked toward second base and quickly realized he had no chance of retiring Menke. Two A's broke to cover first base—pitcher Odom and second baseman Dick Green. There was some confusion about who would receive Epstein's toss. Green seemed to expect Blue to take it, therefore he was not expecting Epstein's throw to come to him. The resulting error (given to Epstein) put Cincinnati runners at first and third base with nobody out. Darrel Chaney, who was 0-for-3 in the World Series, came up next for the Reds. The A's were in trouble, but Odom replied by striking out Chaney. Jack Billingham was the next Cincinnati batter. Al Michaels bluntly told his NBC Radio audience that Billingham was the worst-hitting pitcher on the Cincinnati staff; furthermore, he was not even a reliable bunter. According to form, Billingham struck out swinging. Pete Rose batted next for the Reds. On Odom's first pitch to Rose, Gerónimo stole second base. Odom struck out Rose looking with a pitch at the knees. Rose furiously but fruitlessly argued Mel Steiner's call. It was all for naught, of course. Oakland had escaped the dangerous jam unscathed. Game Three remained locked at 0–0 heading to the bottom of the fifth inning. The first 4½ innings had moved along rapidly, taking just slightly more than an hour to play.

"The fans are still applauding Blue Moon Odom and booing Pete Rose,"[17] declared NBC Radio's Jim Simpson as Oakland prepared to bat in the home half of the fifth inning. Jack Billingham efficiently whiffed the first two A's he faced. Birthday boy and center fielder George Hendrick was caught looking as was catcher Gene Tenace, both on full counts. Billingham now had accrued six strikeouts. The third batter of the bottom of the fifth fared batter, however. Dick Green connected for a single. Again it was on a pitch with the count full. It was a slow-bounding infield hit to the left of the pitcher's mound. Third baseman Denis Menke fielded the ball cleanly, but he had no play at first base. Blue Moon Odom batted next. He had a .121 batting average in 1972. Al Michaels mentioned that both of Odom's RBIs during the regular season were the result of solo home runs. Odom attempted to bunt in his at-bat but struck out. The game remained scoreless as the pitchers continued to dominate. Odom and Billingham had combined for 15 whiffs.

Joe Morgan was no longer limping as he came to the plate to start the Cincinnati sixth inning, but his batting slump continued. A pop out in foul territory to Sal Bando made Morgan 0-for-10 in the 1972 World Series. Bobby Tolan followed Morgan. He struck out on a full count. It was Odom's ninth strikeout—his best total of the season. Again, Johnny Bench had no baserunners to drive in as he stepped into the batter's box. He was called out on strikes by plate umpire Mel Steiner. Odom, who only had struck out 86 batters in 194⅓ innings during the regular season, surprisingly had accrued double digits in whiffs in Game Three.

The top of the Oakland batting order faced Jack Billingham in the bottom of the sixth inning. Leadoff man Bert Campaneris walked on four pitches. It was Billingham's second walk of the game. Matty Alou was up next. A comedy of errors occurred. Alou's bunt attempt was fielded by Bench. His rushed throw to Joe Morgan covering first base pulled Morgan off the bag—at least that was how first-base umpire Frank Umont saw it. Alou was called safe. As Bench began to argue with Umont, center fielder Bobby Tolan noticed that Campaneris had drifted far off second base. Tolan moved from his outfield position toward second base. Morgan's throw to Tolan was slightly off the mark. The ball rolled away from Tolan—and Campaneris advanced to third base. Two errors were charged on the play: one to Bench and one to Morgan. The A's now had runners on the corners with no one out.

When things settled down, Billingham induced Joe Rudi to hit a sharp ground ball to third baseman Denis Menke. Menke tried to tag Campaneris who adroitly slid back to the bag. Menke then fired the ball to first base to retire Rudi. Alou advanced to second base on the play. With first base open and just one out, Mike Epstein was intentionally walked. Sal Bando, riding an awful 5-for-37 streak at the plate, was the next Oakland batter. He hit into a 4–6–3 double play. Like the A's the previous inning, Cincinnati had survived a tricky situation. Two-thirds of the way through Game Three, the score was still tied, 0–0.

Tony Pérez led off the top of the seventh inning for Cincinnati. Al Michaels joked about the lack of hitting thus far in the contest, noting that Pérez had "hit the most prodigious blast of the game—a routine fly ball to left field! Believe it or not, through six innings, that's the longest ball that's been hit in the game."[18] Indeed, Cincinnati's only hit of Game Three had been a broken-bat single by Denis Menke in the second inning that did not leave the infield.

However, Pérez made it two hits for Cincinnati with a leadoff single into left field. Menke was up next. He successfully bunted Pérez to second base. César Gerónimo, hitless in the World Series, was the next Reds batter to face Odom. He finally made good by singling into right-center field. The Reds caught a huge break when Oakland conceded that Pérez was going to score. George Hendrick, mindful of the soggy outfield, did not especially hustle on the damp grass. When Hendrick picked up the ball, he casually threw it sidearm to shortstop Bert Campaneris. Ian MacDonald of the *Montreal Gazette* opined, "Had Hendrick thrown to the plate, Pérez would have been out by 25 feet. Campaneris could have had him easily as well."[19]

Unfortunately for Campaneris and his teammates, the shortstop's focus was trying to keep Gerónimo from advancing beyond first base. He was unaware that Pérez had slipped rounding third base on his way home. Pérez quickly got up and scored while Campaneris, holding the baseball, had his back to the lead runner. [Authors' note: On the NBC Radio broadcast, Jim Simpson twice misidentified the cutoff man on the play as second baseman Dick Green rather than shortstop Bert

Campaneris. Neither he nor his partner Al Michaels ever corrected the mistake.] Catcher Gene Tenace threw his arms up in despair as he witnessed the debacle unfold in front of him. Albeit oddly, Cincinnati had taken a 1–0 lead in Game Three. It was the first time in the 1972 World Series that the Reds had led any game.

After the game, Oakland manager Dick Williams defended his center fielder. "Hendrick made the only play he could," Williams claimed. "The ball was slow in getting out there. Then it nearly stopped on the wet grass. Hendrick was not slow in getting there."[20] Campaneris said, "I did not see Pérez fall down. Nobody said anything to me, so I don't know what to think."[21] One writer, Lawrence M. Stolle, disagreed. He opined that Hendrick had patrolled the outfield throughout Game Three as if he were asleep.

With César Gerónimo now standing on second base, Darrel Chaney flied out to Hendrick. Pitcher Jack Billingham came up next and struck out. (When asked about his 0-for-4 night at the plate with three strikeouts, Billingham would bluntly tell reporters that he was a pitcher, not a hitter.) Odom now had 11 strikeouts, but his team was down by a run heading to the bottom of the seventh inning.

Starter Jack Billingham was still on the hill for the Reds. "[He's] really been magnificent. He's allowed two hits: one a bunt single and one an infield hit. One ball has been hit to the outfield,"[22] opined Al Michaels. Leading off the bottom of the seventh inning was George Hendrick. On the first pitch he saw, Hendrick broke his bat in flying out to Bobby Tolan in shallow left-center field. Gene Tenace then grounded out to shortstop Darrel Chaney. Dick Williams sent in Gonzalo Márquez to bat for Dick Green. It was Márquez's second plate appearance in the World Series. (He had popped out in another pinch-hitting stint in Game One.) Márquez reached base on an infield hit that deflected off Billingham's glove. Mike Hegan then batted for Blue Moon Odom. Speedy Allan Lewis ran for Márquez. Lewis was a brief nonfactor in Game Three. On the first pitch he saw, Hegan flied out to Tolan to end the home half of the seventh inning.

The top of the eighth inning saw the Reds threaten again. Ted Kubiak was now playing second base for Oakland and Vida Blue was now pitching for the home team. Pete Rose led off against Blue. Batting righthanded for the first time in the game, Rose hit a line drive that new second baseman Kubiak speared for the first out. Joe Morgan drew a walk. It was only the second time Morgan had been on base in the 1972 World Series. Bobby Tolan batted next for Cincinnati. Tolan singled into center field, driving Morgan to third base. With one out, Johnny Bench was announced as the next batter. He would have one of

**Tony Pérez was the best hitter for the Reds in the 1972 World Series, batting. 435 (10-for-28) and driving in two runs. Had the Reds won the Series, he would have been a strong MVP candidate. Pérez scored the only run in Game Three (courtesy Cincinnati Reds Hall of Fame).**

the most infamous unproductive at-bats in World Series history. Bench had already struck out twice in Game Three.

Dick Williams chose to replace the ineffective Vida Blue with Rollie Fingers. Fingers quickly jumped ahead 0–2 on Bench. On a 1–2 count, Tolan stole second base, uncontested, on a slow curveball in the dirt. When the count reached 3–2 on Bench, Dick Williams walked to the mound and conferred with Fingers and Tenace. With first base now open, it looked like Williams was ordering Fingers to intentionally walk Bench. He pointed to the plate; he pointed at Tony Pérez in the on-deck circle; he pointed to unoccupied first base. It was all theatrics, however. Fingers later revealed that Williams' broad gestures contradicted what he was actually saying to his players: They were going to pitch to Bench.

In the broadcast booth, Tony Kubek accurately told NBC's large prime-time viewing audience to be on the alert for a trick play.

When he returned to his defensive position behind the plate, catcher Gene Tenace stood erect behind the left-side batter's box. He casually extended his right arm as if he was expecting to receive a routine fourth ball well out of the strike zone from Fingers. Joe Morgan, standing on third base, smelled a ruse. ("Be alert! Be alert!"[23] he shouted at Bench as Fingers went into his windup.) So did third-base coach Alex

Grammas, who later claimed he had seen a similar play in the minor leagues somewhere. "All I got out of my mouth was 'Uh...' and by that time the pitch was on its way,"[24] he told reporters.

The warnings came too late. Bench relaxed—and paid for it. Fingers zipped a pitch that nipped the outside corner. Umpire Mel Steiner signaled strike three. Bench trudged back to the Cincinnati dugout as the sellout and record crowd of 49,410 roared its approval at the A's chicanery. "Bench, I believe, was thoroughly decoyed,"[25] said Jim Simpson on NBC Radio. He had been, indeed. "This is the most interesting 1–0 game I've ever seen,"[26] added Al Michaels. In the official 1972 World Series film produced by MLB, narrator Curt Gowdy called the ploy "an Academy Award-winning performance."[27]

Gene Tenace told reporters afterwards, "When Bench saw me holding my hand out, I think he just gave up. He was surprised, but he didn't say anything. What could he say? It was a perfect pitch."[28]

In *The Sporting News*, columnist Joe Falls marveled at Tony Kubek's prescience. He wrote, "I still don't believe [Kubek] called that fake intentional walk to Johnny Bench. For years, I've been listening to the Bud Wilkinsons tell me what a quarterback is going to do on third-and-four, and many times they're right. But never have I heard anyone [in baseball announcing] expect a play so completely as Kubek did...."[29]

Nearly 40 years later, baseball historian Harold Friend marveled at the audacity of what the Oakland manager did. He wrote, "It was a play that is thought about often, but [one] that is rarely executed. Williams had the guts to pull it off in the World Series: Turn an 'intentional' ball four into strike three."[30]

Tony Pérez, the next batter, *was* intentionally walked to load the bases with two outs. Denis Menke followed Pérez to the plate. He popped out to Ted Kubiak in foul territory to end the inning. Exuberant A's fans in the bleachers threw streamers onto the outfield warning track to celebrate Oakland escaping yet another awkward situation.

Bert Campaneris grounded out to third baseman Denis Menke to start the bottom of the eighth inning for the home team. Matty Alou grounded to shortstop Darrel Chaney for out number two. Joe Rudi batted third for Oakland. He grounded out to Menke as the A's were retired quietly. Jack Billingham had impressively shut out the Athletics through eight innings.

The bottom of the Cincinnati order came to bat in the top of the ninth inning to face Rollie Fingers. César Gerónimo led off by striking out. (Gene Tenace squeezed a foul tip to complete the strikeout.) Darrel Chaney grounded to Mike Epstein at first base for the second out. Jack Billingham was the next batter. The home crowd graciously recognized the Cincinnati starter's excellent pitching through the first eight innings with a prolonged round of applause. Billingham promptly struck out for the third time in Game Three.

Billingham started the bottom of the ninth inning still nursing a slim 1–0 lead. Only three balls had been hit off him that had gotten out of the infield—and all three had been caught by Bobby Tolan in center field. However, when Billingham fell behind 3–0 to leadoff hitter Mike Epstein, Sparky Anderson immediately pulled him for reliever Clay Carroll. Carroll threw a strike to Epstein and then induced a ground ball to Joe Morgan at second base. Sal Bando was the next man up. He drilled a line drive directly at Morgan who made the catch for the second out.

The A's were down to their final out, but before George Hendrick could bat, two teenage interlopers ran onto the field. The attention-seekers each slid into second base before being seized by ballpark security. They offered no resistance whatsoever—even shaking hands with their captors. "They will spend a pleasant night at one of Oakland's not-too-fine establishments, I'm sure,"[31] declared Al Michaels.

When play resumed, Hendrick tapped a 2–0 pitch up the first base line. Carroll fielded the ball and threw to Pérez in time for the third out. Cincinnati had won Game Three, 1–0. Remarkably, through the first three games of the 1972 World Series, the visiting team was a perfect 3–0. That had not happened in any Fall Classic since 1929. That World Series involved the A's too—the Philadelphia Athletics. They beat the Chicago Cubs in five games.

The Reds were pleased to have won Game Three, of course, but they were not happy with numerous things that transpired. "We got a few calls that upset us tonight," Johnny Bench told reporters. "Our ball club is riled up. Now maybe we've worked out our frustrations."[32] Bench was specifically peeved at the call at first base by AL umpire Frank Umont in the top of the sixth inning where the arbiter ruled that Bench's throw had pulled Joe Morgan's foot off first base. (That was Matty Alou's bunt play on which the Reds were charged with two errors.)

Jack Billingham credited the time of day for his eight innings of shutout pitching. "The twilight made the difference for me," he said. "I don't normally strike out that many batters," continued Cincinnati's winning pitcher who fanned seven Oakland A's. "The twilight no doubt helped me."[33]

Cincinnati manager Sparky Anderson was asked what he said to Billingham when he removed his starter from the game in the ninth inning. "I said, 'Hand me the ball,'" replied Sparky. "I never have a conversation with my pitcher when I go out there."[34] Anderson explained the move. "Jack was tired. I should have taken him out when the count [on Mike Epstein] was 2–0, not 3–0." Billingham provided confirmation. "Sparky never says a thing when he comes to get you," he noted. "He just makes a motion and takes the ball."[35]

Of course, Billingham would have preferred to pitch a complete game. "I had already pitched eight strong innings," he told the press "and I didn't want to come out of the game. You never like to leave in a situation like that." Nevertheless, Billingham understood the big picture. "The idea is for the team to win. ... We had our backs against the wall. I wasn't disappointed."[36]

Billingham said the A's batters were constantly falling behind in the count—and that was perfectly all right with him. "They took a lot of strikes low and away," he said. "They were taking an awful lot of them."[37]

Having a National League umpire behind the plate was beneficial to Billingham. "I was throwing a sinker low and away and hitting the outside corner. [The A's] were letting it pass thinking it was a ball. The American League has a higher strike zone."[38] Billingham's perception was generally regarded as accurate. The noticeable difference in how the two leagues' umpires interpreted the strike zone would become fodder for reporters as the 1972 World Series progressed.

Sparky Anderson said he was unaware that Tony Pérez had stumbled between third base and home plate in scoring the game's lone run. "I didn't see him fall down, but that's the way things have been going for us in this Series before tonight,"[39] noted the Cincinnati skipper.

"It was just a pitcher's night," said losing manager Dick Williams. "What else can you say? All I can do is praise Billingham. He pitched an outstanding game. I'm proud of my pitchers, too." Based on the closeness of the first three games of the 1972 World Series, Williams offered this prognostication: "Maybe the rest will be one-run games too."[40]

Reporters were having fun inquiring about the fake intentional walk that embarrassed Johnny Bench. Rollie Fingers was more than happy to fill in all the details and give his views. He said,

> I had never used the play before. The team never did, but I knew what [Dick Williams] meant immediately. When I went into my stretch, I tried to be relaxed. I just came up real nonchalant-like and let the ball go. I couldn't have thrown it better if I took 15 minutes.
>
> When I played in Little League for the Cucamonga 7-Ups 12 years ago, we used to talk about plays like this one, but I never tried it before. We never rehearsed it.
>
> No, it wasn't a low thing to do, and I didn't smile or laugh when Bench struck out.[41]

"John said he was not fooled,"[42] Sparky Anderson insisted. Dick Williams was openly skeptical. He replied, "I don't know if he wasn't fooled, but it worked, didn't it?"[43]

Nevertheless, Bench ruefully told the press after the game, "I guess that makes me look terrible. It makes me look like the goat."[44]

"When your club wins, nobody is the goat,"[45] penned Milton Richman of United Press International. It had been exactly one week since Bench had dramatically homered in Game Five of the NLCS to start Cincinnati's ninth-inning comeback against the Pittsburgh Pirates. No one was talking about that at-bat anymore—only the fake out play in the World Series.

Ian MacDonald of the *Montreal Gazette* wrote, "The Big Red Machine is rolling again. It isn't full gear by any stretch of the imagination, but it is in motion and this World Series will at least go five games."[46]

Confidence returned to the Cincinnati clubhouse. "We are going to take it to them now," said a happy Sparky Anderson. "We know that after the first two games Vida Blue said beating us seemed as easy as beating the Texas Rangers. We're going to run on them every chance we get. And we're going to get our chances."[47]

The less than ideal weather in Oakland prompted Sal Bando to question whether the MLB season should be as long as it presently was. "We're going to get more and more postponements," he warned, "as baseball keeps scheduling the World Series later and later each year."[48]

Bando continued, "We should start the season later and finish it earlier. We get snowed out in April and we either have rain or frost in October for the World Series. The season should be over in September."[49] The folks who agreed with Bando pointed out that some areas of New York state had already experienced heavy snowfalls—and it was only mid–October.

Pete Rose concurred with Bando's sentiments when he was told of them. "I agree," he said. "I would like to see the World Series end by the first of October. I wouldn't mind playing more doubleheaders so we could finish the season earlier. I'd even give up my days off."[50]

Johnny Bench did not seem to care one way or the other. He stated, "Whether it's in October, November or December, I don't care. If it's the World Series, I'll play anytime."[51]

## Box Score: Game #3
### Cincinnati Reds 1, Oakland Athletics 0
Game played on Wednesday, October 18, 1972,
at Oakland-Alameda County Coliseum

| Cincinnati Reds | ab | r | h | rbi | Oakland Athletics | ab | r | h | rbi |
|---|---|---|---|---|---|---|---|---|---|
| *Rose* lf | 3 | 0 | 0 | 0 | *Campaneris* ss | 3 | 0 | 0 | 0 |
| *Morgan* 2b | 3 | 0 | 0 | 0 | *Alou* rf | 3 | 0 | 0 | 0 |
| *Tolan* cf | 4 | 0 | 1 | 0 | *Rudi* lf | 4 | 0 | 1 | 0 |
| *Bench* c | 4 | 0 | 0 | 0 | *Epstein* 1b | 2 | 0 | 0 | 0 |
| *Pérez* 1b | 3 | 1 | 1 | 0 | *Bando* 3b | 4 | 0 | 0 | 0 |
| *Menke* 3b | 2 | 0 | 1 | 0 | *Hendrick* cf | 4 | 0 | 0 | 0 |
| *Gerónimo* rf | 4 | 0 | 1 | 1 | *Tenace* c | 3 | 0 | 0 | 0 |
| *Chaney* ss | 4 | 0 | 0 | 0 | *Green* 2b | 2 | 0 | 1 | 0 |
| *Billingham* p | 4 | 0 | 0 | 0 | *Marquez* ph | 1 | 0 | 1 | 0 |
| *Carroll* p | 0 | 0 | 0 | 0 | *Lewis* pr | 0 | 0 | 0 | 0 |
| **Totals** | 31 | 1 | 4 | 1 | *Kubiak* 2b | 0 | 0 | 0 | 0 |
| | | | | | *Odom* p | 2 | 0 | 0 | 0 |
| | | | | | *Hegan* ph | 1 | 0 | 0 | 0 |
| | | | | | *Blue* p | 0 | 0 | 0 | 0 |
| | | | | | *Fingers* p | 0 | 0 | 0 | 0 |
| | | | | | **Totals** | 29 | 0 | 3 | 0 |

| Cincinnati | 0 | 0 | 0 | 0 | 0 | 0 | 1 | 0 | 0 | — | 1 | 4 | 2 |
|---|---|---|---|---|---|---|---|---|---|---|---|---|---|
| Oakland | 0 | 0 | 0 | 0 | 0 | 0 | 0 | 0 | 0 | — | 0 | 3 | 2 |

| Cincinnati Reds | IP | H | R | ER | BB | SO |
|---|---|---|---|---|---|---|
| *Billingham* W (1–0) | 8.0 | 3 | 0 | 0 | 3 | 7 |
| *Carroll* SV (1) | 1.0 | 0 | 0 | 0 | 0 | 0 |
| **Totals** | 9.0 | 3 | 0 | 0 | 3 | 7 |

| Oakland Athletics | IP | H | R | ER | BB | SO |
|---|---|---|---|---|---|---|
| *Odom* L (0–1) | 7.0 | 3 | 1 | 1 | 2 | 11 |
| *Blue* | 0.1 | 1 | 0 | 0 | 1 | 0 |
| *Fingers* | 1.2 | 0 | 0 | 0 | 1 | 3 |
| **Totals** | 9.0 | 4 | 1 | 1 | 4 | 14 |

E—Morgan (1), Bench (1), Epstein (2), Tenace (1). DP—Cincinnati 1. SH—Menke
(1, off Odom); Alou (1, off Billingham). IBB—Pérez (1, by Fingers); Epstein (1,
by Billingham). SB—Rose (1, 2nd base off Odom/Tenace); Gerónimo (1, 2nd
base off Odom/Tenace); Tolan (1, 2nd base off Fingers/Tenace). IBB—Billingham (1,Epstein); Fingers (1,Pérez). U—Mel Steiner (NL), Frank Umont (AL), Bob
Engel (NL), Bill Haller (AL), Jim Honochick (AL), Chris Pelekoudas (NL). T—2:24.
A—49,410.

# — 12 —

# Game Four

## *The A's Win in a Pinch*

**Date:** Thursday, October 19, 1972
**Site:** Oakland-Alameda County Coliseum, Oakland, California

> "It was fitting that in this bizarre World Series where two base hits [constitutes] a rally, that [Game Four] would end on a string of singles which couldn't break a pane of glass."[1]—Bob Smizik, *Pittsburgh Press*

Game Four of the 1972 World Series was played under cloudy skies. Pregame drizzle had dampened the playing field at the Oakland-Alameda County Coliseum again-despite assurances from the National Weather Service that the remaining ballgames in Oakland on Thursday and Friday would be played under pleasant conditions. There was also a threat of fog in the region. The temperature at game time was in the low fifties. During the game—which began at 5:30 p.m. local time to accommodate national television, of course—the mercury dropped into the high forties. The overcast sky improved the conditions for the hitting compared to the previous game where the twilight made it difficult for the batters to pick up the ball approaching from the mound. Both teams were able to take batting practice for the first time since Game Two. Both teams needed it.

During the NBC Radio pregame show, Al Michaels noted that pitching had been the keynote theme across the first three games of the 1972 World Series. Michaels examined both clubs' cumulative batting records over the first three games of the Fall Classic and saw few offensive bright spots. "Looking at the statistics sheet," he said, "nobody is really having an outstanding Series, with the exception, perhaps, of Dick Green of the Oakland A's who is 3-for-8, and Tony Pérez of the Reds [who is] 5-for-10. But when you go down the list of the starters you see a lot of 1-for-11 and 0-for-10."[2] Each team had a cumulative batting average of just .178. Michaels, however, optimistically suggested that the capable offenses of the Reds and A's would soon come to the forefront and produce a statistical return to the norm. "I have a feeling that things are going to turn around," he said. "We're about due for a 10–4 or 10–5 game."[3]

During the pregame player introductions, Reggie Jackson was no longer using crutches, but he was still walking gingerly as he entered the field with his A's teammates. Despite his absence from the World Series, Jackson received the longest and loudest cheer of any Oakland player. The national anthem was performed by the notable Los Angeles–based vocal group The 5th Dimension.

Seventy-two-year-old Hall-of-Fame pitcher Robert Moses (Lefty) Grove, the ace of the Philadelphia Athletics' pitching staff during the franchise's last dynasty, tossed out two ceremonial first balls. He was a special guest of A's owner Charlie Finley. Finley had generously paid for Grove to be flown to Oakland from his home in Norwalk, Ohio. Grove had been scheduled to do the honors before Game Three, but Tuesday's rainout had complicated the schedule for the dignitaries too. Governor Ronald Reagan was only available on Wednesday, so Grove's moment in the spotlight was bumped to Thursday. He did not mind the delay. Grove, who had a well-earned reputation for surliness in his playing days, was surprisingly more than accommodating to any baseball writer who wanted to interview him during his extended stay in Oakland. Holding court in a hotel lobby, for three days he delighted in telling stories about himself, his old Athletic teammates and adversaries. Prior to the 1972 World Series, Grove had been the last A's pitcher to win a World Series contest—the sixth game of the 1931 Fall Classic. In 1969, Grove was voted the left-handed starting pitcher on MLB's all-time team during pro baseball's centennial celebrations.

The starting pitchers were both lefthanders: Ken Holtzman for Oakland and Don Gullett for Cincinnati. Holtzman had been the winning pitcher in Game One. Gullett had been sidelined for part of the 1972 season with hepatitis which had sapped his strength and reduced the speed of his pitches. Gullett, when healthy, was a hard thrower with a rising fastball. He was making his first appearance in the 1972 World Series. Although he was just 21 years old, Gullett had previous experience in the Fall Classic on his résumé, having pitched in three games against the Baltimore Orioles in 1970 as a teenager. Gullett was a dominant, all-around high-school athlete in South Shore, Kentucky, having once scored 47 points in a basketball game and 11 touchdowns in a football game. As a high-school pitcher, he tossed a seven-inning perfect game, striking out 20 of the 21 batters he faced.

Pete Rose led off Game Four for Cincinnati against the 6'2" Holtzman. He grounded out to Dick Green at second base. Joe Morgan, hitless in 10 World Series at-bats thus far, continued his uncharacteristic struggles. He flied out to Joe Rudi in left field on the first pitch he saw. Bobby Tolan tried to bunt for a base hit. It was not an especially good one. Holtzman fielded the ball but made a bad throw to first baseman Mike Epstein to allow Tolan to reach base safely. Johnny Bench—in the unusual situation of batting with a teammate on base—came up next and looped a single into right field. Tolan was able to scamper to third base on Bench's timely base hit. With Tony Pérez batting, Bench stole second base without drawing a throw. (It was the fifth stolen base by Cincinnati thus far in the World Series.) The Reds squandered their baserunners as Pérez struck out swinging.

Cincinnati had made two defensive changes from Game Three. Hal McRae was now starting in right field for the Reds while Dave Concepción was positioned at shortstop.

Bert Campaneris led off the bottom of the first inning for Oakland against Gullett. Campaneris struck a slow roller near the pitcher's mound on the third base side. Gullett had trouble with his footing. He momentarily slipped on the damp grass, but he still managed to throw out Campaneris at first base. Matty Alou, age 33, was the A's next batter. He lofted a fly ball to short left field. Pete Rose made a fine running catch to retire the former NL batting champion. Al Michaels joked that after making the putout, Rose was hustling back towards his "friends" in the bleachers. Michaels noted that Rose on this night had a mixture of fans and detractors in the Coliseum's left field seats. One banner festooned there proclaimed, "Rose Garden! Go Reds!" A disparaging one declared an altogether different message: "Rose is a Pansy." The A's third batter, Joe Rudi, popped up to shortstop Dave Concepción as Gullett set Oakland down in order. There was no score after one inning of Game Four.

Hal McRae, batting sixth and making his first start in the 1972 World Series, led off the top of the second for the Reds. He had twice been up in the Series as a pinch hitter—and twice gotten a hit. He singled to center field off Holtzman. Noting that McRae was such a reliable hitter, Al Michaels stated that the Reds would love to have him in their everyday starting lineup but had yet to find a position that suited the defensively challenged ballplayer.

Denis Menke followed McRae to the plate. On a missed bunt, McRae was nearly picked off by Tenace, but the Oakland catcher's throw to Mike Epstein at first base was in the dirt. McRae was erased from the basepath when Menke hit into a force play—Sal Bando to Dick

Green—at second base. Green never made a throw to first base. McRae barreled roughly into Green to make a double play impossible. "A finer block you will never see," chuckled Al Michaels on NBC Radio. "If Al Davis of the Oakland Raiders is here, he may have a prospect."[4] Dave Concepción also grounded to third baseman Bando. Menke was forced out at second base. The relay to first base was not in time to retire Concepción. Don Gullett, Cincinnati's best-hitting pitcher, was next up. He hit a ground ball to Dick Green who flipped it to shortstop Bert Campaneris covering second base. Concepción was put out on the 4–6 force play for the third out.

The struggling Sal Bando batted for Oakland to lead off the home half of the second inning. He got a rare base hit into right field off Don Gullett. Mike Epstein was up next. He was 0-for-7 in the World Series thus far, but he had batted .270 during the regular season. He hit a broken-bat looper that was snared by Joe Morgan. Bando had to hustle back to first base to avoid being doubled up. Reggie Jackson's replacement, George Hendrick, was the next man to face Gullett. He grounded to shortstop Dave Concepción. Concepción smoothly stepped on second base for the force out and then threw to Tony Pérez at first base for an inning-ending double play. Game Four was tied 0–0 after two full innings.

The Reds had a quick and quiet top of the third inning. Pete Rose led off. His bunt only went a few inches in front of the plate. Gene Tenace easily threw out Rose at first base. Joe Morgan only saw one pitch from Ken Holtzman. He grounded it to Dick Green at second base for the inning's second out. Bobby Tolan, the next batter, was jammed on an inside pitch. His grounder was tapped to Sal Bando. Oakland's third baseman made the play to Mike Epstein at first base for the third out.

The bottom of the third inning was also a swift one. It began with Gene Tenace batting against Don Gullett. He grounded out to third baseman Denis Menke. Dick Green struck out swinging. (Johnny Bench dropped the ball, but he applied the tag on Green for the putout.) Pitcher Ken Holtzman connected solidly, but his line drive was caught by Pete Rose in left field. Hits were still a scarce commodity for both teams.

Johnny Bench, now 4-for-11 in the 1972 World Series, was the first Red to face Ken Holtzman in the top of the fourth inning. He slapped a 2–0 single up the middle for a base hit—his second of the game. Tony Pérez followed Bench and drove a pitch to deep left-center field. Initially it seemed to be long enough for a home run, but the ball was chased down by George Hendrick in front of the warning track. "That's the longest drive in the two games here in Oakland,"[5] noted Al Michaels. His broadcast partner Jim Simpson added, "That's the biggest example of the fact that the weather here is very damp and the ball is not carrying at all. The ball simply died."[6] The next Red batter, Hal McRae, grounded to Bert Campaneris. It looked like a double-play ball, but the Oakland shortstop had a bit of trouble corralling it and only was able to get Bench on a force play at second base. Denis Menke, who had been in the majors long enough to play for the Milwaukee Braves, lined out to Sal Bando at third base. After 3½ innings, no runs had been scored in Game Four. "It has been anything but an offensive World Series,"[7] conceded Michaels, who had inaccurately predicted a high-scoring contest on NBC Radio's pregame show.

Bert Campaneris, at the top of the batting order, led off the home half of the fourth inning against Don Gullett. He smacked a grounder just inside third base. Denis Menke backhanded the ball as he went to the ground, rose, and still had time to throw out the fleet-footed Campaneris at first base. It was a fine defensive play. Matty Alou drew a four-pitch walk—the first base on balls allowed by the Cincinnati starter. With Joe Rudi batting, Johnny Bench tried to pick off Alou, but his throw to Tony Pérez at first base bounced into right field. The error was properly given to Pérez as Bench's throw was on the mark, but Pérez appeared to take his eye off the ball to glance at Alou. Alou scampered to second base on the miscue. Rudi struck out. Sal Bando was walked intentionally so Gullett could pitch to the lefthanded Mike Epstein. Epstein hit an infield grounder that shortstop Dave Concepción fielded on the on the right side of second base. Concepción had to hurry, but his throw just beat Epstein to first base. The second excellent defensive play of the inning by the Reds had retired the A's.

Cincinnati shortstop Dave Concepción began the top of the fifth by grounding out to Oakland shortstop Bert Campaneris. Pitcher Don Gullett flied out to center fielder George Hendrick who made a routine catch. Pete Rose, only 1-for-13 in the World Series, hit a fly ball to deep right field, but Matty Alou caught it near the foul line for the third out. The first 4½ innings of Game Four had been played in less than an hour. The score was still 0–0. "Today the two teams were able to take batting practice for the first time since Sunday," Al Michaels kidded, "but you'd never know it."[8]

George Hendrick popped out to second baseman Joe Morgan in the shallow outfield grass to start the home half of the fifth inning for Oakland. Next up to face Don Gullett was catcher Gene Tenace. Continuing his unexpected home run tear, Tenace launched the first pitch he saw inside the left field foul pole to give Oakland a 1–0 advantage. It was Tenace's third home run of the Series. (The last man to hit three round-trippers in a World Series was Donn Clendenon of the New York Mets in their upset win over Baltimore in 1969.) "I know a lot of the country's baseball fans are wondering where in the world were [Tenace's] home runs all year," said Monte Moore on NBC's television coverage. "He didn't play much this year. We feel if he had been playing, he's a 20- or 25-home-run-a-year man."[9] Dick Green followed Tenace to the plate, took a cut at Gullett's first pitch to him, and flied out to Hal McRae for the second out of the inning. Ken Holtzman promptly grounded out to shortstop Dave Concepción to end the frame.

As Joe Morgan led off the top of the sixth inning, Jim Simpson told his NBC Radio audience what Cincinnati fans keenly knew: the top of the NL champions' batting order—Pete Rose, Morgan and Bobby Tolan—had not yet scored or driven in a single run during the 1972 World Series. Morgan and Oakland's Mike Epstein were the only two regulars on either team who had not managed a hit. Morgan's slump continued.

He hit a Holtzman pitch off his fists, harmlessly grounding out to Dick Green at second base. Bobby Tolan grounded out to Bert Campaneris. The next Cincinnati batter, Johnny Bench, looked to have gotten a hit off Ken Holtzman, but Matty Alou made a fine running catch in right-center field to snare the knee-high liner to complete a three-up-three-down inning.

Holding a 1–0 lead, Oakland's Bert Campaneris led off the bottom of the sixth inning. His belt sent Pete Rose to the warning track in foul territory where the Reds left fielder made the catch in front of hostile fans. Matty Alou got a big hand for his fine defensive work when he followed Campaneris to the plate, but he swiftly grounded out to Cincinnati third baseman Denis Menke. Joe Rudi slapped a two-out base hit off Gullett into left field to keep the inning alive. Sal Bando followed with another single into left field. Rudi stopped at second base. The two A's were stranded on base as Mike Epstein flied out to Hal McRae in right field. The struggling Epstein had not gotten a hit since Game Five of the ALCS.

Ken Holtzman took the mound for Oakland, but Dick Williams had both Rollie Fingers and Vida Blue warming up in the bullpen in case Holtzman faltered. Tony Pérez opened the top of the seventh inning by flaring a single that dropped into shallow right field. Hal McRae batted next. He popped out to shortstop Bert Campaneris. Denis Menke, who was just 1-for-11 in the World Series, followed McRae. He slapped a grounder back to Holtzman who deftly fielded it and started a 1–4–3 double play. Oakland still led Game Four by a 1–0 score. Al Michaels declared, "Ken Holtzman and Gene Tenace were the big story Saturday in Game One. So far they've been the whole story in Game Four."[10]

**Joe Morgan struggled at the plate in the 1972 World Series, but he ran well when he reached base. He was perfect in steal attempts against Oakland— until Game Seven (courtesy Cincinnati Reds Hall of Fame)**

The bottom of the seventh inning had George Hendrick leading off for Oakland. He struck out swinging. It was Gullett's third whiff of the game. Gene Tenace got an enormous cheer when he followed Hendrick to bat, but he too struck out. Dick Green drove a breaking pitch inside the bag at third base. Pete Rose got to the ball quickly in left field and threw to second base. It was not in time. Green was on the bag with a double. Pitcher Ken Holtzman batted next. He harmlessly popped up to Denis Menke. The first seven innings of Game Four had been played in less than 90 minutes. The home team was ahead by a single run.

In the top of the eighth inning, Oakland manager Dick Williams replaced Mike Epstein at first base with Mike Hegan, the superior glove man. Things began to get worrisome for Oakland starter Ken Holtzman right away. Righthanded batter Dave Concepción beat out an infield hit to Bert Campaneris. It was the fifth hit that Holtzman had allowed to the Reds. Sparky Anderson sent up pinch hitter Julián Javier to bat for pitcher Don Gullett. The A's had a discussion on the mound about how to defend against the bunt they were sure was coming. Javier indeed bunted the first pitch he saw toward third base. It was a good one. Sal Bando fielded it and threw to Hegan at first base to retire Javier. Concepción, representing the tying run, moved to second base with one out.

The next Red batter, Pete Rose, connected solidly. The ball deflected off pitcher Holtzman's glove fortuitously to second baseman Dick Green. Green threw out Rose at first base as Concepción went to third base on the 1–4–3 fielder's choice. With two out, Joe Morgan was the next batter. Holtzman would not face him, however. Dick Williams opted to replace him with Vida Blue.

Blue threw a strike at Morgan's knees. His next pitch was a low one that almost got away from Gene Tenace. Morgan fouled off Blue's third offering. The fourth pitch, high and outside, nearly sailed over Tenace's head. With a 2–2 count, Blue's next pitch just missed the strike zone. He glared disapprovingly at plate umpire Frank Umont. On a full count, Morgan drew a walk. Bobby Tolan came up with runners at the corners. Morgan broke for second base on Blue's first pitch to the Cincinnati center fielder as Tolan lashed a double down the right field line about three feet fair. Concepción scored. Morgan, hustling on the basepaths, beat the throw to the plate with ease. Suddenly Game Four had shifted to Cincinnati's favor. The Reds were ahead, 2–1. Johnny Bench flied out to George Hendrick in center field to end the inning.

The new Cincinnati pitcher was righthander Pedro Borbón. Bert Campaneris grounded out to Dave Concepción. The Red shortstop's throw to first baseman Tony Pérez was slightly off the mark, but Pérez, employing a bit of nifty footwork, retained contact with the bag. Matty Alou followed Campaneris by hitting an easy ground ball to Joe Morgan. Jim Simpson commented, "Borbón has got that sinking fastball doing just what it's been doing for most of the year and for all the World Series—getting men to hit the ball into the ground."[11] Joe Rudi got his second hit of the night. It bounced past a diving Tony Pérez into right field. Rudi was stranded at first base, however, as Sal Bando grounded out to Concepción.

In the top of the ninth inning, Tony Pérez batted first for the Reds. Vida Blue remained on the mound for Oakland. Pérez hit a Blue changeup into right field for a leadoff single. It was Cincinnati's seventh hit of the game. That was all for Blue. Dick Williams brought in Rollie Fingers to try to stop any potential trouble. The move paid immediate dividends. With Hal McRae batting, Fingers caught Pérez leaning. The pickoff throw led to a rundown in which Pérez was tagged out. The scoring of the play was 1–3–4. McRae struck out on three pitches. "In a manner of speaking," said Jim Simpson, "Fingers has thrown four times and has two outs."[12] Denis Menke hit a promising drive to deep left field where both Joe Rudi and George Hendrick converged. It stayed in the ballpark, however. Rudi made the catch to end the top of the final inning.

César Gerónimo replaced Hal McRae in right field for Cincinnati in the bottom of the ninth inning. The Reds were suddenly poised to level the 1972 World Series at two games apiece with the fourth consecutive win by the visiting team—something that had not happened since the 1923 Fall Classic. All they needed were three outs. But the usually reliable Pedro Borbón was unable to shut down the pesky A's in Game Four when it counted the most. Borbón got leadoff hitter Mike Hegan to ground out to Denis Menke at third base, but he then surrendered a one-out single to pinch hitter Gonzalo Márquez that slowly bounded untouched over second base. (Prior to the World Series, a Cincinnati advance scout, Ray Shore, had informed Anderson how to defense Márquez. Shore stated that Márquez had a tendency to hit fly balls into left field, but his ground balls usually went up the middle. Thus, shortstop Dave Concepción should position himself accordingly. But Concepción, another Venezuelan, disagreed. He told Anderson that Márquez usually knocked everything toward the left-side hole and insisted on playing him that way. Anderson wrongly deferred to his shortstop instead of his scout's notes—and his decision cost Cincinnati dearly.)

The fleet-footed Allan Lewis predictably entered the game as a pinch runner for Márquez.

Gene Tenace came to bat next. When the count reached 2–1 on Tenace, Anderson promptly gave Borbón his walking papers for the day. He was removed in favor of righthander Clay Carroll, the man who had superbly saved Game Three and was widely regarded as the best reliever in the NL. Carroll's fine reputation apparently meant nothing to Tenace. Tenace rapped a single too, this one bounced into left field. Lewis stopped at second base. Dick Williams sent up a second pinch hitter, seldom-used Don Mincher, batting for Dick Green, to try his luck versus Carroll.

Mincher had played in the 1965 World Series for the Minnesota Twins when they had lost to the Los Angeles Dodgers in seven games. On July 20, he had come to the A's along with Ted Kubiak in a trade with the Texas Rangers. (It was Mincher's second stint with Oakland, having played with the A's in 1970 and part of 1971.) As a backup first baseman, he had batted just 64 times for Oakland in 1972. Mincher rapped a hit of Carroll too. It fell into center field and drove home the fleet-footed Lewis from second base. Bobby Tolan slipped while fielding the ball, allowing Tenace to take third base on the play. Suddenly Game Four was tied, 2–2, and the home team had runners at first and third with just one out. "This Oakland crowd has gone crazy!"[13] shouted NBC's Curt Gowdy above the deafening din. Dick Williams called upon the speedy

Cincinnati third baseman Denis Menke did little offensively in the 1972 World Series, but he was perfect on defense for the NL champions. Menke committed no errors in the Fall Classic (courtesy Cincinnati Reds Hall of Fame).

Blue Moon Odom to run for Mincher. The move was designed to make a potential inning-ending double play more difficult for the Reds to turn. Odom had been used as a pinch runner 28 times in 1972.

Quick to recognize a positive trend, Williams opted to employ his third pinch hitter of the ninth inning. Ángel Mangual batted for Rollie Fingers. Bob Smizik of the *Pittsburgh Press* wrote, "It promised to be the mismatch of the season. Mangual, a former Pirate farmhand, had been a distinct flop with the A's. So badly had he performed that George Hendrick, a .182 hitter, was starting in front of him."[14]

Williams' faith in Mangual was rewarded with a timely bit of luck. Mangual knocked a slow-moving single into right-center field through a drawn-in infield on the first pitch that Carroll threw to him. (Hal Bock of the Associated Press wrote that Mangual "drilled" a single. That was a bit of hyperbole.) Gene Tenace easily scored the third Oakland run to make the final score 3–2 for the home team. "Had the infield not been drawn in, there was a distinct chance of a double play," Jim Simpson, commented. The A's rushed from their dugout to happily mob Mangual. Instead of the 1972 World Series being level, Oakland now held a commanding 3–1 edge in games—a huge turn of events. The crowd exploded with delight at the sudden and dramatic change of fortunes for the home team.

Sparky Anderson was unimpressed with the game-winning hit. "Mangual didn't even hit the ball," he asserted. "That wasn't a hit; the ball was right in on him. It knocked the bat out of his hands." Anderson then created a new baseball term: "He hit a seeing-eye dog."[15] [Authors' note: Sparky Anderson had an amusing habit of mangling the English language that reporters found endearing. He often chose incorrect words or terms to describe things. Once he observed that an impressively muscular ballplayer looked "like a Greek *goddess*."]

Upon hearing the remarks of the vanquished Cincinnati manager, Mangual was not upset in the slightest. "He's right," said the man with the game-winning RBI. "You have to be lucky in this game. There are nine players out there. You have to hit the ball where no one is." Mangual continued,

> When I hit the ball, the first thing that came to my mind was that it was a double-play ball. I know I've got to run. I didn't even look at the ball. I just put my head down and ran and I prayed that it would go through.[16]

Losing pitcher Clay Carroll, who failed to retire any of the three A's he faced in the ninth inning, felt he had been unlucky in defeat. "I just made one bad pitch the whole inning," he moaned. "That was to Don Mincher. I made a good pitch to Mangual. The ball just seemed to jump off his bat. That's why I don't really feel so bad because they didn't hit me hard. If they had hit me hard, I'd feel worse."[17]

Carroll feared that the surprise turn of events may have quashed his team's championship aspirations. "We had a hell of a chance of coming back to tie the Series," he noted. "We had a one-run lead going into the bottom of the ninth, and then...."[18] Carroll did not finish his sentence; instead he began another: "I'm really disappointed. This was a big game for us. I just blew it. But I'm not going to hold my head down. I'll be ready tomorrow. We'd really like to win this thing but...."[19] Again, Carroll left his thought unfinished.

Despite the unfavorable result of his outing, Carroll—who answered to the nicknames Hawk or Super Hawk because of his hooked nose— philosophically noted, "At least I can say I was in the World Series."[20]

Rollie Fingers got credit for the win for his ninth-inning work for the A's in which he kept the Reds from increasing their lead.

Pete Rose, too, was thoughtful about the stunning defeat his team was just handed. The next day he noted,

> Within a week I've learned everything about baseball that you have to know. One week ago, I was the happiest I'd ever been when Johnny Bench hit that

home run and we beat Pittsburgh to win the National League pennant. I never felt so rotten, so low as I did after losing the game last night.[21]

Winning manager Dick Williams believed he and his team had caught a break after his pitching change in the top of the eighth inning did not pay the expected dividends. "I had a fresh arm in the bullpen," he said, referring to Vida Blue. "I thought he could stop things. He didn't. But in the end, it didn't make any difference."[22]

Sparky Anderson recalled in his autobiography that scout Ray Shore, whose information he ignored in the crucial bottom of the ninth inning, walked silently into his office when Game Four concluded, thumbed through his scouting report to make sure it said what he thought it said, and slammed it onto Anderson's desk. Shore left without saying a word. Anderson admitted Shore was wholly justified in doing so.

After the game, Gene Tenace, who scored the winning run, took time to clarify to the media how his surname should be pronounced. The surprise batting star of the World Series assured all and sundry it was the same as "tennis"—not "ten-ace" as he often heard it said. Then Tenace said, "In Italy, where my grandparents came from, it's 'ten-ah-chi.'" The 26-year-old felt compelled to add, "I don't care what they call me as long as we keep winning."[23] Tenace's name on his birth certificate read "Fury Gino Tennaci."

Tenace delighted in hitting his third home run of the World Series because of something that Sparky Anderson said to the press after his two-homer show in Game One. Anderson, who was normally highly diplomatic, had carelessly described Oakland's catcher as "the kid who hasn't done much before."[24] That remark irked Tenace. "I know Sparky," he said. "I played against him in the minors. It's kind of disappointing to me that he said something like that. I hit fairly well against [his teams] in the minors." Tenace got one of the A's four hits in the decisive ninth inning. It was a single. "I was trying for [another] home run,"[25] he admitted.

One baseball subject that reporters were discussing amongst themselves—and with the World Series participants, too—was the supposed difference between the strike zones depending on which league provided the plate umpire. It was generally believed that NL umpires called more low strikes than their AL counterparts. (For example, in the bottom of the ninth inning, Clay Carroll was visibly upset that the first pitch he threw was not called a strike by AL umpire Frank Umont.) Ralph Bernstein of the Associated Press noted, "Umpires working the Series concede there might be a slight variance because of different techniques, but insist it is so slight that the players should be able to adjust."[26]

"Basically, we wear outside chest protectors and work directly over the catchers," explained AL umpire Jim Honochick. "The National League umpires wear inside protectors and work between the hitter and the catcher in the open hole. We stand up and they crouch. The difference [in strike zones] is strictly human judgment."[27]

Cincinnati's Jack Billingham said he preferred having an NL umpire work home plate in his games because, as a sinker ball pitcher, he tended to get more pitches—even those below the knees—called strikes. Honochick would not go that far. He said a pitch that crosses home plate below the batter's knees is, by rule, always a ball regardless of who is calling balls and strikes. "It's simply judgment, although there's no question that they [NL umpires] get a better look at lower pitches than we do because of their positioning."[28]

The two managers differed over whether or not any of this affected World Series games. Dick Williams believed that it did not. Sparky Anderson said it did, however. "I try to select my pitcher based on the umpire working behind the plate,"[29] he noted.

Joe Morgan's uncharacteristic batting slump continued. After Game Four he was hitless in 13 at-bats in the World Series. Dating back to the end of the NLCS, Morgan was 0-for-17. He had just one hit in his last 22 official at-bats. The next day, when Cincinnati pitching coach Larry Shepard was reminded by NBC's Tony Kubek that his staff had only allowed eight runs in four games, yet the Reds were on the verge of elimination, Shepard replied, "If you had told me this a week ago, I would have laughed at you."[30]

Pittsburgh baseball reporter Bob Smizik was not at all impressed by the closeness of all four games thus far contested in the 1972 Fall Classic. Dominant pitching was simply not his cup of tea. (Perhaps he was embittered that his hometown Pirates were absent from the World Series fun.) In his summary of Game Four, Smizik acerbically wrote in the *Pittsburgh Press*, "The win gave Oakland a 3–1 advantage in games and had baseball people hoping this hitless mess would end [tomorrow] and spare baseball any more embarrassment."[31]

Indeed, Cincinnati's collapse in the ninth inning of Game Four (or Oakland's dramatic comeback, depending on up how one chooses to look at it)—and the quick turnover for the next day's afternoon game—seemed to be a strong indication that the 1972 World Series would not go beyond a fifth game.

Following Game Four, columnist Jim Murray wrote an amusing human-interest piece about three A's players who certainly defied the image of the stereotypical, undereducated professional baseball player. Murray began his column by penning this funny generality:

> Everybody knows a ballplayer, even a World Series star, is an uncouth lout who scratches himself in public, spits a lot, eats with a knife, makes noise drinking, calls girls "broads," and his wife "the old lady." His education stopped in grade school where he learned to fix automobiles and hit curveballs, and the only book he ever read had pictures in it. He doesn't like movies where they wear clothes.[32]

As evidence that this perception was not necessarily true in all cases, Murray happily presented Oakland's Mike Epstein, Mike Hegan, and Don Mincher. Murray noted that Epstein is an alumnus of the University of California, Hegan attended three colleges, and Mincher "wears contacts from ruining his eyes [from] reading."[33] According to Murray, Epstein "knows more big words than William F. Buckley," Hegan is "a master of word games," and Mincher "can probably order in a French restaurant."[34] Murray noted that, despite their ample IQs, the threesome collectively refer to themselves as "the maroons." In order to fit in with the rest of the A's, however, they do their best to pretend they "just came into town on a load of pumpkins."[35]

For fun, however, Epstein, Hegan and Mincher occupied their spare time by compiling a helpful, punny glossary of definitions for words the average ballplayer might not know. Here are some selected samples:

- Enigma: relief for constipation
- Caustic: expensive
- Slander: thin
- Ostentatious: the capital city of Texas, or a resident thereof
- Resonance: where you live
- Omnipotent: a sexual hang-up
- Glossary: an 8 × 10 shiny photo

MLB announced that the gross receipts from the first four games of the World Series totaled $2,240,035.99. The players' share of this amount was 51 percent: $1,142,418.35. As was standard, any receipts from games five through seven would not be included in the players' pool.

After having a chat with Joseph Reichler, a spokesman for Commissioner Bowie Kuhn, Lawrence M. Stolle of the *Youngstown Vindicator* reported that major changes would likely be happening in MLB in 1973. Declining offensive numbers were a concern, according to Reichler. "We are going to try to bolster the batting attack,"[36] he said. The introduction of a special pinch-hitter in the pitcher's spot in the batting order was being seriously discussed. Stolle noted that the rule had been in vogue in the International League for two years and had been perceived as a tremendous success. Reichler told Stolle that both inter-league play and automatic intentional walks would eventually be part of MLB rules too. The AL clubs apparently were strongly in favor of these rule changes while the NL moguls were considerably less enthusiastic.

It was not a good night for the Big Red Machine at the Oakland Coliseum on October 19, nor was it a good night for an Ohio-bred racehorse that had the same name. The four-year-old pacer, owned by Cincinnati baseball fan Barton A. Holl, ran at Hollywood Park in Inglewood, California. Big Red Machine entered the starting gate as a 10:1 longshot—and ran that way, finishing eighth in a ten-horse field.

### Box Score: Game #4
**Cincinnati Reds 2, Oakland Athletics 3**
Game played on Thursday, October 19, 1972,
at Oakland-Alameda County Coliseum

| Cincinnati Reds | ab | r | h | rbi | Oakland Athletics | ab | r | h | rbi |
|---|---|---|---|---|---|---|---|---|---|
| Rose lf | 4 | 0 | 0 | 0 | Campaneris ss | 4 | 0 | 0 | 0 |
| Morgan 2b | 3 | 1 | 0 | 0 | Alou rf | 3 | 0 | 0 | 0 |
| Tolan cf | 4 | 0 | 1 | 2 | Rudi lf | 4 | 0 | 2 | 0 |
| Bench c | 4 | 0 | 2 | 0 | Bando 3b | 3 | 0 | 2 | 0 |
| Pérez 1b | 4 | 0 | 2 | 0 | Epstein 1b | 3 | 0 | 0 | 0 |
| McRae rf | 4 | 0 | 1 | 0 | Hegan 1b | 1 | 0 | 0 | 0 |
| Gerónimo rf | 0 | 0 | 0 | 0 | Hendrick cf | 3 | 0 | 0 | 0 |
| Menke 3b | 4 | 0 | 0 | 0 | Marquez ph | 1 | 0 | 1 | 0 |
| Concepción ss | 3 | 1 | 1 | 0 | Lewis pr | 0 | 1 | 0 | 0 |
| Gullett p | 2 | 0 | 0 | 0 | Tenace c | 4 | 2 | 2 | 1 |
| Javier ph | 0 | 0 | 0 | 0 | Green 2b | 3 | 0 | 1 | 0 |
| Borbón p | 0 | 0 | 0 | 0 | Mincher ph | 1 | 0 | 1 | 1 |
| Carroll p | 0 | 0 | 0 | 0 | Odom pr | 0 | 0 | 0 | 0 |
| **Totals** | 32 | 2 | 7 | 2 | Holtzman p | 3 | 0 | 0 | 0 |
| | | | | | Blue p | 0 | 0 | 0 | 0 |
| | | | | | Fingers p | 0 | 0 | 0 | 0 |
| | | | | | Mangual ph | 1 | 0 | 1 | 1 |
| | | | | | **Totals** | 34 | 3 | 10 | 3 |

| | | | | | | | | | | | | | |
|---|---|---|---|---|---|---|---|---|---|---|---|---|---|
| Cincinnati | 0 | 0 | 0 | 0 | 0 | 0 | 0 | 2 | 0 | — | 2 | 7 | 1 |
| Oakland | 0 | 0 | 0 | 0 | 1 | 0 | 0 | 0 | 2 | — | 3 | 10 | 1 |

| Cincinnati Reds | IP | H | R | ER | BB | SO |
|---|---|---|---|---|---|---|
| Gullett | 7.0 | 5 | 1 | 1 | 2 | 4 |
| Borbón | 1.1 | 2 | 1 | 1 | 0 | 0 |
| Carroll L (0–1) | 0.0 | 3 | 1 | 1 | 0 | 0 |
| **Totals** | 8.1 | 10 | 3 | 3 | 2 | 4 |
| Oakland Athletics | IP | H | R | ER | BB | SO |
| Holtzman | 7.2 | 5 | 1 | 1 | 0 | 1 |
| Blue | 0.1 | 2 | 1 | 1 | 1 | 0 |
| Fingers W (1–0) | 1.0 | 0 | 0 | 0 | 0 | 1 |
| **Totals** | 9.0 | 7 | 2 | 2 | 1 | 2 |

E—Pérez (1), Holtzman (1). DP—Cincinnati 1, Oakland 1. **2B**—Cincinnati Tolan (1, off Blue), Oakland Green (1, off Gullett). HR—Oakland Tenace (3, 5th inning off Gullett 0 on, 1 out). SH—Javier (1, off Holtzman). IBB—Bando (1, by Gullett). SB—Bench (1, 2nd base off Holtzman/Tenace). IBB—Gullett (1, Bando). U—Frank Umont (AL), Bob Engel (NL), Bill Haller (AL), Chris Pelekoudas (NL), Mel Steiner (NL), Jim Honochick (AL). T—2:06. A—49,410.

## — 13 —

# Game Five

### *Produce ... and a Gamble*
### *That Didn't Produce*

**Date:** Friday, October 20, 1972
**Site:** Oakland-Alameda County Coliseum, Oakland, California

> "I don't blame them too much. You have to hand it to
> fans who back their team. But I don't go for this throw-
> ing of fruits and vegetables."[1]—Cincinnati's Pete Rose
> discussing the behavior of some Oakland fans

> "Someone please check the world baseball champion-
> ship and see if it's ticking or has prickles on it, or causes
> lung cancer or something. Two teams handed it back and
> forth here Friday as if it were a satchel of stolen gold and
> the cops were coming."[2]—Jim Murray, syndicated sports
> columnist.

A one-word comment that Cincinnati's Pete Rose made to a Bay Area
reporter after Game One of the 1972 World Series propelled him
into the center of a storm—nothing especially new for the opinionated
Reds superstar. When asked by a San Francisco journalist if he thought
that Oakland's Catfish Hunter was "a super pitcher,"[3] Rose firmly
responded with a brief and brusque negative. "No,"[4] he simply said. This
pithy remark neither sat well with the A's nor their fans.

The San Francisco scribe used Rose's remark as evidence to label
the NL champs from Cincinnati as "crewcut boors" and Rose specifically as insufferably arrogant. Rose tried to backtrack somewhat when
he found himself at the center of an Oakland media storm. He stated
that his comments about Hunter were "really a misunderstanding." He
explained,

> I didn't say he wasn't a good pitcher. Any man who can win 60 games in
> three years has to be a good pitcher. But, in my mind, there have only been

two super pitchers that I've faced: One is Sandy Koufax and the other is Bob Gibson.[5]

Apparently, the entire city from whence the Reds hailed was held in disdain by the locals. "Where's Cincinnati?" asked a huge banner erected outside Oakland's city hall.

Game Five was played on a Friday afternoon, 1 p.m. Oakland time. Of course, this had not been part of the original scheduling plan, but the rainout that pushed Game Three from Tuesday to Wednesday and set the Series back a day potentially created a travel problem if the Oakland-Cincinnati tussle was extended to at least six games. If Oakland won Game Five, the Series would be over, of course. But

Pete Rose holding court in the Reds' clubhouse. Rose became a focal point for angry A's fans after telling a reporter that Catfish Hunter was not a "super pitcher" (courtesy Cincinnati Reds Hall of Fame).

if Cincinnati happened to win on Friday, Game Six, back in Ohio, was slated to be a Saturday game with a 1 p.m. starting time to adhere to the demands of NBC's television schedule. The only way that both teams could be in Cincinnati at the appointed hour would be to play Game Five in Oakland at 1 p.m. Pacific time on Friday and then depart immediately after its conclusion. That is what happened. (To date, Game Five of the 1972 Fall Classic is the last World Series contest to be played on a weekday afternoon. Times had changed quickly. Prior to 1971, Every World Series game in history had been an afternoon game. Oakland owner Charlie Finley had been a very vocal advocate of weekday night games.)

Catfish Hunter, the pitching star of Game Two was back on the hill for Oakland in Game Five, attempting to wrap up the World Series for the hometown A's. On NBC's pregame show, Monte Moore called Hunter "the most consistent pitcher in Oakland A's history"[6] having won nearly 60 regular-season games since 1970. He had not lost a game since August 25 when the Baltimore Orioles beat him, 5–2.

Gary Nolan, Cincinnati's Game One starter, was initially slated by Sparky Anderson to be handed the ball for Game Five, but he was ailing. His arm had tightened up. Instead, facing Catfish Hunter was a Cincinnati righthander who was once lauded as one of the best pitchers in MLB: Jim McGlothlin, who had turned 29 years old two weeks before Game Five. Entering the World Series, however, McGlothlin was arguably the least heralded of Sparky Anderson's pitchers.

In discussing the October 20 pitching matchup, broadcaster Al Michaels described the boyish-looking McGlothlin as having fallen in and out of esteem with the Reds in 1972. (Columnist Jim Murray agreed. He humorously wrote that McGlothlin was a "well-*rusted* pitcher" who gets a start "every other phase of the moon."[7]) McGlothlin had been playing professional baseball since he was a freckle-faced 17-year-old in the California Angels farm system. He married his high school sweetheart at age 19. Utterly unpretentious, as a minor leaguer McGlothlin told a reporter about his family life. "I'm just a hillbilly," he said. "I like John Wayne and country music. Our tastes are simple, and we live within our means."[8]

McGlothlin had been acquired by the Reds after the conclusion of the 1969 season in the same trade that brought Pedro Borbón from the Angels to Cincinnati. (At the time, McGlothlin was considered the more important acquisition.) In 1970, he had the best year of his career, going 14–10. McGlothlin had started both the last MLB game ever contested at Crosley Field, the home ballpark of the Reds from 1912 to June 1970, and the first one they played at new Riverfront Stadium. Biographer Charles F. Faber wrote, "During his first seasons with Cincinnati, McGlothlin had an adequate fastball, good control, an excellent sinker, and a curve with a good snap to it."[9] By late 1972, however, McGlothlin's pitching prowess was noticeably declining. He was shuffled in and out of the Cincinnati starting rotation to the bullpen. He started 21 games and relieved in 10 others, compiling a 9–8 record and a mediocre 3.91 ERA. McGlothlin pitched one inning in Game Three of the NLCS—the top of the ninth—in which he allowed no hits and no runs and faced the minimum three Pittsburgh batters. McGlothlin had not started a game for the Reds in nearly a month—and he had not completed a game since August.

Despite Cincinnati being in a difficult position, oddsmakers declared Game Five to be a tossup. One sports betting operation in Lake Tahoe was curiously offering 11:10 odds on both teams.

During the pregame introductions, Gene Tenace and Catfish Hunter got the biggest cheers from the hometown crowd while Pete Rose was loudly booed. American League president Joe Cronin threw out the ceremonial first pitch from the Commissioner's box. The formally clad Oakland Symphony Orchestra played the national anthem. It was a return engagement, of sorts. They had been chased off the field by the heavy rain and hailstones shortly before they were supposed to perform "The Star-Spangled Banner" on Tuesday night.

Pete Rose was the first Red to face Catfish Hunter in Game Five. After being an offensive force in the NLCS, Rose was a dismal 1-for-15 in the World Series. He wasted no time getting on track, though. Batting lefthanded, he drove the first pitch he saw 400 feet for a home run to right-center field. Rose was the 127th Cincinnati batter to come to the plate in the 1972 World Series—and the first one to hit a home run. Rose, who had homered just six times in 1972, sprinted around the basepaths to give the visitors a 1–0 lead. "That didn't take long," said Curt Gowdy. Be that as it may, Gowdy predicted, "That home run's not going to bother Hunter. He's got a lot of poise."[10] In his autobiography, Hunter remembered thinking otherwise. He sensed Rose's blast as a harbinger of a difficult day ahead. Hunter recalled a charming homespun aphorism his father liked to utter on such occasions: "The sun don't shine on the same dog's ass every day."[11] It was the 11th time in Series history that the first batter of a game had homered. Tommie Agee of the New York Mets had been the last to do it, in Game Three of the 1969 Fall Classic off Baltimore's Jim Palmer.

Joe Morgan followed Rose to the plate, but his ongoing World Series batting woes continued. He promptly tapped a check-swing grounder back to Hunter for the inning's first out. Morgan was now 0-for-14. Bobby Tolan popped up to shortstop Bert Campaneris who called off Dick Green to make the routine catch. Clean-up hitter Johnny Bench struck out swinging on a breaking pitch. Oakland came to bat for the first time in Game Five trailing the Reds by a run.

Bert Campaneris led off for the A's and knocked a soft grounder back to Jim McGlothlin for the first out. Matty Alou grounded out to Darrel Chaney (who was back playing shortstop for the Reds). When Joe Rudi came to bat, the Reds outfielders played him straight away, not expecting him to pull the ball. The defensive positioning made no difference as Rudi went down swinging. "Despite not having pitched in a month, McGlothlin set down the A's one-two-three,"[12] noted an impressed Jim Simpson on NBC Radio.

Tony Pérez batted first in the top of the second inning for Cincinnati. Like Pete Rose the previous inning, Pérez solidly whacked Catfish Hunter's first pitch. It was a double that landed down the left field line. Denis Menke came to bat next and bunted. Hunter fielded the ball and threw to Mike Epstein at first base for the putout. The sacrifice moved Pérez to third base with just one out. César Gerónimo failed to drive Pérez home. He lofted a fly ball that was caught by left fielder Joe Rudi in foul territory about 50 feet behind third base. Pérez was forced to stay put at third base. With two out, shortstop Darrel Chaney was intentionally walked so Hunter could face the ninth man in the Cincinnati order, pitcher Jim McGlothlin, who possessed a .126 lifetime batting average. McGlothlin made contact with Hunter's first offering. His bat broke, but the ball still carried into center field. Fortunately for the A's, it stayed airborne long enough for center fielder George Hendrick to make a fine running catch to retire the Reds. The score remained 1–0 for Cincinnati.

Mike Epstein, 0-for-10 in the World Series, led off the bottom of the second inning for Oakland. He drew a four-pitch walk from Jim McGlothlin. Taking no chances, Sparky Anderson ordered Pedro Borbón to warm up in the Cincinnati bullpen. Sal Bando drove a McGlothlin pitch to deep center field, but Bobby Tolan made the catch for the first out. George Hendrick got a hit that did not travel 50 feet. On a full count he hit a dribbler near the third-base line that was about a foot fair. McGlothlin hustled to field it, but the ball slipped out of his hand when he tried to make his throw to first baseman Tony Pérez. The speedy Hendrick would have likely been safe anyway regardless of McGlothlin's mishap, so the play was properly scored a base hit. Epstein advanced to second base with one out. Gene Tenace was the next batter. (Curt Gowdy noted that Tenace and Yogi Berra were the only two catchers to have hit three home runs in a World Series—and that Berra was present at the Oakland Coliseum for Game Five.) Tenace eclipsed Berra shortly thereafter by launching a three-run homer over the left field fence. The A's had vaulted into a 3–1 lead. On NBC Radio, Al Michaels quipped, "They give a car to the World Series MVP each year. I'd say at this point Gene Tenace is almost in the driver's seat."[13] The message board at the Coliseum announced that Tenace's fourth homer in a single World Series put him among some lofty company: Babe Ruth, Lou Gehrig, Duke Snider and Hank Bauer. In a 1992 interview, Tenace recalled, "I remember looking up at the scoreboard when they made that announcement and thinking, 'I don't belong with those guys!'"[14]

When the game resumed, Dick Green grounded out to third baseman Denis Menke. Catfish Hunter followed Green and struck out to send the game to the third inning.

Amidst loud booing, Pete Rose led off the top of the third inning for Cincinnati. Again he swung at Catfish Hunter's first pitch. Again he connected for a hit. This one was a mere single pulled into right field, however. Joe Morgan failed to move Rose up, popping out to second baseman Dick Green in shallow center field. Bobby Tolan hit a long drive on a 1–2 pitch. He sent it to the opposite field, forcing Joe Rudi to make a difficult leaping catch at the warning track for the second out. Johnny Bench was the next Cincinnati batter. He hit a pitch off his fists that looked to be dropping just beyond the Oakland infielders. Shortstop Bert Campaneris, moving backwards, made a difficult catch to retire Bench.

After making the last putout in the top of the third inning, Bert Campaneris led off the home half. He watched a Jim McGlothlin curveball for a third strike called by plate umpire Bob Engel. Matty Alou flied out to César Gerónimo in right field for the second out. Joe Rudi was awarded first base after being hit by a McGlothlin fastball. Mike Epstein, still hitless in the World Series, batted next. Epstein grounded a 3–0 pitch to Tony Pérez at first base to end the Oakland third inning. The A's failed to increase their 3–1 lead.

The hot Tony Pérez, 8-for-15 in the World Series thus far, led off for the Reds in the top of the fourth inning. NBC Radio's Jim Simpson mentioned that Pérez had homered off Catfish Hunter in the 1966 All-Star Game. Pérez did not homer this time; he grounded out to shortstop Bert Campaneris. However, the next Red batter, Denis Menke, did. His solo homer on a hanging breaking pitch sailed over left fielder Joe Rudi's head into the bleachers to whittle Oakland's lead to a single run, 3–2. César Gerónimo had a lengthy at-bat, fouling off numerous pitches— including sharply lining one into the Cincinnati dugout—before being called out on strikes. Darrel Chaney had a much shorter at-bat, flying out to George Hendrick for the third out of the inning.

Oakland captain Sal Bando led off the bottom of the fourth inning for the home team. Jim McGlothlin had some control issues as Bando walked on a full count. McGlothlin then fell behind George Hendrick 2–0. Cincinnati manager Sparky Anderson opted not to wait any longer. He replaced McGlothlin with Pedro Borbón who was making his fourth appearance in the 1972 World Series. Hendrick bunted. The ball deflected off Borbón's glove toward first baseman Tony Pérez, who relayed the ball to Joe Morgan at first base. Bando advanced to second base on the unusual 1–3–4 sacrifice. Gene Tenace got a huge ovation when he came to the plate. He was intentionally walked—a highly unpopular move with the paying customers. Dick Williams sent up lefthanded Gonzalo Márquez to bat for second baseman Dick Green.

The move paid off. Márquez blooped a single—his third pinch hit of the World Series—into center field. Bando scored and Tenace advanced to third base. Allan Lewis ran for Márquez. Catfish Hunter was the next Oakland batter. His attempt at a squeeze bunt failed when he missed the ball. Tenace was caught in a rundown and tagged out by third baseman Denis Menke. Lewis ran to second base on the botched play. Hunter flied out to Bobby Tolan to end the inning. Still, the score was 4–2 in Oakland's favor. The six runs scored in Game Five already made it the highest-scoring game of the 1972 World Series even though only four innings had been played.

Ted Kubiak entered the game as Oakland's new second baseman. Pedro Borbón was scheduled to lead off the Cincinnati fifth inning. He did not bat. Sparky Anderson sent up pinch hitter Ted Uhlaender instead. Uhlaender grounded out to Mike Epstein at first base. He made an unassisted putout. Pete Rose grounded out to shortstop Bert Campaneris. Joe Morgan, still hitless in the World Series, drew a four pitch-walk off Catfish Hunter. With Bobby Tolan batting, Morgan got a good jump and broke for second base. Tolan slashed Hunter's first pitch into right field. Morgan scored all the way from first base on what amounted to a long Tolan single. Again, the Reds had narrowed the Oakland lead to a single run. Johnny Bench was the next Red in the batting order. Dick Williams decided to remove Hunter and replace him with Rollie Fingers. Fingers was becoming a familiar face to the Reds, having pitched in every 1972 World Series game so far. Tolan quickly stole second base and moved to third base on a pitch that got away from catcher Gene Tenace. (It was scored a wild pitch.) Tolan was stranded at third base, however, as Bench was called out on strikes. Heading to the bottom of the fifth inning, Oakland's defense left the field holding a 4–3 lead over the NL champions despite only having three hits.

Tom Hall was the third Cincinnati pitcher to enter the game. He had pitched two innings in Game Two without allowing a run. Al Michaels said on NBC Radio, "Hall was one of the more valuable Reds [pitchers] this year because he was a short man, a middle man, a long man, and, every once in a while, he made a start."[15] The first A's hitter in the bottom of the fifth, Bert Campaneris, sent a long fly ball to left field. Pete Rose scampered backwards and caught it at the edge of the warning track. Matty Alou, struggling with just one hit in 15 World Series at-bats, was next up. He hit a ground ball to pitcher Hall for the second out. Righthanded Joe Rudi struck out swinging. For the first time since the first inning, Oakland was set down in order.

Tony Pérez grounded out to shortstop Bert Campaneris to start the Reds' sixth inning. Next up was Denis Menke. He went down swinging.

"Boy, is Fingers tough on righthanders!"[16] Al Michaels marveled as Menke headed back to the visitors' dugout. Lefthanded César Gerónimo flied out to Joe Rudi in left field to end the short inning.

Mike Epstein, still hitless in the World Series, led off the home half of the sixth inning against Tom Hall. He hit an easy, two-hop ground ball to Tony Pérez. "One first baseman retires another,"[17] observed Al Michaels. Sal Bando, the A's third baseman, hit a ground ball to his counterpart, Cincinnati's Denis Menke, for the inning's second out. George Hendrick, 2-for-14 in the World Series, popped out in foul ground to Menke. Hall had again breezed through an inning.

Mike Hegan took over at first base for Oakland as the top of the seventh started. Rollie Fingers remained on the mound for Oakland. Cincinnati manager Sparky Anderson sent up pinch hitter Joe Hague to bat for light-hitting shortstop Darrel Chaney. Second baseman Ted Kubiak made a fine, hustling defensive play to retire Hague on a slow ground ball. Another pinch hitter, Dave Concepción, batted for pitcher Tom Hall. On a 3–2 count Concepción flied out to George Hendrick. Switch-hitting Pete Rose, who had two hits in Game Five, batted left against Rollie Fingers. Rose drove Joe Rudi back to the fence, but the left fielder made the catch to end the inning. Time was running out on the Reds if they hoped to bring the World Series back to Cincinnati; they were a run behind and down to their last six outs.

Clay Carroll was the new Cincinnati pitcher for the bottom of the seventh inning. (He was placed in the eighth spot in Cincinnati's batting order; Dave Conception stayed in the game at shortstop for the Reds in the ninth spot.) It was Carroll's fourth appearance of the 1972 World Series. He had been the losing pitcher in Game Four. Gene Tenace, who had singled off Carroll the previous night, grounded to third base. Denis Menke flawlessly fielded it backhanded and easily threw out Tenace at first base. Al Michaels commented, "So many things have happened in this Series that one thing I think that has been overlooked is the play of Denis Menke. He has swept up everything in sight, everything hit his way in the Series."[18]

The next Oakland batter was 30-year-old Ted Kubiak. Kubiak had appeared in two previous games in the 1972 World Series, but he was batting for the first time. He caught a huge break when Carroll slipped on the grass left of the mound attempting to field what should have been a certain out. The play was scored an infield hit. Rollie Fingers, a decent hitter for a pitcher, was up next. He bunted. It was fielded by Johnny Bench who almost became entangled with the charging Denis Menke. Bench still managed to throw the ball to second baseman Joe Morgan, who was covering first base on the play, for the 2–4 putout. The sacrifice moved Kubiak to second base with two out. Bert Campaneris, 3-for-18 in the World Series, batted next. Campaneris was called out on strikes to end the inning. Oakland failed to add to their 4–3 lead.

His club desperately needing a run, Joe Morgan led off the top of the eighth inning against Rollie Fingers. He drew a five-pitch walk. Only Lou Brock had stolen more bases than Joe Morgan in 1972, so the A's looked for Morgan to run. "Morgan is on first base and I'd have to say he is almost a cinch to go,"[19] noted Al Michaels. With Bobby Tolan batting, Fingers made four throws to first base to keep Morgan close. A pitchout did not coax Morgan to go. But, on Fingers' next pitch to Tolan, Morgan stole second base easily. It was his second theft of the World Series. It proved to be an important advancement as Tolan singled to right field, driving home Morgan. Pursuing the ball was right fielder Matty Alou. He was victimized twice. The ball skittered under his glove and he slipped on the outfield grass—despite the lovely sunny afternoon it was still slick from the long stretch of damp days—and Tolan moved to second base. Alou was charged with an error. The exciting game was now level at 4–4. The Big Red Machine's four runs thus far in Game Five matched their total output for the first three Series games.

Johnny Bench batted next. He tried to bunt the first pitch from Fingers—and it caused a brief controversy. The ball bounced straight up in front of Bench and struck him as he began to move toward first base. The Oakland players maintained it had hit Bench in fair territory outside the batter's box, thus Bench should be ruled out for interference. However, plate umpire Bob Engel disagreed, saying Bench was still in the batter's box when the ball struck him—making the play merely a foul ball. The dispute amounted to nothing as Bench grounded sharply to third baseman Sal Bando. Bando held Tolan at second base and threw out Bench for the first out of the inning.

Tony Pérez batted next—and another controversy arose. On a pitch where Pérez struck out, Bobby Tolan tried to steal third base without getting an especially good jump. Catcher Gene Tenace's throw to Sal Bando at third base arrived ahead of Tolan, but umpire Jim Honochick ruled that Tolan's hook slide into the base had eluded Bando's tag. Bando was furious. For the second time in two batters, Oakland manager Dick Williams came onto the field to dispute a call, but Honochick was unmoved. Tolan was safe at third base with two out. Honochick's call did not matter, however, as Fingers struck out Denis Menke to end the Cincinnati eighth inning. Heading into the home half of the eighth inning, the thoroughly entertaining Game Five was tied 4–4.

Matty Alou was Oakland's first batter to face Clay Carroll in the bottom of the eighth. The slick grass came into play yet again. On a ground ball that Cincinnati first baseman Tony Pérez had to move forward and to his right to field, he slipped. While on his stomach, Pérez managed to make an accurate toss to Carroll covering the bag, who almost slipped himself and awkwardly lunged at first base. Umpire Bill Haller correctly called Alou out despite the missteps.

Joe Rudi batted next for Oakland. He lofted a fly ball that Pete Rose momentarily appeared to have trouble finding in the sky. Rose recovered quickly enough to make the catch for the second out. Mike Hegan batted next. A .329 hitter in the regular season, Hegan hit a bounding ground ball toward second base. Joe Morgan had to move to his right to field it. Hegan was deceptively quick and Morgan may have made too casual a throw. On an extremely close play, Bill Haller ruled that Hegan was safe at first. (Television replays backed Haller's call as accurate.) Sal Bando knocked a base hit into center field that advanced Hegan to third base with two out. The sellout crowd was charged up as Dick Williams sent in a pinch hitter to bat for George Hendrick. It was one of the ninth-inning heroes from Game Four—Don Mincher. Sparky Anderson countered by bringing in Ross Grimsley to pitch. Grimsley had been tentatively scheduled to be the Reds' starter in Game Six. The chess match was not yet finished: Williams substituted Ángel Mangual in place of Mincher. Mangual grounded out to Joe Morgan to end the A's threat. After eight innings, Game Five was still deadlocked at 4–4.

Ángel Mangual stayed in the game for Oakland and played center field. César Gerónimo led off the top of the ninth for Cincinnati. The tension in the ballpark was palpable. Gerónimo slapped Rollie Fingers first pitch into right field for a single.

Pitcher Ross Grimsley came up next. Everyone expected him to bunt. Everyone was right. On the first pitch Grimsley saw from Fingers, he bunted. However, it was a poor one. The ball popped high into the air. Fingers sensed an opportunity to make a double play as Gerónimo, he thought, had to stay close to first base. Fingers let the ball fall to the ground in front of him—a perfectly legal play. He then picked it up and threw to second baseman Ted Kubiak covering first base, figuring that Grimsley would quickly be put out and Gerónimo would be caught in a rundown. Things went awry when Fingers' throw to Kubiak was slightly off the mark. Kubiak had to make a desperate lunge to catch the ball and his momentum pulled him away from the bag. Still, Kubiak recovered to apply a tag on Grimsley as the pitcher ran by him. Gerónimo trotted to second base. It was anything but a typical 1–3 putout on a sacrifice bunt. (Fingers had definitely overthought the situation. Gerónimo was well off first base when the ball was in the air. A simple catch followed by doubling Gerónimo off first base was quite probable.) "The Reds have the go-ahead runner at second base," summarized Curt Gowdy on NBC TV. "That's what they were trying to do anyway."[20] Tony Kubek added, "Kubiak has made some good plays at second base. That one may have been a game-saver."[21] On NBC Radio, Al Michaels commented, "Fingers thought he'd be cute—and it cost him."[22]

After the Game, Fingers explained what happened on Grimsley's bunt. He said he heard Tenace yelling at him, "Let it go!" Fingers continued,

> So I decided to let it drop and try to get a double play by throwing to second or first because the baserunner [César Gerónimo] was holding. But I just couldn't find the handle of the ball after it bounced. Then I wanted to get the ball as quickly as I could to Kubiak covering first. I had good footing, but my throw was a little hurried.[23]

Pittsburgh baseball scribe Bob Smizik philosophically noted, "It was a play born of genius, but one that died of butchery."[24]

Dave Concepción was the next Red to bat. He hit a ground ball to Sal Bando, but the Oakland third baseman uncharacteristically botched the play. He did not field the ball cleanly. By the time Bando found the handle, he had to make a rushed throw to first baseman Mike Hegan. It was in the dirt. Hegan did well to prevent the ball from getting by him, but Concepción was safe at first base on Bando's error. The Reds had runners at the corners with one out.

Pete Rose exploited the opportunity by singling into center field. Gerónimo scored easily. Concepción was safe at third base as Ángel Mangual's throw was well off the mark. Rose alertly took second base on the play. Cincinnati was now looking like the advertised Big Red Machine. They had surged into a 5–4 lead. The visitors' dugout suddenly and justifiably became animated. Tony Kubek said, "It's the first time in the Series that we've seen Cincinnati be able to take advantage of their great team speed and force mistakes."[25]

Dick Williams removed Fingers from the game, replacing him with lefthander Dave Hamilton. The 24-year-old rookie from Seattle was making his first World Series appearance. He had compiled a 6–6 record in 1972 with a 2.93 ERA. Hamilton had appeared in 25 games and made 14 starts.

Joe Morgan was the next batter for the rallying visitors. Morgan lofted a high fly ball to Matty Alou in right field. Alou moved forward and to his right to make the catch. Dave Concepción tagged up and tried to score on the play, but Alou unleashed a fine throw to Tenace. The play at the plate was not even close. Concepción was nailed. Plate umpire Bob Engel enthusiastically signaled the third Cincinnati out. Oakland now needed a run to stay alive in Game Five.

Gene Tenace led off the bottom of the ninth inning for Oakland against Ross Grimsley. Tenace drew a five-pitch walk as Sparky Anderson nervously fretted and paced in the visitors' dugout. Ted Kubiak tried to move Tenace to second base with a bunt, but he popped up to Tony Pérez. Pérez made the easy catch 25 feet in front of first base for the putout. Dick Williams sent in Dave Duncan to pinch hit for pitcher Dave Hamilton. (Duncan, with a .218 batting average and 19 home runs in 1972, had been the A's starting catcher for more than half the season—before Gene Tenace took over.) Sparky Anderson responded by changing pitchers. Jack Billingham entered the game. Williams sent in Blue Moon Odom to run for Tenace. Duncan ripped a base hit into left field. Pete Rose gathered the ball near the line. There was no chance to prevent Odom from advancing to third base, so Rose smartly threw to second base to hold Duncan at first. "The A's continue their miraculous pinch hitting,"[26] declared Curt Gowdy above the mounting crowd noise. Like the Reds in the top of the ninth, Oakland had runners at the corners with just one out.

Oakland shortstop Bert Campaneris came to the plate for the fifth time in Game Five. He was 0-for-4 in his first four at-bats. "It's another seat-squirmer here at the Oakland Coliseum,"[27] accurately said Gowdy. With an 0–2 count, Campaneris, on a half swing, lofted a popup into foul territory behind first base. Reds second baseman Joe Morgan moved over to make the catch just past the skin of the infield. He caught the ball, but he stumbled momentarily. Again, the wet grass was a factor. Blue Moon Odom tagged up and daringly attempted to score the tying run. Morgan quickly regained his balance and made an accurate throw to Johnny Bench who applied the tag. Umpire Bob Engel emphatically signaled out.

Odom angrily argued the point, roughly bumping into Engel once he got to his feet, but the game-ending call was clearly correct. (Somehow Odom did not receive a postgame ejection for making contact with the man in blue; nor was he fined or suspended.) Dick Williams rushed to the plate—but only to escort Odom away from Engel. "Boy, will they be second-guessing everything that happened in the ninth inning today!"[28] yelled an excited Al Michaels on NBC Radio. "What happened in the ninth inning bordered on the incredible,"[29] agreed Jim Simpson.

[Authors' note: Blue Moon Odom was ejected five times in his MLB career. Remarkably, three of them were the end result of his arguing plays at home plate. Odom had been ejected once before in 1972, on May 23. In that instance, he hotly disputed umpire Ron Luciano's ninth-inning safe call on California's Mickey Rivers that tied the game. Odom was pitching at the time.]

**In perhaps the most dramatic moment of the 1972 World Series, Cincinnati catcher Johnny Bench applies a tag to Oakland pinch-runner Blue Moon Odom to end Game Five (courtesy Cincinnati Reds Hall of Fame).**

Thus ended one of the most entertaining World Series games ever contested, with the visiting Cincinnati Reds defeating the Oakland A's 5–4. As was the case in the first four games, the margin of victory in Game Five was just one slender run. Ross Grimsley picked up the win in relief. Jack Billingham got the save. Rollie Fingers took the defeat. The riveting game, replete with twists and turns, had taken 146 minutes to play.

Both teams would have to return to Cincinnati's Riverfront Stadium to complete the 1972 Fall Classic. Vida Blue was announced as Oakland's starting pitcher for Game Six. Outside of Sparky Anderson, no one had a clue who would start for Cincinnati in about 18½ hours.

After the topsy-turvy game, Pete Rose elaborated at length about his ongoing battles with the left-field fans at the Coliseum. In Game Four and Game Five, Rose was the target for missile-throwing spectators who peppered the 31-year-old with an assortment of objects. Many were apparently acquired from the produce sections of local supermarkets. With Cincinnati's victory in Game Five now in the books, and the two teams heading back to Ohio to complete the 1972 World Series, Rose was in the proper mood to laugh at all the goings-on. "This was vegetable day," he claimed. "[On] Thursday they were throwing oranges and apples, but today it was tomatoes and eggs. They were big California tomatoes, too. No, none of them hit me, fortunately."[30]

Rose also chuckled at the fickle nature of the outfield customers at the Oakland Coliseum. He attempted to placate the relentless hecklers by tossing five new baseballs into the stands during pregame batting practice—and it worked. He got a standing ovation. "It cost me $15, but it mellowed them," Rose said. "They tossed tomatoes and eggs instead of oranges and apples. There must be a guy out [in the left-field stands] who owns a vegetable store."[31]

There were many talking points from such a dramatic, incident-filled game, but the final play seemed to generate much of the postgame discussion. Many reporters thought that Blue Moon Odom's attempt to score on a relatively shallow fly ball was reckless. Jim Murray was one of them. The acerbic columnist penned, "Blue Moon Odom broke for the plate. He might have been able to beat a throw from Venus De Milo, but he had 90 feet to run ... and the ball had about 100. The mathematics were in favor of the ball."[32]

Oakland manager Dick Williams stated the obvious about the risky, game-ending play: "It was a gamble we took that didn't work." Williams insisted that he had made the decision to send Odom homeward—not third-base coach Irv Noren nor Odom himself. "It was a good play," Williams claimed. "Morgan needed a perfect throw to get John. I'd do the same thing again."[33]

In the Oakland clubhouse, Blue Moon Odom was still insisting he was safe. "I was safe—I know I was,"[34] he told a group of reporters. He had few believers. Even his own manager, Dick Williams sternly noted, "I saw the TV replay twice. That umpire [Engel] called it right."[35]

Sparky Anderson refused to criticize Odom or Dick Williams for sending him on the popup. "I'll never judge anything on the other side," the Cincinnati manager said diplomatically. "I was only hoping that Joe [Morgan] had seen him."[36]

Joe Morgan himself said he was prepared for anything. "I've played this game for eight years [professionally] and nothing is going to surprise me." Johnny Bench praised Morgan for getting the ball to him with a bit of time to spare despite slipping on the wet field after his catch. "I saw [Odom] leave third base in a hurry," Bench said. "When Joe slipped, I knew it could be close. I knew I had to take the ball to him."[37] In a pregame interview prior to Game Six, Morgan told NBC's Joe Garagiola that he had called off his first baseman, Tony Pérez, so he himself could catch the ball. Morgan believed he would have a better chance than Pérez to throw out Odom if the Oakland pinch runner attempted to score.

Bobby Tolan, who finally got on track offensively, said he and his teammates preferred playing in the afternoon sunshine rather than in the hazy Oakland twilight. It provided for better hitting conditions, he explained. "It's better hitting the ball here in the daytime. At Cincinnati [in the first two games] we hit the ball at everybody. Today we hit like we were supposed to hit."[38]

Pete Rose—who had plenty to talk about—told reporters that he and Oakland catcher Gene Tenace had exchanged a few combative words during Rose's at-bat in the top of the seventh inning with two out and no runners on base. After receiving what he thought was a third strike from Rollie Fingers, Tenace threw the ball to third baseman Sal Bando—except that plate umpire Bob Engel called the pitch a ball. Rose took exception to Tenace's action and said to him, "For cripes' sakes! If you're going to keep umpiring like that all the time, why don't you get yourself an indicator?"[39] Rose and Tenace exchanged a couple of more barbs before Rose flied out to Joe Rudi to end the inning.

"I was mad when it happened, but I'm not now," said Rose. "I don't blame Tenace; he wants those pitches. He's trying to do his job, and I'm trying to do mine. That's all."[40] In the Oakland clubhouse, Tenace was not dwelling on the confrontation whatsoever. He said it was all water under the bridge.

Some journalists were openly wondering if Blue Moon Odom would be facing some sort of discipline from Commissioner Bowie Kuhn as a result of the final play of Game Five. (A photo of Odom bumping umpire Engel appeared in many newspapers the following day.) One such scribe was Melvin Durslag of *The Sporting News*. He cynically wrote when the World Series ended,

> Mr. Odom, a baserunner, was tagged out at the plate. Concluding, amazingly, that he was safe, he rammed the umpire [Bob Engel], nailing him with his forearm and chest, staggering him and knocking off his cap.
>
> Normally in baseball this is such an automatic suspension that one asks no questions, other than whether the ban is three days, five, or ten.
>
> There mere fact that the gods from Fifth Avenue were willing to ignore this was luck for Oakland beyond belief.[41]

Other writers began to believe that Cincinnati's overall advantage in speed could make a big difference as the World Series advanced to its conclusion. Lawrence M. Stolle of the *Youngstown Vindicator* penned, "While [Gene] Tenace, with his record-tying four home runs, is the batting hero, [Cincinnati's speed on the basepaths] may drive him to *hara-kiri* next year as a catcher. The Reds, led by Morgan, Tolan and Bench, have swiped eight bases in only nine attempts. In the other one, Dave Concepción was erased while many claim he wasn't tagged...."[42]

With his Reds now back in the hunt, Cincinnati manager Sparky Anderson could be openly magnanimous to his adversary. After the win in Game Five was safely in the books, Anderson told reporters that Dick Williams had done excellent work in managing the A's in first five games of the World Series. "He's done a good job ... he pulls out all the stops," Cincinnati's skipper said of his Oakland counterpart. "He's tough. He's maneuvered his people well and he's kept all the games close. That's the thing I always have to be concerned with—trying to figure out what [Williams] might do."[43]

Of course, with his team heading back to friendly and familiar Riverfront Stadium, Anderson was highly optimistic about Cincinnati achieving a comeback in the Series. "I still say we'll win it in seven,"[44] he predicted. Lawrence M. Stolle concurred. "The magic number is still one for Oakland, but the momentum has shifted to Cincinnati as the Reds come back home for [the] sixth game of the World Series,"[45] he wrote. Stolle, like Anderson, foresaw the Reds triumphing in seven games.

Joe Morgan was just as optimistic. He reminded the media, "I keep telling you fellows that if we get the top of our batting order on base, we'll score runs and win." Morgan continued, "The key is my getting on base. I walked twice and scored twice. Now we need just one more win to tie the Series. We'll get it. We're going to finally prove we're a better club than Oakland."[46]

A United Press International reporter accurately declared that the Reds had extended the 1972 World Series to at least a sixth game "because the Oakland A's stopped producing ninth-inning miracles and made ninth-inning mistakes, instead."[47]

Columnist Jim Murray said Game Five was a thriller for baseball fans to savor because of the plethora of oddball plays and assorted miscues. "It was an exciting game," he wrote. "Mistakes are always exciting. Just ask the guy who makes the mistake of dating his secretary in his mother-in-law's favorite restaurant."[48]

## Baseball Almanac Box Score: Game #5
### Cincinnati Reds 5, Oakland Athletics 4
Game played on Friday, October 20, 1972,
at Oakland-Alameda County Coliseum

| Cincinnati Reds | ab | r | h | rbi |
|---|---|---|---|---|
| Rose lf | 5 | 1 | 3 | 2 |
| Morgan 2b | 3 | 2 | 0 | 0 |
| Tolan cf | 4 | 0 | 2 | 2 |
| Bench c | 4 | 0 | 0 | 0 |
| Pérez 1b | 4 | 0 | 1 | 0 |
| Menke 3b | 3 | 1 | 1 | 1 |

| Oakland Athletics | ab | r | h | rbi |
|---|---|---|---|---|
| Campaneris ss | 5 | 0 | 0 | 0 |
| Alou rf | 4 | 0 | 0 | 0 |
| Rudi lf | 3 | 0 | 0 | 0 |
| Epstein 1b | 2 | 1 | 0 | 0 |
| Hegan 1b | 1 | 0 | 1 | 0 |
| Bando 3b | 3 | 1 | 1 | 0 |

| Cincinnati Reds | ab | r | h | rbi |
|---|---|---|---|---|
| Gerónimo rf | 4 | 1 | 1 | 0 |
| Chaney ss | 1 | 0 | 0 | 0 |
| Hague ph | 1 | 0 | 0 | 0 |
| Carroll p | 0 | 0 | 0 | 0 |
| Grimsley p | 0 | 0 | 0 | 0 |
| Billingham p | 0 | 0 | 0 | 0 |
| McGlothlin p | 1 | 0 | 0 | 0 |
| Borbón p | 0 | 0 | 0 | 0 |
| Uhlaender ph | 1 | 0 | 0 | 0 |
| Hall p | 0 | 0 | 0 | 0 |
| Concepción ph,ss | 2 | 0 | 0 | 0 |
| **Totals** | 33 | 5 | 8 | 5 |

| Oakland Athletics | ab | r | h | rbi |
|---|---|---|---|---|
| Hendrick cf | 2 | 1 | 1 | 0 |
| Mincher ph | 0 | 0 | 0 | 0 |
| Mangual ph,cf | 1 | 0 | 0 | 0 |
| Tenace c | 2 | 1 | 1 | 3 |
| Odom pr | 0 | 0 | 0 | 0 |
| Green 2b | 1 | 0 | 0 | 0 |
| Marquez ph | 1 | 0 | 1 | 1 |
| Lewis pr | 0 | 0 | 0 | 0 |
| Kubiak 2b | 2 | 0 | 1 | 0 |
| Hunter p | 2 | 0 | 0 | 0 |
| Fingers p | 0 | 0 | 0 | 0 |
| Hamilton p | 0 | 0 | 0 | 0 |
| Duncan ph | 1 | 0 | 1 | 0 |
| **Totals** | 30 | 4 | 7 | 4 |

| | 1 | 2 | 3 | 4 | 5 | 6 | 7 | 8 | 9 | — | R | H | E |
|---|---|---|---|---|---|---|---|---|---|---|---|---|---|
| Cincinnati | 1 | 0 | 0 | 1 | 1 | 0 | 0 | 1 | 1 | — | 5 | 8 | 0 |
| Oakland | 0 | 3 | 0 | 1 | 0 | 0 | 0 | 0 | 0 | — | 4 | 7 | 2 |

| Cincinnati Reds | IP | H | R | ER | BB | SO |
|---|---|---|---|---|---|---|
| McGlothlin | 3.0 | 2 | 4 | 4 | 2 | 3 |
| Borbón | 1.0 | 1 | 0 | 0 | 1 | 0 |
| Hall | 2.0 | 0 | 0 | 0 | 0 | 1 |
| Carroll | 1.2 | 3 | 0 | 0 | 0 | 1 |
| Grimsley W (1–1) | 0.2 | 0 | 0 | 0 | 1 | 0 |
| Billingham SV (1) | 0.2 | 1 | 0 | 0 | 0 | 0 |
| **Totals** | 9.0 | 7 | 4 | 4 | 4 | 5 |
| Oakland Athletics | IP | H | R | ER | BB | SO |
| Hunter | 4.2 | 5 | 3 | 3 | 2 | 2 |
| Fingers L (1–1) | 3.2 | 3 | 2 | 2 | 1 | 4 |
| Hamilton | 0.2 | 0 | 0 | 0 | 0 | 0 |
| **Totals** | 9.0 | 8 | 5 | 5 | 3 | 6 |

E—Alou (1), Bando (1). DP—Cincinnati 1, Oakland 1. **2B**—Cincinnati Pérez (1, off Hunter). HR—Cincinnati Rose (1, 1st inning off Hunter 0 on, 0 out); Menke (1, 4th inning off Hunter 0 on, 1 out), Oakland Tenace (4, 2nd inning off McGlothlin 2 on, 1 out). SH—Menke (2, off Hunter); Grimsley (1, off Fingers); Hendrick (1, off Borbón); Fingers (1, off Carroll). IBB—Chaney (2, by Hunter); Tenace (1, by Borbón). HBP—Rudi (1, by McGlothlin). SB—Tolan 2 (3, 2nd base off Fingers/Tenace, 3rd base off Fingers/Tenace); Morgan (2, 2nd base off Fingers/Tenace). WP—Fingers (1). HBP—McGlothlin (1, Rudi). IBB—Borbón (1, Tenace); Hunter (2, Chaney). U—Bob Engel (NL), Bill Haller (AL), Chris Pelekoudas (NL), Jim Honochick (AL), Frank Umont (AL), Mel Steiner (NL). T—2:26. A—49,410.

# — 14 —

# Game Six

## *The Real Reds Finally Show Up*

**Date:** Saturday, October 21, 1972
**Site:** Riverfront Stadium, Cincinnati, Ohio

> "Why was a travel day used to go west but not when the teams were coming east? Silly question. Television, of course, is the answer to that one."[1]—William Leggett, *Sports Illustrated*

> "The famine ended for the Cincinnati Reds—and it may have spelled the beginning of the end for the Oakland Athletics."[2]—Bob Smizik, *Pittsburgh Press*

After Oakland took the first two games of the 1972 World Series at Riverfront Stadium, many baseball fans did not expect the Fall Classic to return to Cincinnati. But home field advantage was proving to be an elusive intangible. Cincinnati responded as champions do by winning two of the three games played in Oakland—necessitating the return of the Reds and A's to Ohio on short notice. Both teams arrived at their Cincinnati hotels at about 2:30 a.m. Eastern time on Saturday, October 21. With the first pitch scheduled for just after 1 p.m.—game time was dictated by television—few players on either team got more than four of five hours of sleep. William Leggett of *Sports Illustrated* commented, "And forthwith, the world's fastest sleepwalkers began rattling around Riverfront Stadium...."[3]

With the legal bookmakers in Nevada listing the Reds as the 6:5 favorites to take Game Six, the mound matchup for Saturday afternoon was Cincinnati's Gary Nolan and Oakland's Vida Blue. Blue, who had been bickering with his manager and owner about being yanked from his team's starting rotation because of his subpar regular season (6–10) and a severe September slump, had been announced as the Game Six starter by Dick Williams—if the ballgame needed to be played—before

Game Five. On the other hand, Nolan's assignment was not nearly so certain. Nolan, who had lost Game One, was penciled in by Sparky Anderson to start Game Five, but soreness and general discomfort in his neck and pitching shoulder caused him to be scratched. He did throw lightly in the Cincinnati bullpen during Game Five, but Nolan would have been considered a longshot to start the sixth game of the World Series. Nolan would try his best, but it would be an effort for him. NBC Radio's Jim Simpson noted that Nolan had loosened up prior to the game at least 10 minutes longer than Vida Blue had.

Despite it being a day game, the ballpark lights were on for its entirety as rain was threatening to fall. The University of Cincinnati Marching Band entertained the full house at Riverfront Stadium before the game and then performed the national anthem.

Shortstop Bert Campaneris led off the game for the A's. He was still being loudly and consistently booed by the Cincinnati faithful because of the ALCS incident with Detroit's Lerrin LaGrow. Broadcaster Monte Moore, working Game Six on NBC Radio, noted that since Game One, when Campy had stroked two hits, he had been struggling at the plate, having gotten just one hit. His batting woes continued as he grounded out to Reds third baseman Denis Menke. Matty Alou, who was also having difficulties at the plate, came up next and grounded out to Joe Morgan at second base. Joe Rudi flied out to right fielder Hal McRae to end the three-up-three-down top of the first. The questionable Gary Nolan was off to a fine start for the Reds in Game Six.

The bottom of the first inning featured both excellent and shoddy defense by Oakland. Pete Rose led off for the home side. He hit a ground ball off Vida Blue to the left side of the infield. It was fielded by Bert Campaneris deep in the hole at shortstop. His long but strong throw nipped Rose at first base for the first out of the inning. The overdue Joe Morgan came up next. He slashed a solid drive to center field that rattled off the wall. Remarkably, it was Morgan's first hit of the 1972 World Series. Ángel Mangual, who was starting for the first time in the Series in place of the slumping George Hendrick, made an error on his throw to the infield, allowing Morgan to move to third base. It was scored as a double for Morgan plus an error on Mangual. (It was the first of two egregious blunders from Mangual in Game Six.)

More terrific fielding by shortstop Bert Campaneris kept Morgan from scoring the game's first run. With Bobby Tolan batting, Oakland third baseman Sal Bando was playing in to prevent Morgan from scoring on a ground ball hit to him. Tolan lofted a bloop popup that would have ordinarily been a routine catch for Bando. But where he had positioned himself for Tolan's at-bat, it was not. Campaneris, however, speedily moved over to make a backhanded catch for the second out—and to hold Morgan at third base. "That was a very, very fine play,"[4] Monte Moore stated on NBC Radio. The next batter, Johnny Bench, lined out to Joe Rudi in deep left field just inside the foul line. Thanks to sparkling defensive plays, Vida Blue had gotten out of an early jam. Game Six was scoreless after one inning.

Mike Epstein, who was a dismal 0-for-12 so far in the 1972 Fall Classic, led off the top of the second inning for Oakland. Gary Nolan got him to strike out swinging. Sal Bando, who was batting .222 (4-for-18) in the World Series, came up next. He got his fifth hit of the Series by lining a single into center field. Ángel Mangual was the next A's batter. He had a memorable plate appearance. A minor controversy ensued when Mangual hit a slow, bounding grounder to Denis Menke at third base. Mangual appeared to have safely beaten Menke's throw to first base. In fact, he had—and umpire Chris Pelekoudas had made the safe signal. Then, abruptly, Pelekoudas reversed his call. He signaled out and pointed to the bag, indicating that Mangual had missed the base! An MLB runner missing first base on an infield grounder was a rarity, to say the least. The call must have been accurate as there was minimal squawking from the visitors' dugout. (The next day, an incredulous Pittsburgh sports journalist called Mangual's costly, head-scratching baserunning gaffe "a monumental rock."[5]) Bando was now standing at second base with two out. Gene Tenace, who had remarkably belted four home runs in the first five games of the World Series, came to bat next. He hit a fly ball. It was very high but not especially deep. Left fielder Pete Rose made the easy catch for the third out.

Tony Pérez flied out to Matty Alou to start the home half of the second inning. Hal McRae was the next batter to face Vida Blue. He had connected for three hits in six at-bats so far in part-time play in the World Series. McRae drove Ángel Mangual back to the warning track, but the center fielder caught the fly ball with no difficulty. Mangual also tracked down a long fly ball hit by third baseman Denis Menke to conclude the inning. The game remained scoreless heading into the third inning.

Oakland's Dick Green led off the top of the third inning by quickly grounding out to shortstop Dave Concepción. Vida Blue was the second Oakland batter. He took a Nolan curveball for a called third strike. Bert Campaneris hit a ground ball back to the mound. It caromed off Nolan, but the Reds pitcher was able to quickly retrieve the ball and underhand it to Tony Pérez at first base in time for the final putout of the inning. The score was still deadlocked, 0–0.

Dave Concepción was the first Red to bat in the bottom of the third inning. Blue caught Concepción looking for his first whiff of the day.

Concepción briefly argued the third-strike call, made by plate umpire Bill Haller, before trudging back to the Cincinnati dugout. (Haller had worked in one previous World Series, the Orioles-Dodgers clash in 1966, but this was his first-ever plate assignment in the Fall classic.) Gary Nolan also struck out. Blue's control abandoned him when he faced the next Cincinnati batter, Pete Rose. He walked Rose on four pitches, all of them low. With Joe Morgan batting, the A's anticipated Rose might try to steal. They were right. Catcher Gene Tenace called for a pitchout. It was executed perfectly; Rose was thrown out at second base by a considerable margin. A third of the way through it, Game Six was still a 0–0 game.

Matty Alou was the first Oakland batter to face Gary Nolan in the top of the fourth inning. He hit a soft popup to Hal McRae in right field for the first out. Joe Rudi propelled a massively high fly ball to Pete Rose in left field for the second out. Monte Moore informed his listeners, "When you see a man like Rudi hit one that high, he's just missed hitting a home run by a fraction of an inch on the baseball."[6] Cleanup hitter Mike Epstein went down swinging for the second time in two at-bats. Oakland had only managed to get one runner on base in the first four innings. Nevertheless, Sparky Anderson, worried about pitcher Gary Nolan and his ailing shoulder, ordered Pedro Borbón to warm up in the bullpen in case Nolan got himself into any trouble. In the NBC Radio booth, Jim Simpson and Monte More joked that the busy Borbón was threatening to set a record for most times warming up in a single World Series.

In the bottom of the fourth frame, Joe Morgan popped out in foul territory to Oakland catcher Gene Tenace. Vida Blue overpowered Bobby Tolan for a strikeout. Blue appeared to be sailing along nicely—until Johnny Bench crushed a line-drive home run to left field. The Reds took the lead in Game Six, 1–0. "Johnny Bench sends 50,000 fans into ecstasy,"[7] said Monte Moore. It had taken 5½ games to achieve, but it was Bench's first RBI of the 1972 World Series. Moments later Moore added, "The pitch was down and away. It was down and Bench sent it away."[8] With the crowd still roaring its approval of Bench's homer, Tony Pérez quietly made the third out of the Cincinnati fourth inning on a routine ground ball to Oakland third baseman Sal Bando.

Whatever concerns Sparky Anderson—and Gary Nolan himself—may have had about Nolan's fitness to continue proved to be valid ones. Oakland orchestrated a rally in the top of the fifth inning. Sal Bando, who had the A's only hit thus far in the game, opened the frame with a single over the head of Cincinnati shortstop Dave Concepción. Nolan briefly righted the ship by getting two A's to make outs. They were loud ones. On an 0–2 count, Ángel Mangual lined out to Pete Rose in very deep left field; Rose snagged Mangual's drive just in front of the wall with a slight leap. Next, Gene Tenace flied out to Bobby Tolan in the deepest section of center field. Jim Simpson commented, "Nolan has to thank his lucky stars someone was there to catch both those balls."[9] Nolan appeared to be out of danger.

Dick Green, however, was luckier with his placement. He drilled a double to center field. It bounced off the wall. Bando scored all the way from first base. Game Six was now tied at 1–1. Green was the last batter Nolan would face in 1972. Nolan departed. Sparky Anderson would later tell reporters he had erred in not replacing Nolan earlier. "I was kicking myself," Anderson said. "I should have gotten Gary out of there sooner. He told me his arm was tightening. There was no reason for him to pitch to Green."[10]

It was not Pedro Borbón who took the mound, however. It was Ross Grimsley—the losing starting pitcher in Game Two and the winner in relief in Game Five less than 24 hours earlier. With the Reds one game away from elimination, Anderson could not afford to be cautious. Nolan, despite being rocked in the fourth inning, was given a round of applause by the Cincinnati fans for a fine season in which he won 15 games for the Reds.

The next batter was Vida Blue, a switch-hitter. He batted right against the lefthanded Grimsley. Blue drew a walk. Bert Campaneris came up. When Grimsley's first pitch was called a ball by Bill Haller, the crowd at Riverfront Stadium was audibly concerned. However, Campaneris popped up Grimsley's next offering. Joe Morgan caught it just behind the pitcher's mound. The Reds were somewhat lucky to be in a tie game heading to the bottom of the fifth inning. With the score level, Gary Nolan would not get a decision in Game Six.

In the home half of the fifth inning, Hal McRae wasted no time sparking Cincinnati's offense. He drove Vida Blue's first pitch off the center field wall for a double. The next Red, Denis Menke, was retired on another great defensive play by shortstop Bert Campaneris. Menke's grounder caromed off Blue's glove. It still had enough steam to reach Campaneris who was playing deep. His throw nipped Menke at first base, but McRae advanced to third base on the fielder's choice. Dave Concepción next hit a fly ball to Ángel Mangual in center field. It was deep enough to score McRae. The sacrifice fly put the Reds back into the lead, 2–1. Blue struck out Ross Grimsley to end the inning.

Matty Alou, who was only 1-for-19 in the World Series, was the first man to bat for Oakland in the top of the sixth. His batting woes continued. Alou lined out to second baseman Joe Morgan. Joe Rudi fared better. He lined a single into left field. Mike Epstein was up next. He hit a ground ball to Tony Pérez. Pérez fielded the ball in front of the bag and had to apply a tag on Epstein to retire him. Rudi moved to second base on the fielder's choice. Grimsley fell behind 3–0 to the next Oakland batter, Sal Bando. He was not permitted to finish the job. Sparky Anderson lifted him in favor of Pedro Borbón. He was making his fifth appearance in the 1972 World Series. Borbón's first toss was a called strike. Bando popped up Borbón's next pitch. Johnny Bench caught it in foul territory. The A's sixth-inning threat had produced nothing on the scoreboard. Cincinnati still held a slim 2–1 advantage.

Pete Rose led off the bottom of the sixth inning. Rose was fooled by a sneaky Vida Blue changeup. He gently popped out to Dick Green. Joe Morgan, who was a disappointing 1-for-18 in the World Series, was the next man to come to bat. He had another unproductive plate appearance. His ground ball, also to second baseman Green, was underhanded to Mike Epstein at first base. Morgan was out by several steps. Bobby Tolan fared better than both Rose and Morgan. He knocked a single into center field just beyond the reach of shortstop Bert Campaneris. Dick Williams sensed trouble was brewing. At his urgent request, the Oakland bullpen suddenly got busy.

Johnny Bench was the next Cincinnati batter. Blue's first two pitches to Bench were balls. Those were the last pitches that Vida Blue threw for Oakland in Game Six. Dick Williams replaced him with 34-year-old righthander Bob Locker who was making his first appearance in the 1972 World Series. Tolan immediately stole second base— his fifth theft of the 1972 World Series. The pitch was a ball to Bench. With the count now 3–0, Bench was intentionally passed. (There was no subterfuge this time; the A's truly intended to walk the Cincinnati catcher, and they did. By baseball's scoring rules, the base on balls was charged to Blue.) Tony Pérez followed Bench to the plate. With both runners moving, Pérez lined a 1–1 pitch to center field for a base hit. Tolan scored. Bench advanced to third base. Cincinnati was now ahead, 3–1. The two-run margin was the largest lead they had enjoyed in any 1972 World Series game so far. Hal McRae grounded into a 6–4 force play to end the inning.

With Pedro Borbón still on the mound, Ángel Mangual put a scare into Red fans by singling to center field to lead off the top of the seventh. Gene Tenace was the next batter. A murmur went through the crowd. The patrons seemed to sense a key moment in the game was at hand. Borbón was up to the occasion and got Tenace to fly out to Bobby Tolan in center field. Dick Green was the next scheduled Oakland batter, but Gonzalo Márquez was inserted into the eighth spot in the Oakland lineup as a pinch hitter—his specialty. Márquez had three pinch hits already in the 1972 World Series, equaling a record already shared by three other players. He did not get a hit this time. Márquez, on a full count, grounded back to Borbón. The Cincinnati pitcher hesitated for a moment—he may have forgotten how many outs there were—and it cost the Reds an inning-ending double play. Mangual was forced out at second, but Márquez beat the throw to first base to keep the inning alive.

Now the wheels started turning in both managers' heads. Dick Williams sent lefthanded batter Don Mincher to the plate to bat for pitcher Bob Locker. Sparky Anderson countered by removing Pedro Borbón from the mound. Lefthander Tom Hall replaced him. Williams reacted to that stratagem by sending Mincher back to the dugout and bringing in Dave Duncan, a righthanded hitter, to bat. The chess match ended with Duncan striking out swinging. The phantom appearance by the veteran Mincher was the last time his name would ever appear in an MLB box score.

Ted Kubiak replaced Márquez in the Oakland lineup and played second base. Dave Hamilton was the new Oakland pitcher as the Reds batted in the bottom of the seventh inning. It would be the biggest inning of the whole World Series for either team. It did not start out to be especially promising for the home team. Denis Menke led off for Cincinnati. He was unsuccessful, popping up to Gene Tenace in foul ground, but Dave Concepción singled to center field. Pitcher Tom Hall was the next hitter. He was obviously going to try to lay down a sacrifice bunt. It turned out to be unnecessary as Concepción stole second base. Hall, now swinging away, struck out. Pete Rose was intentionally walked by Hamilton to get to the struggling Joe Morgan. Morgan was not to be denied this time. He lined a base hit into left field. Concepción scored to make it a 4–1 Cincinnati lead. Rose successfully slid—headfirst, of course—into third base, soiling his pristine white home jersey. Morgan moved up to second base when the throw from Joe Rudi went to third base. Bobby Tolan, the next Reds hitter, drove both runners home with a base hit to right field. It was the third consecutive game that Tolan had driven in a pair of runs. The Reds now led comfortably, 6–1. It was only the second time in the World Series that Cincinnati had scored more than a single run in an inning. The ineffective Dave Hamilton was given the hook by Dick Williams.

Joe Horlen replaced Hamilton on the mound. With Johnny Bench up, Tolan stole second base—prompting Horlen to intentionally walk Bench. A Horlen wild pitch moved the two Cincinnati runners into scoring position. Clearly rattled, Horlen walked Tony Pérez. César Gerónimo was the ninth man to bat in the bottom of the seventh—the first time that many men had come to the plate in any inning of the 1972 World Series. Gerónimo blooped a base hit into left field, scoring two more Reds as the home team assumed a commanding 8–1 lead. A seventh game of the 1972 World Series now seemed a certainty. All five Cincinnati runs in the inning had come with two outs. There was no one warming up in the Oakland bullpen. Horlen was on his own; he would finish the game for the clearly beaten A's. Denis Menke came to bat for the second time in the seventh inning. He also made an out for the second time in the frame with a ground ball to shortstop Bert Campaneris.

Bert Campaneris, who was hitless in his last 15 at-bats, led off the top of the eighth inning for the A's. He grounded out to shortstop Dave Concepción. Matty Alou did the very same thing. Bobby Tolan chased down a lazy fly ball that Joe Rudi lofted into center field. Tom Hall had made short work of the discouraged A's in the eighth inning.

Joe Horlen faced Dave Concepción, the first Cincinnati batter in the bottom of the eighth inning. The home team's shortstop punished Horlen by smacking a triple to center field. Cincinnati pitcher Tom Hall batted for the second time in the game. With two strikes on him, Hall made good contact, but his line drive was deftly snagged by Oakland first baseman Mike Epstein for the inning's first out. Pete Rose came up next and struck out. Joe Morgan got a warm reception when he came to bat after Rose. He hit a ground ball to Epstein who fielded it on his knees. He flipped it to Horlen who beat Morgan to the bag to record the third out. Concepción's triple was wasted. The score was still 8–1 for Cincinnati after eight innings.

"The A's have a long row to hoe, as they say in the cotton fields,"[11] declared the folksy Monte Moore on NBC Radio as the top of the ninth inning got underway. Slumping Mike Epstein grounded out to Tony Pérez at first base. Epstein was now 0-for-16 in the World Series. Pérez made the second putout too, catching Sal Bando's foul popup. Ángel Mangual delayed the inevitable by stroking a base hit into right field. It probably could have been a double, but with his team down by seven runs, Mangual cautiously halted at first base. He was the first Oakland batter to get a hit off Tom Hall, who had retired six A's in a row. Gene Tenace followed with an infield hit that advanced Mangual to second base. Ted Kubiak batted for the first time in Game Six. He bounced a grounder to third baseman Denis Menke. He stepped on third base to force out Mangual and bring a merciful end to what had become a one-sided game. Ross Grimsley got credit for the win despite his short outing in which he only faced five Oakland batters. Vida Blue took the loss. For the fourth time in six autumns, the World Series would require a seventh game.

Dick Williams kept his sense of humor after the lopsided loss. He told reporters, "Sparky was right. He said the Series would go seven—but I don't think he picked the right winner."[12]

After the game, Pete Rose told the press the Reds had seized the momentum of the Series and would not let it go. "When our guys start hitting, they keep hitting for a couple of days," Rose said. "And we're having such an easy time stealing bases that our manager wants everybody to try it. I wouldn't be surprised if we actually steal the final game from Oakland. We've stolen everything else."[13]

Gene Tenace was concerned about the Cincinnati's mounting successes on the basepaths. "The pitchers have got to hold them on," he said. "They're getting walking leads. I haven't been throwing bad. It's kind of tough to spot them a lead halfway down. I realize the pitchers are concentrating on the hitters, but they've got to make their [baserunners] honest, make them stop. But then, I probably should have thrown out a couple of guys today, so it evens out."[14]

As the 1972 World Series approached its climax, passions were running high among some fans and even biased newspaper headline writers. For example, the *Bowling Green (KY) Daily News* began referring to Oakland's slugging catcher as "Tenace the Menace."

Most of the banter was all in good fun, but one fan snapped. According to a United Press International story, a man, described as "a crackpot," was arrested just outside Riverfront Stadium thanks to an anonymous tip forwarded to Cincinnati police and ballpark security. An unknown person had phoned the stadium to report that a man, later identified as 32-year-old Elwood King of Louisville, had threatened to shoot Gene Tenace if he hit another home run against the hometown Reds. (According to another version of the story, a woman who was waiting in line to buy a standing-room ticket for Game Six, heard another person nearby state that Tenace would not leave the ballpark alive if he hit another home run. She then alerted a policeman.) Through the first five games of the World Series, Tenace had slugged four round-trippers. He did not connect for one in Game Six. King was arrested as he tried to enter the stadium—and he did have a concealed firearm and a bottle of whiskey in his possession.

The Oakland catcher was not told about the scary situation until after the game had concluded. "You're kidding!" said the disbelieving Tenace when he was apprised of the gunman's threat to his life. "You mean to say he is going to kill me? And what are the police planning to do with him? Turn him loose tomorrow?"[15] Tenace was placed under FBI protection for the remainder of the World Series. [Authors' note: In a 2014 article that appeared on a website for Reds fans, Andrew Shinkle wrote that Tenace claimed he was informed of the death threat after Game Two—not after Game Six. In a 1992 interview with the *Los Angeles Times*, Tenace said the threat arrived after Game One. These timelines clearly contradict the media reports from 1972. Perhaps Tenace misremembered the sequence of events. Be that as it may, in a 2017 MLB documentary, Tenace said he received a letter of apology from King a decade after the death threat was made—while he was playing for St. Louis in the 1982 World Series. King informed Tenace that he had turned his life around after doing time in prison. Regardless of the dispute about the details, Shinkle accurately described the incident as "a shameful moment in Reds fandom."[16]]

In the next day's Sunday newspapers, sports writers were heralding the arrival of the *real* Cincinnati Reds—not the bunch who had been struggling mightily to generate offense, not the team that had only scored 11 runs in the 1972 World Series prior to Game Six. One of them was Bob Smizik of the *Pittsburgh Press*. "Yesterday's win was accomplished in typical Cincinnati style," wrote the scribe, "a style that was absent for the first five games."[17]

The suddenly hot Bobby Tolan came under some criticism from the A's for his unabashed attempt to steal bases when Cincinnati had assumed a large lead in Game Six. "That's bush league," said Blue Moon Odom. "He better not try that on me. How long has he been in the majors?"[18]

Tolan begged to differ. "Running is part of my game," he sincerely noted. "If I don't run, I can't make money for my club. Why should I take away part of my game? Just because we're winning by a big score doesn't mean we don't need more runs. In the World Series you need all the runs you can get."[19] The Reds had stolen 11 bases in the World Series and had only been caught twice. Both times had been on pitchouts.

Near the end of the NBC Radio broadcast of Game Six, Monte Moore noted, "Each year they pick an outstanding player of the World Series. There's quite a race. If the Reds win [the Fall Classic] it looks like Bobby Tolan has moved into the driver's seat."[20] Much would depend on how Tolan performed in crucial Game Seven the following afternoon, of course.

For Cincinnati to win the 1972 World Series, they would have to defeat the A's for the third consecutive game. Gene Tenace proved he was a much better baseball player than a baseball statistician. Prior to Game Seven, Tenace reputedly told Johnny Bench that Oakland had not lost three straight games during the entire 1972 season. That was far from the truth. In fact, the AL champions had dropped three games in a row on *six* different occasions in 1972! This included a four-game Oakland losing skein that extended from August 6 through August 9.

Despite his team frittering away its 3–1 lead in the World Series, Oakland owner Charlie Finley remained optimistic even as the momentum of the 1972 Fall Classic perceptibly shifted toward the Reds. He told a reporter from the *New York Times*,

> My wife whispered to me in the eighth inning how I never did accomplish anything the easy way, how I always have to do it the hard way. We haven't done anything the easy way all year. We do it the hard way. I guess that calls for seven games. It is a little frustrating and a little disappointing [to lose a two-game lead in the World Series], but we're not the least bit discouraged.[21]

Oddly, recent baseball history favored the A's going into Game Seven at Riverfront Stadium: The previous four times that a World Series had required a seventh game, the visiting team had won it each time.

## Box Score: Game #6
### Oakland Athletics 1, Cincinnati Reds 8
Game played on Saturday, October 21, 1972, at Riverfront Stadium

| Oakland Athletics | ab | r | h | rbi | Cincinnati Reds | ab | r | h | rbi |
|---|---|---|---|---|---|---|---|---|---|
| *Campaneris* ss | 4 | 0 | 0 | 0 | *Rose* lf | 3 | 1 | 0 | 0 |
| *Alou* rf | 4 | 0 | 0 | 0 | *Morgan* 2b | 5 | 1 | 2 | 1 |
| *Rudi* lf | 4 | 0 | 1 | 0 | *Tolan* cf | 4 | 2 | 2 | 2 |
| *Epstein* 1b | 4 | 0 | 0 | 0 | *Bench* c | 2 | 2 | 1 | 1 |
| *Bando* 3b | 4 | 1 | 2 | 0 | *Pérez* 1b | 3 | 0 | 1 | 1 |
| *Mangual* cf | 4 | 0 | 2 | 0 | *McRae* rf | 3 | 1 | 1 | 0 |
| *Tenace* c | 4 | 0 | 1 | 0 | *Gerónimo* rf | 1 | 0 | 1 | 2 |
| *Green* 2b | 2 | 0 | 1 | 1 | *Menke* 3b | 4 | 0 | 0 | 0 |
| *Marquez* ph | 1 | 0 | 0 | 0 | *Concepción* ss | 3 | 1 | 2 | 1 |
| *Kubiak* 2b | 1 | 0 | 0 | 0 | *Nolan* p | 1 | 0 | 0 | 0 |
| *Blue* p | 1 | 0 | 0 | 0 | *Grimsley* p | 1 | 0 | 0 | 0 |
| *Locker* p | 0 | 0 | 0 | 0 | *Borbón* p | 0 | 0 | 0 | 0 |
| *Mincher* ph | 0 | 0 | 0 | 0 | *Hall* p | 2 | 0 | 0 | 0 |
| *Duncan* ph | 1 | 0 | 0 | 0 | **Totals** | 32 | 8 | 10 | 8 |
| *Hamilton* p | 0 | 0 | 0 | 0 | | | | | |
| *Horlen* p | 0 | 0 | 0 | 0 | | | | | |
| **Totals** | 34 | 1 | 7 | 1 | | | | | |

| | | | | | | | | | | | | | | |
|---|---|---|---|---|---|---|---|---|---|---|---|---|---|---|
| Oakland | 0 | 0 | 0 | 0 | 1 | 0 | 0 | 0 | 0 | — | 1 | 7 | 1 |
| Cincinnati | 0 | 0 | 0 | 1 | 1 | 1 | 5 | 0 | × | — | 8 | 10 | 0 |

| Oakland Athletics | IP | H | R | ER | BB | SO |
|---|---|---|---|---|---|---|
| *Blue* L (0–1) | 5.2 | 4 | 3 | 3 | 2 | 4 |
| *Locker* | 0.1 | 1 | 0 | 0 | 0 | 0 |

| Oakland Athletics | IP | H | R | ER | BB | SO |
|---|---|---|---|---|---|---|
| Hamilton | 0.2 | 3 | 4 | 4 | 1 | 1 |
| Horlen | 1.1 | 2 | 1 | 1 | 2 | 1 |
| **Totals** | **8.0** | **10** | **8** | **8** | **5** | **6** |
| Cincinnati Reds | IP | H | R | ER | BB | SO |
| Nolan | 4.2 | 3 | 1 | 1 | 0 | 3 |
| Grimsley W (2–1) | 1.0 | 1 | 0 | 0 | 1 | 0 |
| Borbón | 1.0 | 1 | 0 | 0 | 0 | 0 |
| Hall SV (1) | 2.1 | 2 | 0 | 0 | 0 | 1 |
| **Totals** | **9.0** | **7** | **1** | **1** | **1** | **4** |

E—Mangual (1). **2B**—Oakland Green (2, off Nolan), Cincinnati Morgan (1, off Blue); McRae (1, off Blue). **3B**—Cincinnati Concepción (1, off Horlen). HR—Cincinnati Bench (1, 4th inning off Blue 0 on, 2 out). SF—Concepción (1, off Blue). IBB—Bench 2 (2, by Blue, by Horlen); Rose (1, by Hamilton). SB—Tolan 2 (5, 2nd base off Locker/Tenace, 2nd base off Horlen/Tenace); Concepción (1, 2nd base off Hamilton/Tenace). CS–Rose (1, 2nd base by Blue/Tenace). WP—Horlen (1). IBB—Blue (1, Bench); Hamilton (1, Rose); Horlen (1, Bench). U—Bill Haller (AL), Chris Pelekoudas (NL), Jim Honochick (AL), Mel Steiner (NL), Bob Engel (NL), Frank Umont (AL). T—2:21. A—52,737.

# — 15 —

# Game Seven

## *19 Mustaches Win*

**Date:** Sunday, October 22, 1972
**Site:** Riverfront Stadium, Cincinnati, Ohio

> "[Dick] Williams, accused of overmanaging, moved his men around as if he were playing chess. And for the most part, he made the right moves."[1]—Associated Press

> "When you tell people someday a team with Johnny Bench, Tony Pérez, Joe Morgan, Bobby Tolan and Pete Rose on it lost [a World Series] to [a team with] Dick Green, Ángel Mangual, Tim Cullen and Gene Tenace on it, people are going to frown and say, 'Let's see, was that the one that was fixed?'"[2]—columnist Jim Murray

With rain threatening all afternoon, the 1972 baseball season concluded at Cincinnati's Riverfront Stadium on Sunday, October 22 with the climactic and dramatic seventh game of the World Series. For the twelfth time since 1955, the Fall Classic required the full seven games before a winner could be decided. Uniquely for 1972, however, it was the sixth time in those seven games where the margin of victory was one solitary run.

The A's made some notable lineup changes for this critical game: Ángel Mangual, as he did in Game Six, played center field, but Dick Williams moved him up to the second spot in the Oakland batting order. Gene Tenace batted in the cleanup spot and played first base as the hitless Mike Epstein was finally benched. (Epstein was not at all happy about being left off the Oakland starting lineup.) Matty Alou, batting just .048, was dropped from the second spot in the Oakland order down to sixth. Dave Duncan assumed Tenace's position behind the plate and batted seventh. (Duncan was the most hirsute of the hairy A's, having both a mustache and a beard.) Bob Hertzel would write that Duncan

**185**

behind the plate was better defensively for the A's with "the Reds having stolen everything but Tenace's World Series MVP trophy."[3] How the myriad of changes would work out was anyone's guess. One unidentified Oakland player told Monte Moore that at the end of the game "our coats will either be drenched with champagne or tears."[4] Moore also pointed out that the projected difference between a winning player's World Series share in 1972 and a losing player's was going to be in the neighborhood of $8,000, so any game-deciding mistakes made in Game Seven would literally be costly ones.

Reggie Jackson and Pete Rose each brought his respective team's lineup to home plate. Mel Tormé performed "The Star-Spangled Banner" for the edgy capacity crowd. Taking their defensive positions, the Reds ran onto the field to an enormous cheer. The start of Game Seven game was momentarily delayed when a banner that had become entangled around the left-field foul pole was ordered removed by the umpiring crew. The tension was palpable inside Riverfront Stadium.

Rain was falling gently onto the ballpark's artificial turf when Jack Billingham threw the first pitch of Game Seven to A's shortstop Bert Campaneris. He swung and softly lofted the ball to César Gerónimo in shallow right field. Gerónimo made the routine catch for the first out. The slumping Campaneris was now hitless in his last 20 World Series at-bats dating back to Game Two. Ángel Mangual was the next Oakland batter to face Billingham.

On a 1–0 pitch, Mangual belted a line drive into right-center field that looked to be a routine catch for Bobby Tolan. It was not. He casually ran toward it—then suddenly leaped with his catching hand extended. To the dismay of the crowd, the ball ticked the top of Tolan's glove, sailing by him and bouncing to the wall. By the time it was retrieved, Mangual was standing on third base. Monte Moore, working on NBC Radio, was shocked at how a seemingly simple catch had been botched. "Bobby Tolan, I believe, misjudged a blast off the bat of Ángel Mangual," he excitedly declared. "It's an error on Tolan and the A's get the first break of the seventh game!"[5]

The following batter, Joe Rudi, flied out to shallow left field. Pete Rose made the catch. His accurate peg to the infield dissuaded Mangual from trying to score. It was a huge out—and the crowd recognized it with a loud cheer for Rose. There were now two out and the Reds seemed poised to avoid the consequences of Tolan's awful gaffe.

However, the A's caught their second break of the inning when Gene Tenace's ground ball hit a seam in the artificial surface and bounced over the head of Cincinnati third baseman Denis Menke who was playing deep. (Menke, like Tolan, got merely the edge of his glove

Bobby Tolan is shown scoring one of his two runs in Cincinnati's 8–1 victory in Game Six. However, Tolan is largely remembered for two costly defensive miscues in Game Seven (courtesy Cincinnati Reds Hall of Fame).

on the ball.) Mangual scored easily on what was properly ruled a base hit, albeit a lucky one. Because of Tolan's error, the run, of course, was unearned. Sal Bando struck out swinging on a curveball well out of the strike zone to end the inning. Nevertheless, the two freakish occurrences had given the visitors a fortuitous 1–0 lead after half an inning in the biggest game of the 1972 baseball season. It was the first lead Oakland had held in any game since their comeback win in the ninth inning of Game Four. The baseball gods seemed to be favoring the Oakland A's.

The usually sure-handed Tolan later tried to explain his ill-timed misplay in the outfield. "I thought Mangual's fly ball was sinking," he ruefully recalled, "but it wasn't. I just tipped it. It just took off."[6] It certainly was an uncharacteristic defensive blunder. Tolan had only made four errors during the regular season and had compiled a sparkling fielding percentage of .990.

Pete Rose led off the bottom of the first inning. The switch-hitter was batting lefthanded against Blue Moon Odom. Rose beat out an infield hit that was rapped to second baseman Dick Green. Rose narrowly beat Green's throw to Gene Tenace, according to Jim Honochick. The AL umpire's call on the bang-bang play was hotly disputed—especially by Odom. It was much ado about nothing, though, as Odom regained his composure and coaxed Joe Morgan into hitting into a double play. Bert Campaneris, fielded the sharply struck ground ball, stepped on second base, and threw to Tenace to complete the twin killing. Bobby Tolan then grounded to first baseman Gene Tenace who tossed the ball in plenty of time to Odom who was covering first base on the play.

The struggling Matty Alou, possessing just one measly hit in 21 World Series at-bats, was at least creative in his plate appearance. He attempted to bunt the ball over pitcher Jack Billingham's head. He did. However, Reds shortstop Dave Concepción—who was getting rave reviews for his defensive prowess by baseball writers who had just discovered him—got a favorable bounce off the artificial turf. Concepción got to the ball in time to throw out Alou at first base. Dave Duncan, who had 19 home runs in the regular season for Oakland, drew a four-pitch walk off Billingham. Dick Green was the next Oakland batter. He knocked his sixth hit of the Series into left field. Duncan, a slow runner, stopped at second base. Pitcher Blue Moon Odom came to bat. Odom tried to bunt twice and hit two foul balls. Odom did not swing at Billingham's third pitch—a ball—but catcher Bench alertly picked off Dave Duncan who had drifted too far off second base. A long rundown resulted. For a moment, Duncan and Green were standing on second base simultaneously. Duncan vacated the base—even though he was entitled to it as the lead runner—and was tagged out in the chaos. Shortly thereafter, Odom hit a foul popup that Johnny Bench skillfully chased down for the third out. Bench made a splendid, one-handed running grab on the play and earned a huge cheer from his admirers.

Johnny Bench, the defensive hero of the top of the second inning, led off the bottom half for Cincinnati. With the excited crowd clapping rhythmically, Bench lined out to Oakland shortstop Bert Campaneris who was playing deep. The next Red batter, Tony Pérez, hit a long fly to Joe Rudi who was driven to the warning track in left field. He then made one step toward the infield and hauled in the fly ball for the second out. "Odom hasn't fooled the first two batters in the second inning,"[7] Monte Moore noted in his radio commentary about the well struck balls. Denis Menke batted next for Cincinnati. Menke had been the best defensive player for the Reds in the World Series, but he had been a disappointment at the plate, only managing two hits. His total remained at a pair as he grounded out to third baseman Sal Bando. Oakland still led Game Seven, 1–0, after two complete innings.

Bert Campaneris batted for the second time in the game to lead off the third inning. Campaneris hit a slow chopper that third baseman Denis Menke fielded in front of shortstop Dave Concepción. His throw to Tony Pérez allegedly beat the speedy Campaneris to first base—but the A's had their doubts. Oakland first-base coach Jerry Adair was furious at the second close call made by Jim Honochick that had gone against the visitors in Game Seven. Dick Williams came onto the field to join the heated discussion, but Honochick's call stood, of course, and Campaneris was out. On NBC Radio, Monte Moore commented that no one could question the integrity of the World Series umpiring as the three most debated calls in the 1972 World Series had been made by AL umpire Jim Honochick—and all three had gone against the AL champion Oakland A's. Ángel Mangual gently popped up to second baseman Joe Morgan for the second out of the inning. Joe Rudi then hit a ground ball to Menke. This time there was no doubt about his throw beating the runner to the bag. Rudi was out easily to end the top of the third.

César Gerónimo led off the bottom of the third inning. He had three hits in his previous 16 World Series at-bats. He hit a ground ball to first base. Gene Tenace fielded it and beat Gerónimo in a footrace to the bag for the first out. Dave Concepción, who had connected for four hits in 10 at-bats in the Series, was up next for Reds. Concepción lofted a 3–1 changeup to Joe Rudi in left field for a routine out. Pitcher Jack Billingham batted next. Odom fell behind the Cincinnati hurler 2–0 in the count but then tossed three straight strikes. The inning was over. Odom had faced the minimum nine Reds through three frames. Oakland maintained its 1–0 advantage in Game Seven.

Gene Tenace faced Jack Billingham to start the Oakland half of the fourth inning. Billingham whiffed Tenace on a breaking ball out of the strike zone and got a big cheer from the tense Riverfront Stadium crowd. Sal Bando came up next for the A's. He slapped a hot ground ball to Denis Menke. The Cincinnati third baseman made a fine play on a ground ball that short-hopped him. He threw to Tony Pérez for the second out. "Denis Menke sucks up another tough one over behind third base,"[8] Monte Moore told his radio audience. Matty Alou batted next. NBC statistician Alan Roth provided a bit of trivia: Alou was the only Series regular who had not yet struck out. At least that positive streak continued, but Alou's overall batting trouble persisted. He grounded out to Joe Morgan at second base to end the inning as bright sunshine broke through the cloud cover in Cincinnati.

The enthusiastic crowd, who had taken to mimicking the pennant-waving throngs in Oakland, kept up a continuous din between innings. Pete Rose faced Blue Moon Odom to start the home half of the frame. He drove a long fly ball to deep center field. Ángel Mangual had a long run, but he chased down Rose's blast for a tough putout. Manguel's catch was a fine one, requiring him to reach high to snag it while moving. "Rose really put some timber on that one,"[9] Monte Moore said. Joe Morgan came up after Rose. He drew a walk. The crowd became vocal, fully expecting some excitement on the basepaths from Cincinnati's biggest base-stealing threat. Bobby Tolan came to the plate. Morgan got a good jump, broke for second base on the second pitch to Tolan, but Dave Duncan threw him out with an excellent toss. (Interestingly, Morgan got a significant round of applause as he trotted back to the home dugout, despite making an out. Apparently, the home crowd admired his moxie.) Afterward, Dick Williams would emphasize that Duncan throwing out Morgan at second base was the key play of Game Seven—and perhaps the entire World Series—as it sent a message to the Reds that they could no longer run at will and would have to work to earn every run.

Tolan eventually drew a walk from Odom, making Morgan's failure to steal second base even more glaring. Tolan himself had stolen 42 bases during the 1972 regular season—and he had pilfered five more in the World Series—but he did not get a chance for a theft in this instance. Johnny Bench followed Tolan to the plate. Cincinnati's catcher was not in the batter's box very long. On the first pitch, Bench popped out to third baseman Sal Bando in foul territory over the visitors' dugout.

Dave Duncan led off the top of the fifth inning for Oakland. He struck out swinging on three pitches. It was Jack Billingham's third strikeout of Game Seven. All his victims had been righthanded batters who chased curveballs for strike three. Next up was Dick Green who challenged Denis Menke at third base. Menke had to backhand Green's ground ball and rush a throw. It was slightly off the mark, but Tony Pérez was able to apply a tag to Green as he strode toward first base. Dick Williams questioned first-base umpire Jim Honochick briefly, but he accepted the out call without much fuss. Menke was still perfect in the fielding department for Cincinnati. Blue Moon Odom went down on strikes, too—also failing to connect with a Billingham curveball. Halfway through Game Seven, Oakland was ahead, 1–0.

Tony Pérez was the first Cincinnati batter in the home half of the fifth inning. Pérez lined a standup double into left field to energize the crowd who were looking for something to cheer. It was just the second hit that Blue Moon Odom had surrendered to the Reds in Game Seven, but it prompted a flurry of activity in the Oakland bullpen. Two usual starting pitchers, Ken Holtzman and Catfish Hunter, both started to get loose. (The double was Pérez's tenth hit of the World Series; he had gotten at least one hit in all seven games—the only player on either team to have done so.) Denis Menke batted next as the Riverfront Stadium faithful became louder in anticipation of a Cincinnati rally. Menke went down on strikes, however. He tried to check his swing, but it did not matter. Plate umpire Chris Pelekoudas ruled that Odom's pitch had nipped the corner for strike three. César Gerónimo was the next Cincinnati batter. He walked on four pitches to put runners at first and second base with one out. Dave Concepción followed Gerónimo to the plate. The count reached 2–1 on Concepción when A's manager Dick Williams decided to remove his starter for Catfish Hunter.

It was a rare relief appearance for Hunter who had only appeared once in a game as a non-starter in 1972. The move did not surprise him. In his autobiography, Hunter recalled being summoned to relieve Odom. "Why not?" he wrote. "We weren't playing any eighth game."[10] Hunter promptly walked Concepción to load the bases. (The base on balls, by baseball's scoring rules, was charged to Odom.) Hal McRae, who had a .444 batting average in the Series (4-for-9), entered the game to pinch hit for Jack Billingham. Hunter recalled what happened:

> McRae belted my first pitch 400 feet to deepest center field. All I could think of was "Not now! Not a grand slam in the World Series!" But Mangual, back to the wall, made the catch. Pérez tagged up and scored. Then [Pete] Rose drilled a ball deep to right-center. Again, Mangual hauled it in. Nobody said a word [to me] in the dugout.[11]

McRae's drive missed clearing the fence by about ten feet. Even though he had driven in the tying run, McRae slammed his helmet in frustration when he returned to the Cincinnati dugout. The two long drives had only resulted in one run for the Reds and a pair of loud outs to conclude the fifth inning. Nevertheless, the score was now tied, 1–1. Neither starting pitcher would figure in the decision. Jim Simpson theorized on NBC Radio that both Sparky Anderson and Dick Williams would have been content that their respective starters had lasted as long as they did in Game Seven.

Having been lifted for a pinch hitter, Jack Billingham was no longer on the mound for the Reds as the A's prepared to bat in the top of the sixth inning. Jim Simpson briefly summarized how impressive the Cincinnati righthander had been in his five innings of work in Game Seven. Billingham had pitched five innings, gave up just one unearned run, allowed only two base hits while striking out four A's and walking just one. He had retired the last 10 Oakland batters he faced. Simpson neglected to mention another positive stat: In the two appearances Billingham had made in the 1972 World Series, he had not surrendered a single earned run to the AL champions in 13⅔ innings.

Pedro Borbón, making his sixth appearance of the World Series, was now pitching for the Reds. Bert Campaneris led off for Oakland. He broke a horrible batting slump—0-for-21—by rapping a single into center field. Campaneris moved to second base on a sacrifice bunt by Ángel

**Hal McRae was a valuable substitute for the Reds in 1972. He barely missed launching a grand slam home run in Game Seven off Catfish Hunter, but his deep drive was merely a long sacrifice fly (courtesy Cincinnati Reds Hall of Fame).**

Mangual. Joe Rudi's ground ball to Joe Morgan resulted in a fielder's choice. Rudi was put out at first base, but Campaneris was now standing at third base with two out.

Gene Tenace was up next. He ripped an off-speed pitch from Borbón into left field. Pete Rose chased the ball down in the corner and relayed it to the infield, but not before Tenace was safely standing at second base with an RBI double. "Gene Tenace has had some kind of World Series,"[12] said Jim Simpson. NBC's Curt Gowdy agreed, noting that "Tenace had now driven in nine of Oakland's 15 runs in the World Series." Allan Lewis was sent into the game by Dick Williams to run for Tenace. Tenace's World Series was over. (After the game, Tenace diplomatically stated that he was not overly bothered that he was being deprived of a chance to hit a record-breaking fifth World Series home run. However, when he spoke privately to William Leggett of *Sports Illustrated*, Tenace sang a different tune: "I couldn't believe I was coming out.")[13] Williams—focusing on winning the game and the Series above all else—was more concerned about scoring another run and replacing Tenace at first base with Mike Hegan than what might happen when Tenace next came to bat. As Tenace trotted off the field, many of the Cincinnati fans in the record Riverfront Stadium crowd of 56,040 applauded him in a knowledgeable display of respect. Many were also undoubtedly aware of the death threat Tenace had received.

Pedro Borbón clearly did not have his good stuff in Game Seven. Sal Bando was the next Oakland batter. He belted an RBI double to center field. Again, Bobby Tolan was a factor. He came up lame on the play near the warning track, collapsing in pain, or else he might have been able to catch the ball. Twice in 1972 Tolan had endured Achilles tendon injuries. He was hobbling badly. At first, it appeared that Tolan was too injured to continue, but he was bandaged and returned to the field. Lewis scored easily on the play. The A's were now in front by two runs, 3–1. Clay Carroll replaced the ineffective Borbón on the mound for Cincinnati. Matty Alou was intentionally walked. Dave Duncan was the next Oakland batter—and the trouble mounted for the Reds. Duncan reached first base on a fielding error by shortstop Dave Concepción. Further damage was averted, however, when Dick Green struck out swinging.

Dick Williams now went about the important business of protecting his club's two-run lead. UPI baseball reporter Vito Stellino wrote, "The ironic thing is that this is the same Williams who left Jim Lonborg in to get belted for seven runs in the seventh game of the 1967 World Series when he managed the Boston Red Sox."[14]

In the bottom of the sixth, Mike Hegan took over at first base for Oakland. Joe Morgan popped out to shortstop Bert Campaneris. The ailing Bobby Tolan struck out swinging against Catfish Hunter. Johnny Bench should have been the third out of the inning. He hit a routine ground ball to Campaneris, but the Oakland shortstop's throw pulled Mike Hegan off first base. Umpire Jim Honochick called Bench safe— although Hegan argued that he had applied a tag to Bench. Tony Pérez was the next Red to bat. Representing the tying run, Pérez drew a base on balls. A wild pitch to Denis Menke moved Bench and Pérez up 90 feet to third and second base. Catfish Hunter was clearly not his usual sharp self. However, Hunter got out of the jam when Menke flied out to Matty Alou in right field. Oakland maintained its 3–1 advantage in Game Seven.

Bobby Tolan was removed from the game before the top of the seventh inning began. César Gerónimo was shifted from right to center field. George Foster was inserted into right field and took Tolan's spot in the Cincinnati batting order. Catfish Hunter led off against Clay Carroll. Hunter walked on four pitches. Bert Campaneris successfully dropped a sacrifice bunt that was fielded by Carroll who threw to first base. Hunter was now standing at second base with one out. Ángel Mangual was the next Oakland batter. Mangual grounded out to Denis Menke at third base. Hunter could not advance on the play. Sparky Anderson removed Carroll from the mound in favor of Ross Grimsley—the winner of the last two games (and the loser of Game Two). Grimsley was the fourth Red pitcher of Game Seven. His first task was to intentionally walk Joe Rudi. He then struck out Mike Hegan to end the top of the seventh. The score remained 3–1 for Oakland after 6½ innings.

Cincinnati sent the bottom third of their batting order to the plate in the bottom of the seventh. Catfish Hunter had an easy time with the first two Reds who strode to the plate. César Gerónimo struck out on the minimum three pitches, chasing a breaking ball for the third strike. Dave Concepción whiffed on four pitches. Another curve ball provided strike three. Ted Uhlaender batted for Ross Grimsley. He fared better than Gerónimo and Concepción, but Uhlaender still lined out to Joe Rudi in left field as the Reds went down in order. After seven innings, Cincinnati was still trailing Oakland by a pair of runs—and they had only managed two hits in Game Seven. Time was fast running out on the Big Red Machine.

With Grimsley out of the game, Tom Hall became the fifth Cincinnati pitcher of the afternoon. He had an efficient eighth inning. Sal Bando, whose double had driven in Oakland's third run, struck out swinging on a breaking pitch with the count full. Matty Alou, sporting a lifetime .310 batting average, grounded the first pitch he saw back to Hall for the second out, running his hitless streak to 18 consecutive unproductive at-bats. Dave Duncan struck out swinging on three pitches. Having quickly stifled the A's in the top of the eighth, Hall was given a large cheer by the crowd of 56,000 as he made his way to the home team's dugout.

Pete Rose led off the bottom of the eighth for the home team. He singled into center field. That was the last pitch that Catfish Hunter threw in 1972. He had not been especially dominant, but he had been good enough to stifle the Cincinnati offense and give his club a chance to take the lead. Rose's single was the only hit that he surrendered in Game Seven. Hunter recalled in his autobiography, somewhat inaccurately, "Every ball the Reds hit looked like it had been launched by NASA. 'I know you're getting guys out, Cat,' Dick [Williams] said, 'but you're damn near scaring me to death. I gotta make a change.'"[15]

Lefthander Ken Holtzman came into the game. Joe Morgan ripped a double past Mike Hegan into right field. The ball nearly hit Rose, leading off first base, who had to dive to get out of its way. Precious seconds were lost in Rose's trip around the basepath. Rose considered trying to score on the play, but he abruptly changed his mind and had to hustle back into third base. Morgan thought he had hit an RBI triple. Instead he was forced to halt at second base with Rose occupying third base. It was something that did not appear in the box score and was not widely discussed among the media, but Rose later called it a key point in the game.

The Reds had runners at third and second with nobody out. Julián Javier was announced as a pinch hitter for George Foster. Dick Williams countered by sending Rollie Fingers into the game to replace Ken Holtzman. Anderson countered that move by sending Joe Hague up to bat for Javier. Hague missed his chance to be a hero by popping out on the first pitch to Bert Campaneris in shallow center field. Johnny Bench was the next batter. Dick Williams opted to intentionally walk Bench for the third time in the World Series—even though the Cincinnati catcher was the potential go-ahead run. It was a gutsy move. (Melvin Durslag of *The Sporting News* described Williams' gambit as "directly in conflict with the oldest law of strategy."[16])

After the World Series concluded, Oakland's top scout, Al Hollingsworth, told a reporter from *The Sporting News*, "I'll admire Williams until the day I die for having the courage to walk Bench. It was one of the greatest gambles ever seen. Williams stuck his neck out."[17]

Tony Pérez came up with one out. He hit a fly ball to Matty Alou in right field. It was deep enough to bring in Pete Rose on a sacrifice fly. Joe Morgan also moved up to third base. The Reds were now down by only a single run, but there were now two out. Denis Menke came to the plate. On a 2–2 pitch, Johnny Bench stole second base uncontested. With the count full, Menke popped up to Joe Rudi in shallow center field. The A's left the field with a slim 3–2 lead after eight full innings.

Joe Hague remained in the game in right field for Cincinnati as the ninth inning began. Dick Green led off. He stuck out swinging against Tom Hall. It was Hall's third strikeout of the game. Pitcher Rollie Fingers was the second batter of the top of the ninth. It was the sixth game of the 1972 World Series that Fingers had appeared in, but this was his first at-bat. He grounded out to Denis Menke at third base. Oakland shortstop Bert Campaneris came to bat with two out. He knocked a single into center field. It was the sixth Oakland hit of the game. Ángel Mangual followed Campaneris. He flied out to César Gerónimo in center field. The seventh game of the World Series was moving to the bottom of the ninth inning with Oakland ahead, 3–2.

César Gerónimo was the leadoff batter in the home half of the ninth. On a 1–2 pitch, Gerónimo popped out to shortstop Bert Campaneris for the first out. Dave Concepción was the next Red batter. He grounded out to second baseman Dick Green. Cincinnati was down to their last out. Rolling the dice one final time, Sparky Anderson sent up Darrel Chaney, 0-for-7 in the World Series, to pinch hit for pitcher Tom Hall. He was hit on the foot by a Fingers pitch. Chaney took first base. In this incredibly tight World Series, it was highly fitting that the potential winning run would come to bat in the bottom of the ninth inning with two out. The batter was Cincinnati's favorite son: Pete Rose. He was 2-for-4 thus far in Game Seven—and he had made good contact the two times he had been retired. On the first pitch he saw from Fingers, Rose made good contact again. He sent Joe Rudi retreating to the wall in left-center field in a hurry, but the ball was not propelled deeply enough. Rudi stopped, moved forward slightly, caught the ball with plenty of room to spare—and the Oakland A's were the World Series champions of 1972. Rose had been the last Red retired in Game One as well, eight days earlier.

Rudi happily said decades later, "I was over there and got the ball. We were just jumping up and down, screaming. We couldn't believe that we had won the World Series against the Big Red Machine."[18]

When Joe Rudi clutched the final out of the game it marked some notable milestones: It was the first MLB championship for the A's franchise since 1930 when Connie Mack's mighty Philadelphia Athletics were the kings of professional baseball. More importantly to contemporary fans in California, it was the first overall championship in any major sport for any Bay Area team. With the Hairs having defeated the Squares, Bob Hertzel, with his tongue firmly planted in his cheek, wrote many years later, "The age of innocence died right there on the field in Riverfront Stadium that Sunday afternoon."[19]

Charles O. Finley, who had been heckled by Cincinnati fans, danced merrily on the visitors' dugout at Riverfront Stadium where he exchanged long kisses with his wife, Shirley. Not long afterwards, Dick Williams did the same with his wife. Norma Williams was shown on television weeping with joy. Her husband would appear on the cover of the November 4 edition of *The Sporting News* alongside the caption "The Conqueror." Finley would be named the publication's Man of the Year for 1972. Finley made sure the cover was duly reprinted in the 1973 Oakland A's media guide.

Upon seeing the Commissioner's Trophy on a table in the visitors' clubhouse, Dick Williams said it was an eyeful. He told the NBC television and radio audience. "I saw one of these five years ago [when managing the 1967 Red Sox to a World Series loss against St. Louis]. It's nice to see my captain holding it this time."[20] On the team's flight home, when some of the players requested miniatures of the trophy for themselves, Charlie Finley generously announced he was buying full-sized replicas for the entire A's roster of players and on-field personnel. Finley's generous side was also prominent when he picked up the sizable tab for the A's whole office staff—even the switchboard operator—to travel to Cincinnati to watch the final two games of the World Series in person.

"This is a much better club than I had in Boston in 1967," Williams expounded. "Remember there was Carl Yastrzemski who had the greatest year I've ever seen any player have. Jim Lonborg had a phenomenal year, winning the Cy Young Award. Reggie Smith and José Santiago did excellent work—but this team has depth."[21]

Finley told *The Sporting News* that the A's win was also for and celebrated by fans of the team in the locales it used to call home. He said, "We've received lots of telegrams, maybe 400, wishing us well in the Series. We still have lots of fans in Philadelphia, and, yes, we got wires from Kansas City, too. There were good fans there, just not enough of them."[22]

Finley also declared, "This is the greatest day of my life. None of you can appreciate what this means to me." When asked what the second-greatest day was, Finley responded, "That was when my wife accepted my proposal. Wait ... you better make this my second-greatest thrill. My wife might not like it the other way."[23]

The *Calgary Herald*'s headline writer came up with a clever one to recap Game Seven and the World Series as a whole: "Game, set and match—as in Tenace." The *Herald* also ran a photo of manager Dick Williams applying a playful kiss on Tenace's left cheek. The headline on a sidebar story claimed the 1972 Fall Classic had been won by "19 mustaches."

An unnamed scribe from the Herald News Services encapsulated the AL champions' unexpected triumph this way:

> The A's, who migrated to California from Kansas City four years ago after moving from Philadelphia 13 years before that, were solid underdogs when the Series began. They had lost their best hitter, Reggie Jackson, and best lefthanded relief pitcher, Darold Knowles, through injuries and were rated colorful but questionable in the manner vaguely resembling the old New York Mets.[24]

"We didn't exactly overpower [the Reds]," Sal Bando summarized in the postgame tumult. "Their pitching was good, too. But they didn't have to face Reggie Jackson. If they held us down with Reggie in the lineup, I'd be willing to give them more credit."[25]

Jackson himself weighed in on his absence in the Series. "The Reds were favored to walk through us because I wasn't playing," he noted. "But the guys stuck together—maybe the word is 'united.'"[26]

"The trophy belongs right here," declared winning manager Dick Williams. "It's a beautiful thing," he emphasized as he pointed to it. There were tears in his eyes. Before emotion overtook him, Williams managed to bark out a sarcastic comment: "I overmanaged!" He also graciously said, "Neither club is better than the other."[27] (In the November 4 edition of *The Sporting News*, Melvin Durslag wryly commented, "As you know, only a loser ever overmanages. A winner makes moves of genius dimension.")

Bobby Tolan believed the key moment in Game Seven came in the home half of the eighth inning when the Reds had Joe Morgan on sec-

Often accused of over-managing, Dick Williams masterfully guided his underdog Athletics over Cincinnati in seven games to win the World Series for the first time since 1931. Chief among his wizardly moves was the memorable fake intentional walk on Johnny Bench in Game Three. When a team ekes out a victory by a single run, praise often goes to the manager. The A's played nine one-run games in the 1972 postseason, winning seven of them (Doug McWilliams/National Baseball Hall of Fame and Museum).

ond base and Pete Rose on third base with no one out. Tolan should have followed Morgan in the batting order, but he had been removed from the lineup by manager Sparky Anderson because he was hobbling. Joe Hague batted instead. With a chance to be a hero, Hague had an unproductive at-bat, popping out to shortstop Bert Campaneris. Cincinnati scored just once in the eighth inning, leaving the tying run on base. "As far as I'm concerned, there went our World Series." Tolan said. "I feel it was my fault. I let the fans down—and I have no excuse."[28] Tolan also philosophically proffered the idea that Oakland was predestined to win the Fall Classic, a fatalistic statement that probably would not have pleased his teammates or his manager.

"The season is over, gentlemen," Bobby Tolan declared to a collection of reporters gathered around him, "and I'm going to take a long vacation. I'm tired. I need a rest. I have nothing else to say."[29]

However, veteran sports scribe Sam Lacy of the *Baltimore Afro-American* did have something to say—and it was highly critical of Tolan. Lacy wrote the following scathing assessment of Cincinnati's center fielder in the October 28 edition of his newspaper:

> Bobby Tolan may have escaped the label of bum because he is a great actor. Tolan misplayed two balls off Oakland bats which should have been caught. And both resulted in enemy runs.
>
> In the first inning, Tolan overran Ángel Mangual's drive for a three-base error. Mangual scored moments later.
>
> Then in the sixth, he pulled up as trying to avoid hitting the wall on a fly ball by Sal Bando. It appeared to this observer that Bobby blew a more-than-routine, though not difficult play because he didn't trust the warning track which helps outfielders locate danger. In what seemed an afterthought, Tolan dropped to the ground clutching the back of his leg. After it was wrapped, he returned to his station.
>
> It marked the first time this writer has seen an acute muscle pull treated by bandaging.

Joe Morgan, who got just three hits in his 24 Series at-bats, also personally accepted his share of blame for Cincinnati's defeat. "I was very disappointed that I didn't get on base in the first three games. This team depends on me and I let them down."[30] Still, Morgan managed to deflect some criticism to the Cincinnati pitching staff and how they allowed Gene Tenace to repeatedly get the best of them. "I'm a little disappointed that our pitchers let him do as much damage as he did," he said. He then conceded, "Oakland never quit. They deserve to be world champions."[31]

A disappointed Sparky Anderson told the press that he figured his club should have won the World Series in six games, having blown Game Four in Oakland. Nevertheless, in typical sportsmanlike fashion, Anderson praised the winners and added, "My guys don't have to hang their heads about anything—and they know it."[32] In his autobiography written 26 years after the A's beat the Reds, Anderson declared,

> Everybody says the Cincinnati-Boston World Series in 1975 was the best in history. I don't. I'll always maintain that the best Series I was ever involved in was the 1972 World Series against Oakland. That's because those were the two of the finest ballclubs to go against each other you'll ever see in I don't know how long.[33]

Anderson also added, "Oakland was a much better ballclub than the 1970 Baltimore team that beat us. In fact, Oakland was the best team I ever managed against."[34]

William Leggett of *Sports Illustrated* was not so kind in his assessment of the vanquished. He mocked Cincinnati losing the World Series twice in the span of three autumns. He wrote, "Anytime the Reds get into the Series, National League rooters know enough to hand their betting money to their wives."[35]

Jim Murray also kicked the Reds while they were down, emphasizing their inability to win baseball's premier event. He wrote in his October 23 syndicated column, "As is its custom, Cincinnati lost a World Series here on Sunday. It's a tradition in Cincinnati. The team keeps coming home saying, 'Oops! Sorry about that!' It's the one that wakes up in the corner saying, 'Where am I?' while someone waves smelling salts under its nose."

Baseball revels in its numbers, and there never is a shortage of World Series statistics for fans to digest. The 1972 Fall Classic was no different in that respect than any other. Altogether, the two teams combined to break or tie 32 different World Series records. Of course, some of the "records" were minutiae of the highest order: Fewest balks committed (0), fewest shutouts by one team (Oakland, 0), fewest triples by one team (Oakland, 0), and most at-bats in one inning (Denis Menke, 2). Others were more substantial: Most hits by a pinch hitter (Gonzalo Márquez, 3), and best fielding percentage by a third baseman (Denis Menke, 1.000; 29 chances without an error).

Gene Tenace was at the forefront of making baseball history, of course. It was determined that Tenace had set a new record for slugging percentage in a seven-game World Series. His .913 slugging average eclipsed Babe Ruth's .900 mark set back in 1926. (Ruth's New York Yankees lost that World Series in an upset to the St. Louis Cardinals.) Tenace also set marks for most home runs in the first game of a World Series (2), most home runs in a World Series (4) and for homering his first two at-bats. Tenace, who was referred to by John G. Griffin in a UPI article as "an obscure bench-warmer for Oakland until mid-season,"[36] outhomered the entire Cincinnati roster by a 4:3 ratio. He was rightfully named the World Series MVP by *Sport* magazine. His prize was a snazzy new sports car—a noticeable upgrade on the 1972 Oldsmobile he presently drove. "It couldn't happen to a better guy,"[37] insisted Sal Bando, Tenace's roommate and victorious A's captain.

In 1988, while being interviewed for Catfish Hunter's biography, Tenace recalled something that the injured pitcher Darold Knowles had said on the team bus as the A's were traveling to Riverfront Stadium for Game One of the World Series. "I've got a prediction," Knowles sated. "I had a dream last night. I'm predicting that either Gene Tenace or George Hendrick is going to be the MVP of the Series."[38]

"Now, remember this was before the first pitch was even thrown," Tenace noted. "I just said, 'I hope you're right, because if one of us wins the MVP [Award], it means we won the Series.'"[39]

With the World Series championship and the MVP Award in his pocket, Tenace could afford to be generous—even to the man who threatened his life before Game Six. "I really feel sorry for somebody like that," he told a reporter. "The man really has a problem of some kind."[40]

During the eighth inning, Dick Williams was seen talking to Charlie Finley near the owner's box seat. When a reporter asked him what the conversation was about when the game's outcome was still very much in doubt, Williams smiled and replied, "I just wanted to make sure the champagne wasn't frozen. After all, it had been on ice for three days."[41]

One Oakland scribe made a point of praising the much-maligned owner of the A's. Ed Levitt wrote in his October 23 column in the *Oakland Tribune*,

> Charlie Finley. Remember him?
> He's the guy who gets knocked in the press for doing things wrong.
> Poor Charlie. He's so stupid he became a millionaire. And the guy is so out of tune with the times he won a World Series yesterday. And Charlie Finley is so ruthless he cried because his Oakland team won perhaps the greatest honor in sports.[42]

The A's owner received a congratulatory telegram from Ronald Reagan. The governor of California sent his "warmest congratulations" to Finley and his club. Reagan praised the team for their "coolness under pressure and their tremendous will to win."[43]

The 1972 World Series featured generally excellent pitching. On the negative side, the two teams set a new low mark for combined batting average for a seven-game Series: a meager .209. (Remarkably, each team individually compiled a .209 average! Even odder, both teams had .295 slugging percentages!) Oakland only scored as many as four runs once in the seven Series games—and that occurred in Game Five, a game the A's lost! Despite generally strong pitching throughout the seven games, there was no complete game thrown by a pitcher on either team. That was a first—but it was the start of a trend, too. A long time would pass from Steve Blass going the full nine innings against Baltimore in Game Seven of the 1971 World Series until there was another complete game tossed in a Fall Classic: Luis Tiant of the Boston Red Sox next did it in Game One of the 1975 World Series when he shut out Sparky Anderson's Reds, 6–0.

A few baseball writers dwelled on the upset aspect of the seven games. Lowell Reidenbaugh of *The Sporting News* reminded his readers,

> These were the A's who, before the start of the World Series, were accorded virtually no chance against the Reds. It would be the foremost mismatch, chuckled the cognoscenti, since the lions took on the Christians.
>
> As an extra, it was hinted slyly that the National League pair-up of the Reds and the Pirates would have provided a greater spectacle since, after all, they were the two most formidable baseball clubs in Bowie Kuhn's fiefdom.
>
> The monumental mismatched never materialized....[44]

In the end, this World Series was decided by the surprising A's— without Reggie Jackson or Darold Knowles—outplaying the Reds in key situations. Al Abrams of the *Pittsburgh Post-Gazette* saw Game Seven— and the 1972 Fall Classic as a whole—this way:

> It is not unusual for a super sports spectacle such as a World Series to weave a suspenseful drama of triumph around an underdog. Neither is it unusual for the fickle fates to smile upon comparative unknowns and single them out as kings while slighting the great.
>
> Just as everybody was writing them off, the swinging A's of Dick Williams reverted to their old script in this Series—tough pitching and undistinguished players rising to the heights.
>
> Fury Gene Tenace, hardly a household name when this October began, haunted the Reds once again. The author of four home runs in the first five games was content with a single and a double yesterday, driving in two of the three runs. He also played first base like a Hal Chase until taken out of the game for a pinch runner in the sixth.
>
> The other unknown who stood out this afternoon was Ángel Mangual ... who made several fine catches in the outfield. [He] also scored the A's first run.
>
> If anyone would have told me that Gene Tenace would hit more home runs in the Series than Johnny Bench (4:1) and that the Ángel in the A's out-field would outplay the classy Bobby Tolan in center field ... even for one day.... I would have begged, borrowed ... got money whichever way I could to bet him they wouldn't.[45]

## Box Score: Game #7
### Oakland Athletics 3, Cincinnati Reds 2
Game played on Sunday, October 22, 1972, at Riverfront Stadium

| Oakland Athletics | ab | r | h | rbi |
|---|---|---|---|---|
| Campaneris ss | 4 | 1 | 2 | 0 |
| Mangual cf | 4 | 1 | 0 | 0 |
| Rudi lf | 3 | 0 | 0 | 0 |
| Tenace 1b | 3 | 0 | 2 | 2 |
| Lewis pr | 0 | 1 | 0 | 0 |

| Cincinnati Reds | ab | r | h | rbi |
|---|---|---|---|---|
| Rose lf | 5 | 1 | 2 | 0 |
| Morgan 2b | 3 | 0 | 1 | 0 |
| Tolan cf | 2 | 0 | 0 | 0 |
| Foster rf | 0 | 0 | 0 | 0 |
| Javier ph | 0 | 0 | 0 | 0 |

| Oakland Athletics | ab | r | h | rbi |
|---|---|---|---|---|
| *Hegan* 1b | 1 | 0 | 0 | 0 |
| *Bando* 3b | 4 | 0 | 1 | 1 |
| *Alou* rf | 3 | 0 | 0 | 0 |
| *Duncan* c | 3 | 0 | 0 | 0 |
| *Green* 2b | 4 | 0 | 1 | 0 |
| *Odom* p | 2 | 0 | 0 | 0 |
| *Hunter* p | 0 | 0 | 0 | 0 |
| *Holtzman* p | 0 | 0 | 0 | 0 |
| *Fingers* p | 1 | 0 | 0 | 0 |
| **Totals** | 32 | 3 | 6 | 3 |

| Cincinnati Reds | ab | r | h | rbi |
|---|---|---|---|---|
| *Hague* ph,rf | 1 | 0 | 0 | 0 |
| *Bench* c | 3 | 0 | 0 | 0 |
| *Pérez* 1b | 2 | 1 | 1 | 1 |
| *Menke* 3b | 4 | 0 | 0 | 0 |
| *Gerónimo* rf,cf | 3 | 0 | 0 | 0 |
| *Concepción* ss | 3 | 0 | 0 | 0 |
| *Billingham* p | 1 | 0 | 0 | 0 |
| *McRae* ph | 0 | 0 | 0 | 1 |
| *Borbón* p | 0 | 0 | 0 | 0 |
| *Carroll* p | 0 | 0 | 0 | 0 |
| *Grimsley* p | 0 | 0 | 0 | 0 |
| *Uhlaender* ph | 1 | 0 | 0 | 0 |
| *Hall* p | 0 | 0 | 0 | 0 |
| *Chaney* ph | 0 | 0 | 0 | 0 |
| **Totals** | 28 | 2 | 4 | 2 |

| | | | | | | | | | | | | | |
|---|---|---|---|---|---|---|---|---|---|---|---|---|---|
| Oakland | 1 | 0 | 0 | 0 | 0 | 2 | 0 | 0 | 0 | — | 3 | 6 | 1 |
| Cincinnati | 0 | 0 | 0 | 0 | 1 | 0 | 0 | 1 | 0 | — | 2 | 4 | 2 |

| Oakland Athletics | IP | H | R | ER | BB | SO |
|---|---|---|---|---|---|---|
| *Odom* | 4.1 | 2 | 1 | 1 | 4 | 2 |
| *Hunter* W (2–0) | 2.2 | 1 | 1 | 1 | 1 | 3 |
| *Holtzman* | 0.0 | 1 | 0 | 0 | 0 | 0 |
| *Fingers* SV (2) | 2.0 | 0 | 0 | 0 | 1 | 0 |
| **Totals** | 9.0 | 4 | 2 | 2 | 6 | 5 |
| Cincinnati Reds | IP | H | R | ER | BB | SO |
| *Billingham* | 5.0 | 2 | 1 | 0 | 1 | 4 |
| *Borbón* L (0–1) | 0.2 | 3 | 2 | 2 | 0 | 0 |
| *Carroll* | 1.0 | 0 | 0 | 0 | 2 | 1 |
| *Grimsley* | 0.1 | 0 | 0 | 0 | 1 | 1 |
| *Hall* | 2.0 | 1 | 0 | 0 | 0 | 3 |
| Totals | 9.0 | 6 | 3 | 2 | 4 | 9 |

E—Campaneris (1), Tolan (1), Concepción (1). DP—Oakland 1. 2B—Oakland Tenace (1, off Borbón); Bando (1, off Borbón), Cincinnati Pérez (2, off Odom); Morgan (2, off Holtzman). SH—Mangual (1, off Borbón); Campaneris (2, off Carroll). IBB—Alou (1, by Carroll); Rudi (1, by Grimsley); Bench (3, by Fingers). SF—McRae (1, off Hunter); Pérez (1, off Fingers). HBP—Chaney (1, by Fingers). SB—Bench (2, 2nd base off Fingers/Duncan). CS—Morgan (1, 2nd base by Odom/Duncan). WP—Hunter (1). HBP—Fingers (1, Chaney). IBB—Fingers (2, Bench); Carroll (1, Alou); Grimsley (1, Rudi). U—Chris Pelekoudas (NL), Jim Honochick (AL), Mel Steiner (NL), Frank Umont (AL), Bill Haller (AL), Bob Engel (NL). T—2:50. A—56,040.

## *Editorial*

The following editorial ran in the *Pittsburgh Post-Gazette* on Monday, October 23, 1972, under the headline "The 'Mod Squad' Wins"*:

In clean-cut, organized baseball they stood out like a sore thumb. The players wore colorful mustaches (some even had beards), their splashy green and gold uniforms were derided as "softball outfits," players quarreled openly with each other and even with their manager (Dick Williams), and everybody openly beefed about the eccentric club owner, Charlie Finley.

Yet, this oddball, "disorganized" baseball club scrapped its way to the top by winning the World Series four games to three over the Cincinnati Reds in one of the tightest duels in the history of the game. (In only one game was the difference between the two clubs greater than one run.) Here was a multi-transfer club (from Philadelphia to Kansas City to Oakland) which even with this year's hot team usually had great yawning spaces in the stands as Oaklanders stayed away *en masse*.

Baseball, which has striven hard to maintain a sedate image, will never be the same again. How, for example, can American Legion baseball continue to insist that players in its tournaments may not be long hairs or wear mustaches?

Pittsburghers didn't know whether to laugh or cry in seeing the Mod Squad tweak the carburetor out of the Big Red Machine which barely had overcome us in a two-out, ninth-inning situation in the National League playoffs. How could this happen to the winner of the presumably superior National League?

But the A's have been such a joke for years that even National League fans must cheer at seeing these perennial underdogs come out on top for once. And particularly because their flamboyant way of doing things is a good tonic for America right now, and [it] may be the best thing in years for the fading image of baseball itself.

---

## — 16 —

# Let the Celebrations Begin

### *Party Time in Oakland*

"Talent wins games, but teamwork wins championships."
—Michael Jordan

"Winning solves everything."—Tiger Woods

With victory comes the inevitable influx of fair-weather fans. With the Swingin' A's triumph over the Reds in the 1972 World Series, Oakland was miraculously transformed into a baseball-mad metropolis—proving that winning is indeed everything and the only thing to a great many people. The city's AL club that required numerous discount-ticket-price promotions to draw a million fans to its home games in 1972 was suddenly an object of tremendous civic pride. The celebrations in and around Oakland began in earnest immediately after the last putout was made by Joe Rudi approximately 1,837 miles and three time zones away at Riverfront Stadium. It was, after all, the first time a team from the Bay Area had won all the marbles in any of the four major professional sports.

According to a United Press International news story, "This industrial city of 362,000 on the eastern shores of San Francisco Bay went bananas Sunday night over a baseball team." The report continued,

Nearly 35,000 persons tried to crowd into Oakland International Airport to greet their returning diamond heroes. However, only slightly more than 12,000 were able to squeeze into the terminal

In contrast, a canned sardine would probably feel liberated.

Thousands more milled around the outside of the terminal and traffic was backed up two miles on an access road from Nimitz Freeway. Police finally sealed off the airport to all traffic.

At least 1,000 rooters broke through police barricades and spilled onto the airport apron to surround the A's chartered plane after it landed. This delayed welcoming ceremonies inside the terminal for more than one hour.

"Never saw anything like it. Just fantastic," said Oakland mayor John Reading.

Phil Mumma of the Oakland Port Authority was a bit more explicit.

"You might think the Beatles or the Rolling Stones were here," said Mumma. "This crowd is four times larger than the one which greeted President Nixon at the Oakland airport a few weeks ago. This is the best thing that ever happened to Oakland."[1]

The overflow crowd had its patience tested when the A's airplane was nearly 50 minutes late in arriving. The passionate crowd passed the time by chanting, "We want the A's!"[2] over and over again.

The continuous din became downright deafening when the A's finally made their way into the packed terminal. Horns blared. Homemade banners fluttered. (One poetic sign read "Rain or Shine, We'll Beat Cincinnati All the Time." The placard with the cleverest pun was perhaps one that read "Big Game Hunter.") People screamed and shouted. Many brought large supplies of adult beverages to share with their fellow well-wishers. There were accounts of several smitten women fainting at the mere sight of their newly discovered mustachioed baseball heroes.

The crowd included A's supporters from as far as 200 miles distant. "Modesto Loves Joe Rudi and the A's" declared one banner. Other fans identified themselves as having traveled from Fresno, Oroville and Sacramento for the spontaneous, happy gathering.

A few of the A's were called upon to make speeches. Some were more eloquent than others. Gene Tenace simply said, "Thank you very much."[3] Catfish Hunter merely bellowed, "We're number one!"[4] several times. A smiling Joe Rudi spoke even less—simply and silently giving two thumbs up to the boisterous demonstration of newfound civic affection.

Sal Bando gushed, "We've brought a world championship to a championship town." Mike Epstein excitedly blurted, "Let's keep this trophy for the next ten years."[5] Don Mincher humbly said, "I hope this night never ends."[6]

Not too surprisingly, the injured but always talkative Reggie Jackson had the most to say to the assembled throng. Among other observations, Jackson noted, "With all the odds against this team, it's a great feeling that they were able to pull together to win it."[7]

Charles O. Finley was feted in several locales in the months following his team's World Series triumph. The people of La Porte, Indiana (where Finley resided) honored him with a special civic dinner that drew 2,200 people. Another dinner in Gary, Indiana (where Finley had lived for three decades) drew an enthusiastic crowd of 900. According to the January 6, 1973, edition of *The Sporting News*, the Oakland Chamber of Commerce was planning a party for Finley and the team in mid–January. The Indiana Society of Chicago declared Finley to be "Hoosier of the Year" for 1972. Finley was thoroughly enjoying the tributes. "I haven't always been so popular,"[8] he dryly noted.

The A's owner came up with a novel way to milk a few more dollars from his championship team: He had a long-playing record album released titled *Finley's Heroes*. (Copies for sale can be found on eBay!) Narrated by Monte Moore, it contained interviews and audio highlights of the 1972 A's remarkable campaign. It ended with Charles O. Finley's comments to reporters after Game Seven of the World Series:

> I can honestly say it's the happiest day of my life. I'm so happy for the players, the manager, the coaches, and my family. It's something that's been well worth waiting for. I'm just so tremendously proud of the great job that this team did. They beat one hell of a great team. Cincinnati is one of the greatest teams in baseball, without a question. But I have to tell you, the A's are even better.[9]

# Under the Knife

"It was frightening. Was Johnny going to die?"[1]—Reds Broadcaster Al Michaels

Unbeknownst to most of the baseball world was the scary personal situation that Cincinnati catcher Johnny Bench unexpectedly faced in August 1972.

The Reds were undergoing routine physical exams that month, which included x-rays. The 24-year-old Bench was quietly told that further x-rays of him were required. The perceptive Reds superstar knew something had to be amiss for this sort of special treatment. He insisted on being told what was wrong. He was informed that his x-ray showed a spot on his right lung—always a troubling revelation. Indeed, the second round of x-rays confirmed there was some sort of growth about an inch or so in diameter. The only good news was that it was deemed to be a very new growth, so the club's medical staff told Bench his necessary surgery to remove it could be postponed until after the 1972 baseball season had concluded. Only the team and Johnny's family knew about his health problem.

Reds broadcaster Al Michaels recalled, "Johnny was just going about his business. There was nothing to indicate there was anything out of the ordinary."[2]

Remarkably, Bench played as well as ever for Cincinnati for the next two months. He won his fifth consecutive Gold Glove and his second NL MVP award. Through it all, he did occasionally wonder if his MLB career might come to a screeching end in 1972. Of course, he also worried about his survival in general. In a 2019 MLB documentary, Bench admitted that when he came to bat in the ninth inning of Game Five of the NLCS against Dave Giusti, he mentally noted that it might be his final plate appearance in the majors. His home run and the Reds' dramatic comeback win against the Pirates guaranteed Bench would have a chance to play in his second World Series.

A few days after his 25th birthday on December 7, Bench underwent a two-hour operation at Christ Hospital in Cincinnati under the direction of Dr. Luis Gonzalez. The growth on Bench's lung was the size of a marble, but it was deemed to be benign and was removed. Reds team physician Dr. George Ballou told the media, "The lesion was found in the fissure between the lower and upper lobes of the right lung, and as a consequence, it was only necessary to remove a small amount of lung tissue."[3]

Bench's parents and his brother and sister were present at the hospital during the surgery. Johnny's father, Ted, gratefully told reporters on behalf of himself and his wife, "Our prayers and the prayers from people all over the nation have been answered. We want to thank everyone for their prayers for our son."[4]

*The Sporting News* thought so little of Bench's surgery that it carried no story about it whatsoever. Its only mention was in the caption of a photo in the January 6, 1973, edition that showed Bench decorating a Christmas tree in his apartment shortly after being released from the hospital.

The surgery did take a toll, though. Bench recalled, "They cut the bone. They cut the rib. They cut the tissue. They stapled me across the chest. I never was Johnny Bench again."[5]

For someone who was never at his peak again after 1972, Bench did all right. He won five more Gold Gloves from 1973 through 1977 to increase his string to 10 straight years. He garnered MVP votes in 1973, 1974, 1975, 1977, 1979 and 1980, finishing as high as fourth twice. Although Bench never again clouted 40 home runs in a single season, he hit at least 22 in seven of the eight years following his surgery. In 1974 he led the NL in RBIs with 129. Bench was named the World Series MVP in 1976. Many baseball historians consider Johnny Bench to be the greatest catcher of all time. The authors of this book concur.

# Aftermaths

"I can't tell you how good of a player [Sal] Bando was or how good of a player Joe Rudi was or how good of a player Gene Tenace was, or Campaneris. You throw in a Hall of Fame reliever and a Hall of Fame starter...."[1]—Pete Rose reflecting on the 1972 Oakland A's 45 years later

The 1972 World Series—and the entire hard-fought postseason—was a welcome shot in the arm for baseball, but MLB was starting to lose its battle with professional football as the premier sports attraction in America. This trend irked a great many veteran sports scribes who cherished the grand old game and everything it had once meant to the country. In the November 4 issue of *The Sporting News*, columnist Joe Falls could not understand why this trend was occurring. He thoughtfully wrote:

> Baseball differs from football in that it is primarily a game of individuals and it is here that baseball—and NBC—shine so brightly. How could football ever give us those closeup shots of Rollie Fingers with that waxed mustache of his staring in at the plate? Or Catfish Hunter with his walrus-type mustache and all that hair sticking out from the back of his cap? It can't.
>
> They can show us the coaches in football and players along the sidelines and sometimes they can zero in and show us the players under those helmets and behind those face bars.
>
> But no way can football match the individualism you get from baseball—the look of intensity on Pete Rose's face as he stands at the plate, the iron-hard glare in the eyes of Dick Williams as he stares out at the field....

Despite Cincinnati's disappointment of losing the World Series for the second time in three years, there was a bright side to the bitter taste of defeat: It also meant the Reds were legitimately a National League powerhouse. However, they were not quite yet the formidable Big Red Machine—a finished project that would win two consecutive World Series in 1975 and 1976. Some personnel changes were necessary for the final step to achieving true greatness. Bobby Tolan was the biggest name to depart the Reds. It was an acrimonious parting.

Tolan's catastrophic Game Seven of the 1972 World Series seemed to produce bad karma that extended into the following year. Tolan's 1973 batting average plummeted to a dismal .206. Moreover, he became something of a malcontent in the clubhouse whose negativity hurt team chemistry. Tolan also engaged in some very public disagreements with Reds management, who were still unhappy about his January 1971 Achilles tendon injury that had occurred in a charity basketball game in Kentucky. (Although he was playing on a team that had been organized by other Cincinnati players, the activity technically violated the terms of Tolan's contract. The basketball team was dissolved shortly after Tolan was hurt.) Tolan sealed his fate by bolting from the Reds for two days in August, and by growing a beard—an obvious violation of longstanding team policy barring facial hair. The fed-up Reds suspended Tolan on September 27. His banishment lasted for the remainder of the year—which included the 1973 NLCS. The heavily favored Reds lost to the New York Mets who had won 17 fewer games than Cincinnati had during the regular season. *The Sporting News* reported in its October 27, 1973, edition, "If Tolan … is still wearing a Cincy uniform next season, it's because [Bob] Howsam was unable to find a taker. And that isn't likely to happen. It's a cinch more than one major league club is willing to gamble he'll become the player he was."

Indeed, Tolan was traded to the San Diego Padres for pitcher Clay Kirby at the end of the 1973 season. Sparky Anderson called the demise of Bobby Tolan as a Red the single biggest failure of his nine-year tenure as the Cincinnati manager. "I take full blame for the situation that came up in 1973 with Bobby Tolan," said Anderson. "I consider this my greatest failure as a manager because I sensed what was happening to him, saw it develop, and did not take the time to do something about it early in the crisis."[2] In a 2017 article for Redlegnation.com, journalist John Ring wrote,

> For whatever reason, Bobby Tolan is never at any of the Reds functions, in which several former Reds players attend. Maybe the Reds don't invite him. Maybe they haven't reached out to him. Or maybe Bobby doesn't want to attend. He's 75 years old now, but 1973 was a long time ago.[3]

By 1973, the talented Dave Concepción had emerged as Cincinnati's shortstop of choice. (An unlucky injury—a broken left fibula suffered during a game versus Montreal on July 22—sidelined him for the second half of 1973. He was batting .287 at the time and had 22 stolen bases in 89 games. Concepción's absence was arguably a major factor why the Reds were upset by the Mets in the NLCS.) A healthy Concepción returned to the Cincinnati lineup in 1974. He played in 160 games and was beginning to be heralded as the NL's best shortstop. Thus, former starter Darrel Chaney—who was the same age as Concepción—was shifted to a reserve role. By 1976, Chaney had been traded to Atlanta.

Hal McRae's last game for Cincinnati was Game Seven of the 1972 World Series. (His lone at-bat in that contest was a 400-foot sacrifice fly hit off Catfish Hunter to tie the game.) In December, McRae was traded along with once-promising but injury-plagued pitcher Wayne Simpson to the Kansas City Royals for pitcher Roger Nelson and outfielder/pinch hitter Richie Scheinblum. The two ex–Royals made very little impact with the Reds, but McRae's move to Kansas City turned out to be very positive for him. McRae wanted to play every day. With the very strong Cincinnati lineup, McRae was likely only going to be a part-timer. Thus, he had more opportunity to be a regular with the Royals than with the Reds. McRae also benefited from the timely new DH rule that would come into vogue in the AL starting in 1973. "The trade breathed new life into McRae's career; he developed into one of the most reliable designated hitters in the American League," wrote biographer Thomas J. Brown, Jr. Indeed, McRae stayed with the Royals until July 1987. He was a three-time All-Star in Kansas City. Six times he batted over .300.

George Foster, the man who scored the NL pennant-winning run for Cincinnati, surprisingly spent almost all of 1973 in the minor leagues. However, he played in 106 games in 1974. In essence, he replaced the departed Bobby Tolan in the Cincinnati outfield. With another new outfielder, Ken Griffey, added to the Reds in 1974, Dan Driessen became the replacement for third baseman Denis Menke, who had been traded to Houston after the 1973 season. (Menke played his last MLB game in July 1974.) Pete Rose moved to third base for the Reds in 1975. The pieces of the dominant Big Red Machine were now in place. Sparky Anderson claimed years later that if Cincinnati's starting pitching had been as dominant as his regular eight players, the Reds could have won 130 games per year in their heyday.

Pitcher Ross Grimsley balked at Cincinnati's strict rules for deportment. He rebelled by wearing his hair long and challenged Sparky Anderson's authority on such matters. Anderson requested that Grimsley be traded after the 1973 season. He was dealt, along with minor-leaguer Wally Williams, to the Baltimore Orioles. The Reds picked up three players in the deal, the most notable was Merv Rettenmund, one of baseball's best and most reliable utility players.

In 1975 the Cincinnati Reds were a dominant bunch. They won 108 games to finish 20 games ahead of the distant second-place Dodgers.

After ousting Pittsburgh in three straight games in the 1975 NLCS, Cincinnati famously won an unforgettable seven-game World Series against Boston—their first Fall Classic victory since 1940. The following season they won "only" 102 regular-season games and waltzed through the 1976 NLCS (versus Philadelphia) and the World Series (versus the New York Yankees) without dropping a single contest. No team had done that since the interleague playoffs had started in 1969—and no team has enjoyed a perfect postseason since the '76 Reds. In Game Two of the 1976 World Series, the losing pitcher for New York was a familiar face to the Reds from 1972: Catfish Hunter. Hunter tossed a complete game, but he gave up a walk-off, RBI single to Pete Rose in the bottom of the ninth inning.

By winning two consecutive World Series, the Reds became the first NL team to accomplish that special feat since John McGraw's New York Giants of 1921 and 1922. "It's a tough ballclub, this Big Red Machine,"[4] said NBC's Joe Garagiola, stating an obvious fact, just before the Commissioner's Trophy was presented. Johnny Bench appeared on the November 1 cover of *Sports Illustrated* alongside the caption "How good are the Reds?" It was a question that was being pondered by baseball buffs. When Joe Morgan was asked by Tony Kubek if he thought the 1976 Reds ought to be ranked among the best baseball clubs ever assembled, he swiftly replied, "I don't see how you can have a much better team."[5] Sparky Anderson, always a stickler for deportment, told the television audience that he was most proud of how professional and classy his team was. Ron Fimrite of *SI* described the tone of Anderson's post–Series comments to the media,

> It was time for Anderson to explain how he had come to be such a genius. But he is a skilled practitioner of false modesty who forever downplays his contributions to his team's achievements. He preferred to emphasize his occasional mistakes, to apologize for his abysmal ignorance, to construct an image of himself as the father, proud yet confused, of a gifted child.[6]

All good things must come to an end, though. The nearly invincible Reds of the mid–1970s became beatable by the end of the decade. Tony Pérez, Cincinnati's all-time leader in RBIs at the time, was traded to Montreal before the 1977 season. It was a move that upper management regretted very quickly because Pérez had been a quiet leader in the clubhouse as well. His absence was felt. Pete Rose, still a force at age 38, signed with the Philadelphia Phillies in 1979, lured by a four-year deal that paid him $3.2 million. Very good Los Angeles Dodger teams won the NL West and league pennants in both 1977 and 1978. The last vestiges of Cincinnati's Big Red Machine played in the 1979 NLCS, where they bowed out to the Pittsburgh Pirates in the minimum three games.

Sparky Anderson was not Cincinnati's manager in 1979, having been surprisingly fired by new general manager Dick Wagner on November 27, 1978. Even though Johnny Bench and Joe Morgan had both missed large chunks of the 1978 season due to injuries, the Reds were only 2½ games in arrears of the Dodgers at season's end. Nevertheless, Wagner wanted to shake up his team by replacing most of Anderson's longtime coaching staff. Anderson objected—and he got the ax too, even though he still had a year left on his contract. The team had just returned from a goodwill trip to Japan when Anderson was told to meet Wagner at a Los Angeles hotel. He thought he was going to be apprised of the club's attempts to sign some notable free agents for 1979. Instead, he was told by Wagner that his services were no longer required by the Cincinnati Reds.

Anderson's firing was wildly unpopular in Cincinnati, of course. An effigy of Wagner was burned in front of Riverfront Stadium. Sack upon sack of fan mail arrived at Anderson's home in California offering support and thanking him for a job well done. Joe Morgan was notified about Anderson's dismissal with a 6 a.m. phone call. Morgan was so shocked by the news that a few minutes later he personally called Anderson to find out if he had dreamed the whole thing. Morgan was especially irked at the timing. He told reporters that if the club intended to fire Anderson, it should have been done before the Japan trip. Nevertheless, the 44-year-old Anderson handled his sudden dismissal in a classy manner. He said he was pleasantly surprised and flattered by all the attention and affection he was getting. As for getting the pink slip, Anderson told *The Sporting News*, "It was a decision made by the front office. That's all I want to say. When I return to Cincinnati with another club, I'll walk with my head up, my shoulders back. I'll be proud."[7] Almost immediately, Anderson had half a dozen offers to manage other MLB teams, but he was not about to make a hasty career decision, knowing full well that he could return to the game just about any time he chose. All the other MLB managers were aware of it, too. Kansas City Royals manager Whitey Herzog told his colleagues at a 1979 preseason get-together that they had all better be on their toes because there was an unemployed white-haired fellow in California—and every MLB general manager had his telephone number. Anderson never did return to Cincinnati as a rival manager. He was hired in June 1979 to pilot an AL club, the Detroit Tigers. Interleague play would not start until 1997—two years after he had retired.

Anderson was replaced in Cincinnati in 1979 by John McNamara, who had managed the Oakland A's in 1970. (Dick Williams had replaced him in 1971!) The head-scratching headline that ran above *The Sporting*

*News* story announcing Anderson's firing read, "Reds Look to McNamara for Higher Standard." It was a lofty goal; the standard Anderson had set in his nine seasons with Cincinnati was a tough act to follow. Anderson's record at the helm of the Reds was 863–586–1. His winning percentage was .596. He had guided the Reds to five divisional titles, four NL pennants and two World Series championships. In the four seasons the Reds did not win the NL West under Anderson's stewardship, they finished second three times—each time behind talented Dodger clubs that advanced to the World Series.

The next postseason appearance for the Reds occurred more than a decade afterward, in 1990. (That year, after eliminating Pittsburgh in six games in the now best-of-seven NLCS, Cincinnati scored a huge upset in defeating the Oakland A's in four straight games, avenging their surprise loss in the 1972 World Series.) In 1990, Sparky Anderson was in his 12th season as manager of the Detroit Tigers. He had led them to a fantastic 1984 season culminating in a World Series triumph. During the victory celebrations, Anderson commented, "I have to be honest. I've waited for this day since they fired me in Cincinnati. I think they made a big mistake when they did that. Now no one will ever question me again."[8] In the 1984 World Series, the Tigers defeated the San Diego Padres in five games. In a way, it was a rematch of the 1972 Fall Classic: Managing the Padres was none other than Dick Williams! Anderson was a success in Detroit. His regular-season totals were 1331 wins and 1248 losses, for a .516 winning percentage. No Tiger manager in the club's storied history—which dates back to 1901—has won more games than George (Sparky) Anderson.

In Oakland, Charlie Finley made some notable off-season moves after the team's 1972 World Series triumph. First baseman Mike Epstein was traded in December 1972 to the Texas Rangers for journeyman pitcher Horacio Piña. It was Oakland's intention to move Gene Tenace to first base on a permanent basis. (Epstein became something akin to a non-person. His 1972 stats for the regular season and postseason were deliberately not listed in the A's 1973 media guide!) Epstein was irked by the trade. "What is shocking is that I am going from a good ballclub to a bad ballclub," he said. "I am going from the best ballclub in the world to the worst in the world."[9]

It was hardly a comment that won friends and fans for Epstein in Texas, but it was typical of him. According to one biographer, Epstein was "a capable power hitter ... but never quite hit well enough to offset his frequent strikeouts, poor defense, and big mouth."[10] Indeed, Epstein was a difficult player to manage and was often his own worst enemy. A first baseman in the Baltimore farm system, Epstein had been named

*The Sporting News* minor league player of the year in 1966 and was the sport's most heralded prospect when he was elevated to Baltimore in 1967. But the Orioles already had Boog Powell well established at first base. When the Orioles tried to convert Epstein to an outfielder in spring training, he balked at the idea—and he was not very good there. In its May 6, 1967, issue, *TSN* referred to Epstein as "a potential superstar with no place to play." Epstein was demoted to the minors, but he refused to report. He was traded to Washington shortly thereafter. At the time of Oakland's 1972 triumph, Epstein had only been with the A's for two seasons. He only played 27 games for the Rangers in 1973 before being traded to California. By the midway part of May 1974, the quickly fading Epstein was out of the majors.

In a good move, Oakland acquired Bill North from the Chicago Cubs in a November 1972 trade for pitcher Bob Locker. Locker, age 34, would win only 10 more games in his career. North was only a fair hitter and had very little power, but the speedy 24-year-old capably covered a lot of ground in center field. Once, versus the Chicago White Sox, North made an unassisted double play! Twice North led the AL in stolen bases while with the A's. During spring training 1973, the promising George Hendrick and Dave Duncan were traded to the Cleveland Indians for catcher Ray Fosse and shortstop Jack Heidemann. Fosse had a solid 1973 season with Oakland, playing in 143 games. In June 1974 in Detroit, Fosse suffered a severe neck injury trying to break up a clubhouse fight between Bill North and Reggie Jackson—and his career wet into a tailspin. Heidemann never played a game for the A's.

Allan Lewis, the speedy pinch-running specialist, had an uncertain future in Oakland and MLB. A journalist for the *New Castle News* wrote five weeks after the World Series ended,

> Lewis, you may remember, is Charlie Finley's "Panamanian Express." He can fly around the bases, but [he] can't do much of anything else. Actually, he scored the run that gave the Oakland A's their championship in the final game of the World Series when he replaced Series hero Gene Tenace on the basepaths in the sixth inning, but shortly thereafter he was sent to Iowa of the American Association from where [any team] can now pick him up for the $25,000 draft price.[11]

Lewis ended up returning to the A's in 1973. He appeared in 35 games that season—but never once batted. (Dick Williams once wryly commented, "[Lewis] is a switch-hitter. He batted .300 last year: .150 lefthanded and .150 righthanded."[12]) Lewis, however, did score 16 runs as a pinch runner. He stole seven bases and was caught four times. He never played in the majors again after 1973.

The core of the A's stayed together—feuding frequently amongst each other most of the way—to win two more World Series titles to make it three straight crowns from 1972 through 1974. Despite the team's obvious talent and penchant for winning, the terrific Oakland ballclub was often not given the credit or respect it deserved. Prior to the 1974 World Series against Los Angeles, Dodger outfielder Bill Buckner remarkably claimed there was not a single member of the two-time defending champions who would be a regular in L.A.'s starting lineup. That comment only served to motivate the A's. Oakland handily beat the Dodgers in five games. After the decisive victory, Dick Green, who starred defensively in that World Series, walked away from the game when his request for a $20,000 raise was flatly turned down by Charles O. Finley. After his retirement from baseball, Green operated a moving van business in Rapid City, South Dakota, for many years.

To casual observers, Finley came across as an eccentric owner who was generally harmless. However, one October, an episode involving an A's utility infielder showed Finley to be a vindictive and cruel autocrat. A biographer wrote, "[The] 1973 World Series finally turned Finley into a national pariah, an identity he would never overcome."[13] Thirty-year-old Mike Andrews, who had played second base and shortstop for Dick Williams in Boston, was the focus of Finley's wrath.

Andrews had started the 1973 season with the Chicago White Sox. Batting just .201, he had been released on July 16. Andrews was acquired by the A's from the Chicago White Sox—at Williams' request—at the July 31, 1973, deadline so he could play in the postseason if the A's got there. They did. During Game Two of the World Series in Oakland, Andrews committed two costly errors in the top of the 12th inning in which the visiting New York Mets scored four runs to win the game and level the World Series at a game apiece. Finley was so miffed by the pair of errors that he coerced the likable Andrews into signing a false affidavit, drawn up by team physician Harry R. Walker, saying that he had "a bicep groove tenosynovitis of the right shoulder."[14] (In layman's terms, it is the inflammation of the sheath that covers a muscle tendon at the front of the shoulder.) This way, Andrews could be removed from the A's World Series roster and be replaced by promising rookie Manny Trillo. Andrews refused at first, but he eventually did as he was told—allegedly being promised a contract for the 1974 season as a reward for his cooperation—and promptly flew to his home in Boston.

Andrews' Oakland teammates were appalled by the goings-on, as was manager Dick Williams. Sal Bando told the media, "That's a joke. I've seen some bush things on this club, but this is going too far." Reggie Jackson told the media that the A's, as a group, were considering boycotting the remainder of the World Series, but they softened their stance to a conspicuous visual display of support for Andrews. The players wore his #17 on their uniform sleeves during Game Three. (Jackson, like almost all of the A's, had longstanding grievances with Finley. After his 1969 season in which he hit 47 home runs, Jackson was hoping for a substantial pay raise. Instead, Finley battled with him fiercely over any increase whatsoever. Jackson recalled, "I told [catcher] Dave Duncan that Finley treats his black players like niggers. Dave told me not to feel worried or hurt because Finley treats his white players like niggers, too."[15])

Commissioner Bowie Kuhn was not buying the injury malarkey and promptly reinstated Andrews. A letter Kuhn sent to Finley denying the A's request to replace Andrews with Trillo, included the following reprimand: "I might add that the handling of this matter by the Oakland Club has had the unfortunate effect of unfairly embarrassing a player who has given many years of able service to professional baseball...."[16]

When Andrews appeared as a pinch hitter in the eighth inning of Game Four, the sympathetic New York fans at Shea Stadium warmly gave him standing ovations *before and after* he grounded out. (Finley and his wife may have been the only people in the ballpark not on their feet. They remained seated in their field-level box.) Finley responded by ordering Williams not to play Andrews in the rest of the World Series. Oakland won the 1973 Fall Classic in seven games; a healthy Reggie Jackson was the MVP.

Finley uniquely showed his displeasure about his players' support of Andrews by issuing cut-rate World Series rings to them. The 1973 version had no diamond, only an ersatz emerald where the one-carat diamond had been set in the 1972 ring. Finley was not present for the presentations. He stayed home in Chicago and delegated the duty of handing out the rings to the team's traveling secretary, Jim Bank. What especially irked several players was that Finley had promised the team after the 1973 ALCS victory over Baltimore that if they won the World Series against the New York Mets, their 1973 rings would be more extravagant than their 1972 rings. Catfish Hunter indignantly declared he had seen high school rings that were more impressive.

Mike Andrews never played in another MLB game. In a story that ran in the November 24, 1973, edition of *The Sporting News*, Andrews bitterly told reporter Ron Bergman,

> I definitely wish it never would have happened. That's probably what I'll be asked about for the rest of my life. I put in some pretty good years in the major leagues to be remembered for something like this. Besides, it took away from the World Series.

Disgusted by the Andrews fiasco, Dick Williams quit his position as the A's manager five days after the World Series ended, walking away from the final two years on his contract that paid him $70,000 annually. Alvin Dark became Oakland's new manager in 1974. This was not a new job for him; Dark had managed Finley's Kansas City A's in 1966 and 1967. Ron Bergman of *The Sporting News* noted that manager Hank Bauer had also been rehired by Finley after seven years had elapsed. The writer joked, "By this timetable, Bob Kennedy [Oakland's 1968 pilot] will manage the A's in 1975."[17]

Williams managed four other MLB clubs from 1974 until partway through the 1988 season: the California Angels, Montreal Expos, San Diego Padres and Seattle Mariners.

Whatever goodwill Charles O. Finley's quirky promotions and oddball personality had gained him over the years all vanished with the Mike Andrews affair. From that point onward, Finley was generally reviled in baseball circles. A picture of Andrews—with his back to the camera—was featured on the cover of the November 3, 1973, issue of *The Sporting News*. In one of several stories about the sordid mess in that publication, Art Spander wrote that the 1973 World Series had been

> ...taken over by a lean, white-haired man, King Charles the First, who delights in pastel colors, panic decisions, and a lot of backwoods ideas he thinks are cute, and [they] might be if they didn't involve grown men and thousands of dollars.
>
> By the time the Series reached the seventh game ... a lot of people weren't rooting for the Mets or the A's. Rather, they were rooting against Finley.

Oakland again led the AL in wins in 1975 with 98 to capture the club's fifth consecutive divisional crown, but they were quickly dispatched in three straight games in the ALCS by the Boston Red Sox by scores of 7–1, 6–3 and 5–3 in which Carl Yastrzemski was the star performer. Just like that, the dynasty of the Swingin' A's came to an end. Bob Valli of the *Oakland Tribune* wrote in its October 8 issue, "Charles O. Finley's goal of matching the New York Yankees' dynasty of five straight championships was snapped two short of its target."

In 1976, Oakland was still competitive, finishing second in the AL West, just 2½ games behind the ascending Kansas City Royals. However, the coming of free agency at the end of 1975—and Charlie Finley's refusal to pay high salaries—decimated the former champions. Catfish Hunter, who was uniquely declared a free agent when Finley had neglected to honor a key clause in his 1974 contract, had already fled. He jumped to the Yankees in 1975.

Finley traded away Reggie Jackson and Ken Holtzman during

spring training of 1976. Sal Bando, Gene Tenace, Bert Campaneris, Rollie Fingers and Joe Rudi all became free agents that autumn. Earlier in 1976, Finley had attempted to sell Rudi and Fingers to the Boston Red Sox for $1 million apiece, and Vida Blue to the New York Yankees for $1.5 million. MLB commissioner Bowie Kuhn reacted with an extraordinary decision: Kuhn invoked the seldom-used "best interests of baseball" veto clause in his contract to nullify Finley's deals which were widely perceived as "fire sales." Finley, in response, filed a $10 million lawsuit against both Kuhn and MLB, claiming restraint-of-trade. Not accepting defeat gracefully, Finley ordered A's manager Chuck Tanner not to use Rudi, Blue or Fingers until further notice.

Things came to a head minutes before a May 27 home game versus Minnesota. The rest of the Oakland players informed manager Tanner that they would refuse to take the field for that day's game if the three players in limbo were not reinstated. Facing a forfeit and the loss of that day's gate, Finley, via telephone from Chicago, gave in to the players' demand. Still, one can only wonder how the prolonged absence of three such players from the Oakland lineup had adversely affected their chances to win the close AL West divisional race in 1976.

On July 7, 1976, Finley was a guest on *The Tonight Show*—a rarity for a baseball magnate—and told Johnny Carson he was confident he would win his lawsuit since there had been many other notable player-for-cash transactions in MLB history dating back to the Boston Red Sox selling Babe Ruth to the New York Yankees in January 1920. Finley lost. The court ruled that MLB's commissioner had the authority to determine what was in the best interests of the sport—including the nullification of player trades.

At the end of the 1976 season, Finley—who was rumored to be trying to move the A's to Washington, D.C.—figured out a new way to anger the Bay Area baseball fans: He fired popular longtime broadcaster Monte Moore. Apparently, Moore was terminated for the high crime of going on a postseason cruise to Mexico with his wife and several of the A's players. Upon his return in early November, Moore found a notice in his mail from Blue Cross informing him that his health insurance, which had always been covered by the team, had been canceled because he was no longer on the club's payroll. The startled Moore promptly made phone calls to the A's business office in hopes of getting an explanation. When he finally got to speak to Finley, Moore got more than he bargained for; he got an earful from the boss.

Finley went on a profanity-filled tirade, berating Moore for "fraternizing with the players"—which had never been a problem in the past. (Moore routinely flew with the team on road trips.) Three players subsequently filed for free agency, however; perhaps Finley bizarrely blamed Moore for that development. "He never said I was fired in those words. He just hung up," the perplexed Moore stated in Ed Levitt's column in the December 8 issue of the *Oakland Tribune* where the startling news was first reported. "If being taken off the payroll means I'm fired, I guess I am."[18]

Levitt was appalled by the shabby treatment Moore had received. He wrote, "That was it. Fifteen years of working for Charlie Finley and he doesn't even give you an explanation, a goodbye, a handshake. You're just through."[19]

Moore, a devoutly religious man, had never missed a single broadcast since being hired by Finley in 1962 to call Kansas City A's games. He calculated the total—including preseason and postseason ballgames— to be 2,640. (Amazingly, Moore had had 15 different on-air partners in his 15 seasons as the A's primary announcer!) Moore's apparent dismissal generated plenty of shock and public outrage among the dwindling local fanbase. "How Finley knifed a house man" blared one headline in a San Francisco daily. *The Sporting News* ran a similar one: "Moore's Loyalty Receives Its Reward—Finley's Ax." In the *TSN* article, Moore stated, "I'm not going to blast Charlie over this.... I've never had a contract, [but] I think I deserve a little better than this after 15 years."[20] Eventually, Finley rescinded his unpopular decision. Moore— who is credited with coining the term "dinger" as a synonym for a home run—remained with the A's in some capacity as an announcer through the 1980 season, and again from 1988 through 1992.

In 1977, Oakland dramatically dropped to the bottom of the AL West standings with a 63–98 record. (Embarrassingly, even the expansion Seattle Mariners finished half a game ahead of them.) Home attendance plummeted to just 495,599—far and away the worst figure in MLB. An Oakland home game on August 19 versus Cleveland drew only 2,700 paying customers on a lovely Friday night.

Home attendance for the A's in 1978 rose by about six percent to 526, 999, but it was still last in the majors by a quarter-million people. By 1979 the average home crowd at the Oakland-Alameda County Coliseum was a pitiful 3,787 as the team attracted only 306,763 fans for the whole season. As fewer and fewer people in the Bay Area began to care about the A's, Finley completely stopped advertising the team. "Charlie hasn't spent one red cent on promotion," complained pitcher Bob Lacey. "I've never been asked to speak anywhere. Nobody knows who we are."[21]

That year, an early-season, three-game series versus the unglamorous Seattle Mariners drew a grand total of 4,806 fans. The nadir was the chilly night of Tuesday, April 17, when an announced "crowd" of 653 people watched Oakland beat Seattle, 6–5. (The true attendance was quite likely even smaller, as the AL tabulates attendance by tickets sold—not by turnstile count. During lulls in the game, Oakland first baseman Dave Revering did a rough head count and calculated there were only about 200 spectators present in the huge stadium.) Journalist Tom Weir did some arithmetic and wrote in *The Sporting News*, "If the average attendance of 3,290 continues, it will be about May 1 before the A's total gate equals San Francisco's Opening Day count of 56,196."[22] Critics began calling the poorly supported club the Triple-A's.

Certainly, Oakland was not close to being a pennant contender in 1979—the team was 1–9 after 10 games—but the awful attendance was primarily because of one person. "It's a revolt against [Charlie] Finley," claimed Robert Nahas, one of the poohbahs in charge of events at the city-owned Oakland-Alameda County Coliseum. "He's the most complex individual I've ever dealt with."[23] Designated hitter Mitchell Page concurred. "There are nothing but negative thoughts around here,"[24] he told Weir. (There was one positive on the 1979 A's: The team had an exciting 20-year-old rookie outfielder named Rickey Henderson who stole 33 bases in the 89 games he played.)

*Sports Illustrated*'s Ron Fimrite had fun discussing the positive aspects of the A's attendance woes in the May 21, 1979, edition. He wrote,

> The A's fan suffers none of the myriad inconveniences that afflict spectators in more populous stadiums. He can park his car as near to the Coliseum as the players do, and he can purchase a ticket at the last possible moment—if he can find a booth open. Once inside, the odds on catching a foul ball are much better than anywhere else. He can easily locate friends in the park, and he is likely to have his own personal vendor of soft drinks, beer and comestibles. He is very much like a guest at an exclusive party.[25]

Other people weren't laughing. Visiting teams, entitled to 20 percent of the gate at all MLB games, were finding that their share of the measly receipts at the Oakland Coliseum were not coming close to covering their traveling and lodging expenses. An unnamed executive from an AL team located in the Midwest bluntly told Fimrite, "It would be cheaper for us to forfeit all our games out there."[26]

Exasperated, the City of Oakland sued Finley for $1.5 million in lost income, plus $10 million in punitive damages. The lawsuit, claiming that Finley was not living up to his basic obligations to operate an MLB team properly and do his best to sell tickets, maintained that Finley's non-promotion of the team had cost the facility hundreds of thousands of dollars in lost parking and concession fees. "He has done the utmost to conceal his team from the public,"[27] said the lawsuit. Meanwhile, Finley had a sweetheart rental deal at the Coliseum. It was only costing him $125,000 to use the facility for the 1979 season. Ever hateful of paying high salaries, Finley did not have any player on the 1979 A's who made $100,000—even though that was approximately the average MLB salary that season.

Everything about the A's of the late 1970s seemed small-time and amateurish. On Opening Day versus the Minnesota Twins, the scoreboards and sound system at the Coliseum were on the fritz. No dignitary was on hand to throw out a ceremonial first pitch—so the plate umpire Derryl Cousins performed the duty. The radio station carrying A's games in 1979 was KXRX, a tiny 5,000-watt operation located in San Jose. Its signal was largely inaudible to fans in the Bay Area after nightfall. (It was, however, clearly a step up from the tiny 10-watt, student-operated college radio station that briefly carried A's games in 1978.) Just 12 hours before the first pitch on Opening Day, Finley got around to hiring an announcer, Red Rush, to call Oakland's games on radio. He had twice been employed as part of the A's broadcast team—once in 1965 (when the team still played in Kansas City) and once in 1971. Team souvenirs available at the Coliseum that season were comically outdated. Fimrite reported,

> Sales are apparently less than brisk at the souvenir stands; last week the concessionaires were offering buttons celebrating Ken Holtzman, who last pitched for the A's in 1975; and Dal Maxvill, who has not played in the majors since that year.[28]

Finley was seldom seen at the ballpark anymore; he was noticeably absent from Opening Day for the first time in his 19 years of owning the club—and just about every other A's home game in 1979, too. He preferred to stay in his hometown of Chicago and keep a low profile. This was quite a contrast from the team's World Series years when, *Sports Illustrated* joked, that the middle initial in Charles O. Finley's name stood for "omnipresent."

By the middle of 1980, Finley had had enough of MLB—and MLB had certainly had enough of Charles O. Finley. On August 23 it was announced that Finley had agreed to sell the A's to Walter A. Hass, Jr., the president of the Levi Strauss clothing company and two of his family members. They intended to keep the team in Oakland. Finley got $12.7 million in the transaction. The following year, the A's qualified for postseason play for the first time since 1975.

At the press conference announcing the sale, Finley used the opportunity to make a long farewell speech from baseball in which he pleasantly recounted what *The Sporting News* called "his innovative baseball career." However, he did take shots at Bowie Kuhn and the new financial realities of MLB. He told reporters,

> The main reason I am leaving baseball is that I can no longer compete financially. During the time we were winning championships, survival was a battle of wits. We did alright then. But it's no longer a battle of wits, but how much you have on the hip. I can no longer compete. I am going to have to leave baseball because of these idiotic, astronomical salaries.[29]

Finley returned to Chicago and spent his remaining years quietly running his insurance company. When Finley died of heart and vascular ailments in 1996 a few days before what would have been his 78th birthday, his obituary in the *Washington Post* accurately described him as "one of baseball's most cantankerous executives and innovators."[30] This was undeniably true. The obit also prominently mentioned that, under his ownership, the superb Oakland A's had won three consecutive World Series from 1972 through 1974 mostly by cultivating homegrown talent. Only the New York Yankees had ever achieved that feat. This was undeniably true, too.

In penning Finley's SABR biography, Mark Armour noted, "It is impossible to write about the great 1970s Athletics ... without presenting Finley as the star of the show; the baseball team, even the games themselves, often seemed a sidelight to some other story. This is exactly how Finley wanted it."[31] Armour also wrote, "For a man who spent 20 years in the game and won three championships, he left very few friends in the game."[32] Indeed, in a 2017 MLB-TV documentary titled *The Swingin' A's*, Vida Blue said of Charles O. Finley, "I hate to speak ill of the dead, but the guy was out of his mind."[33]

# — 19 —

# Gone Too Soon

The 1972 World Series was played half a century ago. With the inexorable passing of time, it is natural that many participants from that World Series have died. Both teams' managers have been deceased for more than a decade. Five of the six umpires who worked the seven hard-fought games are gone too, the lone exception being Bill Haller who celebrated his 87th birthday in February 2022. Many of the players no longer with us left this earthly realm after having lived reasonably long lives. However, three members of the A's and one Red departed far too quickly. They are worthy of special mention.

Oakland first-base coach **Jerry Adair** had a previous connection with manager Dick Williams. Adair was a member of the 1967 pennant-winning Boston Red Sox that Williams had managed. Often referred to as one of the best athletes ever to come out of Oklahoma State University, Adair played varsity college basketball on a team that defeated Wilt Chamberlain's Kansas Jayhawks in 1957—a rarity. Adair was a bit of a latecomer to baseball, but he was a natural at the sport. He was especially adroit with the glove. In one stretch, as a second baseman with the Baltimore Orioles, Adair went 458 chances without committing an error. Midway through the 1967 season, he was acquired by the Red Sox. Jim Lonborg, the ace of the Boston Sox staff, noted that getting Adair "was like adding a gem to a beautiful necklace. He did such a magnificent job for us. He was a quiet guy around the clubhouse. He was so invaluable, older and more experienced."[1] Adair became known as Mr. Clutch among his teammates for his timely hits and defensive gems. (He finished 15th in AL MVP voting.) Adair's batting average dropped severely in 1968, however. At season's end he was left unprotected by Boston and he was taken in the 1969 expansion draft by the Kansas City Royals. Sadly, by early 1970, Adair's six-year-old daughter, Tammy, was in the last stages of terminal cancer, causing Adair to miss most of spring training. She died on April 9. Adair was released from the Royals a month later after batting just .148 in seven games. He was notified just as he was about to board an airplane for a road trip. Adair was embittered by the circumstances and that the Royals had not taken his family crisis into account. He never played another MLB game. In 1972, Adair's old manager, Dick Williams, hired him for the Oakland A's where he coached on the three consecutive A's teams that won the World Series. By 1976, Adair was out of baseball. In 1981, Adair's wife died of cancer. In 1987, Adair himself died of liver cancer. He was 50 years old.

**Jim (Catfish) Hunter** was undeniably one of the best MLB pitchers of the 1970s. Hunter was the first pitcher to win 200 games before his 31st birthday since 1915. In 1974 he was so dominant that teammate Reggie Jackson said that Hunter deserved "the Cy Young Award, the Most Valuable Player Award, the Academy Award, and the kitchen sink."[2] After winning free agency in 1975 in a historic decision because A's owner Charles O. Finley neglected to honor parts of Hunter's contract, the righty from Hertford, North Carolina, signed with the New York Yankees. Within a short time, he revitalized a franchise that had been in decline for a decade. He pitched for New York through the 1979 season, retiring at the fairly young age of 33 because he was financially secure, and he desired to spend a simple life with his family back in the same rural small town where he had grown up. He was elected to the Hall of Fame in 1987. Yankee owner George Steinbrenner noted, "Catfish Hunter was the cornerstone of the Yankees' success over the last quarter-century. We were not winning before Catfish arrived. He exemplified class and dignity and he taught us how to win."[3] In September 1998, during one of his frequent hunting forays, Hunter suddenly experienced difficulty lifting his rifle. A medical examination confirmed the worst: Hunter had ALS—better known to North Americans as Lou Gehrig's disease. Incurable and insidious, the malady snuffed out Hunter's life within a year. His last public appearance was in mid–March 1999 at a Yankee spring training game. He had to apologize to autograph seekers for being unable to sign his name. Hunter was just 53 years old when he died on September 9, 1999. He left behind his wife of 33 years, three children and a grandchild. Hunter was buried in Cedar Wood Cemetery in Hertford. It is located just behind the field where he had starred as a high-school pitcher.

**Gonzalo Márquez** claimed he had been born in 1946 when he first signed a professional baseball contract. Venezuelan birth records, however, show he was actually six years older. (Shaving several years from one's age was so common among prospects from Latin America that it was almost expected by the pro teams that employed them.) Thus, Márquez was an old MLB rookie—age 32—when he played for Oakland in the 1972 World Series. He got one of the three A's key pinch hits in the bottom of the ninth inning of Game Four that dramatically turned the game around. Márquez played for both Oakland and the Chicago Cubs in 1973 and one more season with the Cubs in 1974. A lefthanded batter, Márquez compiled a .235 batting average with one homer and 10 RBI in his 76-game MLB career. Márquez made the most of the 1972 postseason, getting five hits in eight at-bats. He is the answer to an obscure baseball trivia question: On May 5, 1973, Márquez was the most recent lefthanded second baseman to appear in an MLB box score. Once Márquez left the majors—and even while he was under contract to MLB teams—he played until 1984 in the Venezuelan Winter League. On December 19, 1984, Márquez was killed in an automobile accident as he and two sons were returning home from a baseball game in Valencia (Venezuela's third-largest city). They had stopped to buy sandwiches at a roadside food stand. Shortly after they had left the eatery, a drunk driver slammed into the Márquezes' vehicle. Although his two sons both survived the tragic mishap, Gonzalo Márquez did not. He was 44 years old.

By the time he started Game Five of the 1972 World Series at age 29 for Cincinnati, **Jim McGlothlin**'s career was noticeably in decline. The following year, 1973, McGlothlin seemed to lack energy. He started just

Seldom-used Cincinnati pitcher Jim McGlothlin was the surprise starter in Game Five of the 1972 World Series. He gave up four runs in three innings, but the Reds mounted a late rally to win the crucial game (courtesy Cincinnati Reds Hall of Fame).

nine games for the Reds before being traded to the Chicago White Sox in August.

McGlothlin made only one start and four relief appearances for Chicago in the remainder of the 1973 season. McGlothlin's baseball career was over before his 30th birthday, although he did not know it yet. He bought 12 acres of farmland in Kentucky's Boone County and started a country ham business in the offseason with a neighbor. The White Sox did not offer McGlothlin a contract for 1974. In February 1975, McGlothlin was diagnosed—wrongly, it turned out—with stomach cancer. However, an operation for the stomach cancer that was not there showed that McGlothlin had been stricken with a rare form of leukemia. It was incurable. "I'm supposed to be six feet under," he said in an interview that May when he was wan and about 45 pounds below his playing weight, "but I never considered dying."[4] McGlothlin's neighbors and former Cincinnati teammates contributed to help cover his mounting medical expenses. Johnny Bench organized a benefit show at a Kentucky supper club and even sang at the event. Pete Rose established the optimistically named Jim McGlothlin Speedy Recovery Fund. The Cincinnati Reds contributed $1,000 to it from a fund to honor Fred Hutchinson, a former manager who had died of cancer in 1964 at age 45. When news of McGlothlin's illness was made public, the retired pitcher was overwhelmed with sacks of fan mail from baseball fans and well-wishers everywhere. He told a reporter he read every letter received and that the fans' kind messages helped him cope. Nevertheless, McGlothlin passed away at his home two days before Christmas in 1975. He left behind a wife, two daughters and a son. He was only 32 years old.

# Ranking the Fall Classic

## *So How Good Was the 1972 World Series?*

"It [is] not best that we should all think alike; it is differ-ence of opinion that makes horse races."—Mark Twain

"Never in the 69-year history of this hoary event has unconventionality prevailed as it did this time. And the unconventionality doesn't even take into consideration (a) the owner of the A's, who, for steadiness, hardly will remind you of Lloyds of London, (b) the addled opera-tion he runs, and (c) the appearance of his hairy forces."[1]
—Melvin Durslag, *The Sporting News*

The modern version of the World Series has been around since 1903. Counting the 2020 World Series, there have been 116 installments of the Fall Classic. (There should have been 118, but both the 1904 and 1994 seasons sadly ended without a proper climax to the MLB season.) Where does the 1972 World Series rank in terms of greatness?

To adequately answer such a question requires a tremendous amount of analysis and insight. There are both tangibles and intangibles to consider. Shortly after the Los Angeles Dodgers upended the Tampa Bay Rays in 2020, ESPN undertook an effort to rank every World Series from #1 to #116. It used four criteria to create its list from the best Fall Classic ever contested (1975) to the worst (1919):

- "Game leverage index," created by Baseball-Reference.com. It measures how close a game is on a play-by-play basis and how likely the next play is to shift each team's chances of winning it. For example, a World Series game that is tight for nine innings and won by a walk-off hit in the 10th inning will rate much higher than one in which a team jumps ahead early and runs away with it thereafter.
- "Championship leverage index," from The Baseball Gauge,

created by its owner Dan Hirsch. This calculation is similar to game leverage index, except that it also factors in how close a particular World Series was on an overall basis. Thus, a seven-game World Series will rate considerably higher on the list than a four-game sweep would.

- How memorable the Fall Classic was. A good example is the 1988 Dodgers-A's matchup. It was not a particularly closely fought World Series (Los Angeles won it in five games), but as ESPN's Sam Miller notes, "[It] produces instant recall for one inning alone." Of course, this criterion is a completely subjective one and, therefore, it can be heavily influenced by personal bias.
- How historically significant it was, and how satisfying that history is. This criterion, like the one above, is totally comprised of human judgement. Thus, there is an inherent danger with it: As older World Series fade into distant memory or are forgotten altogether, this can skew the results. Accordingly, it will favor Fall Classics that people who compiled the list can actually remember experiencing.

Given all these factors, the 1972 World Series finished a respectable 14th in ESPN's ratings. It finished eighth in the "championship leverage" department and seventh in the "game leverage" category. Sam Miller writes, "Aside from an 8–1 blowout in Game Six, the other six games were each decided by one run, and the clubs finished with identical batting averages and slugging percentages. The great Rollie Fingers pitched in all six close ones, his only 'blemish' being the failure to preserve a one-run lead for a five-inning save [in Game Five]"[2]

One interesting point to note is that of the 13 World Series that finished ahead of the subject of this book in ESPN's rankings, seven of them have been played since the A's and Reds clashed in the autumn of 1972. Therefore, just after it was contested, the 1972 World Series would have rated as the seventh-best of the first 69 Fall Classics.

The 1972 World Series is indeed a forgotten gem.

# Team Batting and Pitching Statistics, 1972 World Series

## 1972 World Series
### Composite Hitting Statistics

| Name | Pos | G | AB | H | 2B | 3B | HR | R | RBI | Avg | BB | SO | SB |
|---|---|---|---|---|---|---|---|---|---|---|---|---|---|
| *Matty Alou* | of | 7 | 24 | 1 | 0 | 0 | 0 | 0 | 0 | .042 | 3 | 0 | 1 |
| *Sal Bando* | 3b | 7 | 26 | 7 | 1 | 0 | 0 | 2 | 1 | .269 | 2 | 5 | 0 |
| *Vida Blue* | p | 4 | 1 | 0 | 0 | 0 | 0 | 0 | 0 | .000 | 2 | 1 | 0 |
| *Bert Campaneris* | ss | 7 | 28 | 5 | 0 | 0 | 0 | 1 | 0 | .179 | 1 | 4 | 0 |
| *David Duncan* | c-1 | 3 | 5 | 1 | 0 | 0 | 0 | 0 | 0 | .200 | 1 | 3 | 0 |
| *Mike Epstein* | 1b | 6 | 16 | 0 | 0 | 0 | 0 | 1 | 0 | .000 | 5 | 3 | 0 |
| *Rollie Fingers* | p | 6 | 1 | 0 | 0 | 0 | 0 | 0 | 0 | .000 | 0 | 0 | 0 |
| *Dick Green* | 2b | 7 | 18 | 6 | 2 | 0 | 0 | 0 | 1 | .333 | 0 | 4 | 0 |
| *Dave Hamilton* | p | 2 | 0 | 0 | 0 | 0 | 0 | 0 | 0 | .000 | 0 | 0 | 0 |
| *Mike Hegan* | 1b-5 | 6 | 5 | 1 | 0 | 0 | 0 | 0 | 0 | .200 | 0 | 2 | 0 |
| *George Hendrick* | of | 5 | 15 | 2 | 0 | 0 | 0 | 3 | 0 | .133 | 1 | 2 | 0 |
| *Ken Holtzman* | p | 3 | 5 | 0 | 0 | 0 | 0 | 0 | 0 | .000 | 0 | 0 | 0 |
| *Joe Horlen* | p | 1 | 0 | 0 | 0 | 0 | 0 | 0 | 0 | .000 | 0 | 0 | 0 |
| *Catfish Hunter* | p | 3 | 5 | 1 | 0 | 0 | 0 | 0 | 1 | .200 | 2 | 1 | 0 |
| *Ted Kubiak* | 2b | 4 | 3 | 1 | 0 | 0 | 0 | 0 | 0 | .333 | 0 | 0 | 0 |
| *Allan Lewis* | pr | 6 | 0 | 0 | 0 | 0 | 0 | 2 | 0 | .000 | 0 | 0 | 0 |
| *Bob Locker* | p | 1 | 0 | 0 | 0 | 0 | 0 | 0 | 0 | .000 | 0 | 0 | 0 |
| *Angel Mangual* | of-2 | 4 | 10 | 3 | 0 | 0 | 0 | 1 | 1 | .300 | 0 | 0 | 0 |
| *Gonzalo Marquez* | ph | 5 | 5 | 3 | 0 | 0 | 0 | 0 | 1 | .600 | 0 | 0 | 0 |
| *Don Mincher* | ph | 3 | 1 | 1 | 0 | 0 | 0 | 0 | 1 | 1.000 | 0 | 0 | 0 |
| *Blue Moon Odom* | p-2 | 4 | 4 | 0 | 0 | 0 | 0 | 0 | 0 | .000 | 0 | 3 | 0 |
| *Joe Rudi* | of | 7 | 25 | 6 | 0 | 0 | 1 | 1 | 1 | .240 | 2 | 5 | 0 |
| *Gene Tenace* | c-6,1b-1 | 7 | 23 | 8 | 1 | 0 | 4 | 5 | 9 | .348 | 2 | 4 | 0 |
| **Totals** | | | 220 | 46 | 4 | 0 | 5 | 16 | 16 | .209 | 21 | 37 | 1 |

## 1972 World Series
### Composite Hitting Statistics

| Name | Pos | G | AB | H | 2B | 3B | HR | R | RBI | Avg | BB | SO | SB |
|---|---|---|---|---|---|---|---|---|---|---|---|---|---|
| Johnny Bench | c | 7 | 23 | 6 | 1 | 0 | 1 | 4 | 1 | .261 | 5 | 5 | 2 |
| Jack Billingham | p | 3 | 5 | 0 | 0 | 0 | 0 | 0 | 0 | .000 | 0 | 4 | 0 |
| Pedro Borbón | p | 6 | 0 | 0 | 0 | 0 | 0 | 0 | 0 | .000 | 0 | 0 | 0 |
| Clay Carroll | p | 5 | 0 | 0 | 0 | 0 | 0 | 0 | 0 | .000 | 0 | 0 | 0 |
| Darrel Chaney | ss-3 | 4 | 7 | 0 | 0 | 0 | 0 | 0 | 0 | .000 | 2 | 2 | 0 |
| Dave Concepción | ss-5 | 6 | 13 | 4 | 0 | 1 | 0 | 2 | 2 | .308 | 2 | 2 | 1 |
| George Foster | of-1 | 2 | 0 | 0 | 0 | 0 | 0 | 0 | 0 | .000 | 0 | 0 | 0 |
| César Gerónimo | of | 7 | 19 | 3 | 0 | 0 | 0 | 1 | 3 | .158 | 1 | 4 | 1 |
| Ross Grimsley | p | 4 | 2 | 0 | 0 | 0 | 0 | 0 | 0 | .000 | 0 | 2 | 0 |
| Don Gullett | p | 1 | 2 | 0 | 0 | 0 | 0 | 0 | 0 | .000 | 0 | 0 | 0 |
| Joe Hague | of-1 | 3 | 3 | 0 | 0 | 0 | 0 | 0 | 0 | .000 | 0 | 0 | 0 |
| Tom Hall | p | 4 | 2 | 0 | 0 | 0 | 0 | 0 | 0 | .000 | 0 | 1 | 0 |
| Julian Javier | ph | 4 | 2 | 0 | 0 | 0 | 0 | 0 | 0 | .000 | 0 | 0 | 0 |
| Jim McGlothlin | p | 1 | 1 | 0 | 0 | 0 | 0 | 0 | 0 | .000 | 0 | 0 | 0 |
| Hal McRae | of-2 | 5 | 9 | 4 | 1 | 0 | 0 | 1 | 2 | .444 | 0 | 1 | 0 |
| Denis Menke | 3b | 7 | 24 | 2 | 0 | 0 | 1 | 1 | 2 | .083 | 2 | 6 | 0 |
| Joe Morgan | 2b | 7 | 24 | 3 | 2 | 0 | 0 | 4 | 1 | .125 | 6 | 3 | 2 |
| Gary Nolan | p | 2 | 3 | 0 | 0 | 0 | 0 | 0 | 0 | .000 | 0 | 3 | 0 |
| Tony Pérez | 1b | 7 | 23 | 10 | 2 | 0 | 0 | 3 | 2 | .435 | 4 | 4 | 0 |
| Pete Rose | of | 7 | 28 | 6 | 0 | 0 | 1 | 3 | 2 | .214 | 4 | 4 | 1 |
| Bobby Tolan | of | 7 | 26 | 7 | 1 | 0 | 0 | 2 | 6 | .269 | 1 | 4 | 5 |
| Ted Uhlaender | ph | 4 | 4 | 1 | 1 | 0 | 0 | 0 | 0 | .250 | 0 | 1 | 0 |
| **Totals** | | | 220 | 46 | 8 | 1 | 3 | 21 | 21 | .209 | 27 | 46 | 12 |

## 1972 World Series
### Composite Pitching Statistics

| Name | W | L | G | GS | CG | S | Sh | IP | ERA | H | SO | ER | BB |
|---|---|---|---|---|---|---|---|---|---|---|---|---|---|
| Vida Blue | 0 | 1 | 4 | 1 | 0 | 1 | 0 | 8.2 | 4.15 | 8 | 5 | 4 | 5 |
| Rollie Fingers | 1 | 1 | 6 | 0 | 0 | 0 | 0 | 10.1 | 1.74 | 4 | 11 | 2 | 4 |
| Dave Hamilton | 0 | 0 | 2 | 0 | 0 | 2 | 0 | 1.1 | 27.00 | 3 | 1 | 4 | 1 |
| Ken Holtzman | 1 | 0 | 3 | 2 | 0 | 0 | 0 | 12.2 | 2.13 | 11 | 4 | 3 | 3 |
| Joe Horlen | 0 | 0 | 1 | 0 | 0 | 0 | 0 | 1.1 | 6.75 | 2 | 1 | 1 | 2 |
| Catfish Hunter | 2 | 0 | 3 | 2 | 0 | 0 | 0 | 16.0 | 2.81 | 12 | 11 | 5 | 6 |
| Bob Locker | 0 | 0 | 1 | 0 | 0 | 0 | 0 | 0.1 | 0.00 | 1 | 0 | 0 | 0 |
| Blue Moon Odom | 0 | 1 | 2 | 2 | 0 | 0 | 0 | 11.1 | 1.59 | 5 | 13 | 2 | 6 |
| **Totals** | 4 | 3 | 22 | 7 | 0 | 3 | 0 | 62.0 | 3.05 | 46 | 46 | 21 | 27 |

## 1972 World Series
### Composite Pitching Statistics

| Name | W | L | G | GS | CG | S | Sh | IP | ERA | H | SO | ER | BB |
|---|---|---|---|---|---|---|---|---|---|---|---|---|---|
| Jack Billingham | 1 | 0 | 3 | 2 | 0 | 1 | 0 | 13.2 | 0.00 | 6 | 11 | 0 | 4 |
| Pedro Borbón | 0 | 1 | 6 | 0 | 0 | 0 | 0 | 7.0 | 3.86 | 7 | 4 | 3 | 2 |
| Clay Carroll | 0 | 1 | 5 | 0 | 0 | 1 | 0 | 5.2 | 1.59 | 6 | 3 | 1 | 4 |
| Ross Grimsley | 2 | 1 | 4 | 1 | 0 | 0 | 0 | 7.0 | 2.57 | 7 | 2 | 2 | 3 |
| Don Gullett | 0 | 0 | 1 | 1 | 0 | 0 | 0 | 7.0 | 1.29 | 5 | 4 | 1 | 2 |
| Tom Hall | 0 | 0 | 4 | 0 | 0 | 1 | 0 | 8.1 | 0.00 | 6 | 7 | 0 | 2 |
| Jim McGlothlin | 0 | 0 | 1 | 1 | 0 | 0 | 0 | 3.0 | 12.00 | 2 | 3 | 4 | 2 |
| Gary Nolan | 0 | 1 | 2 | 2 | 0 | 0 | 0 | 10.2 | 3.38 | 7 | 3 | 4 | 2 |
| **Totals** | 3 | 4 | 26 | 7 | 0 | 3 | 0 | 62.1 | 2.17 | 46 | 37 | 15 | 21 |

The following players were on the 1972 World Series rosters but did not participate in any of the seven games:

**Cincinnati:** Bill Plummer (catcher), Wayne Simpson (pitcher) and Ed Sprague (pitcher)

**Oakland:** Tim Cullen (infielder) and Dal Maxvill (infielder)

## APPENDIX B

# Studs and Duds:
# The Best and Worst Performers

"Productivity is never an accident. It is always the result
of a commitment to excellence, intelligent planning, and
focused effort."—Paul J. Meyer

"It's failure that gives you the proper perspective on success."—Ellen DeGeneres

"I really hate to talk about that [1972] World Series because
I made the last out."[1]—Pete Rose

In any championship series in any sport, there are performers who
excel when it counts the most and those who put on a less-than-
stellar show in the limelight. The 1972 World Series had its share of
heroes and zeroes too. Here are the participants for both teams at each
extreme.

## Cincinnati's Studs

- Tony Pérez was the only player on either team to hit safely in
  all seven Series games. He ended up batting .435 (10 hits in 23
  at-bats) along with drawing four bases on balls. By any measure,
  Tony Pérez had a fine World Series.
- Pitcher Jack Billingham was quietly superb in the Series. In 13⅔
  innings pitched, Billingham did not allow an earned run. He
  struck out 11 batters and picked up a win and a save. He could
  hardly have done anything more on the mound to give his team
  a chance to win.
- Denis Menke did not do much offensively in the seven games—
  he batted a paltry .083 (2-for-24) with six strikeouts—but he
  was absolutely solid at third base throughout the World Series.
  Menke committed no errors in 29 chances.

**Tom (The Blade) Hall provided solid relief pitching for the Reds during the 1972 World Series. In 8⅓ innings over four games, the svelte Hall allowed no earned runs (courtesy Cincinnati Reds Hall of Fame)**

- Hal McRae did not play all that much in the Series, but when he did, he contributed mightily. McRae batted .444 (4-for-9), scored a run, and had two RBIs.
- Tom Hall pitched 8⅓ innings of relief over four games and did not surrender an earned run in any of his outings. The Blade struck out seven batters. In Game Six he earned a save.
- Don Gullett compiled a very respectable 1.29 ERA in seven innings of work.

## Cincinnati's Duds

- Joe Morgan never got on track offensively in the World Series. He batted a miserable .125 (3-for-24), although two of his three hits were doubles. He did draw six walks, but his stolen base total of two was a disappointment.
- In Game Seven, Bobby Tolan committed the costliest and most egregious error of the World Series and suffered an untimely injury that allowed what turned out to be the winning run to score. Tolan did eventually get seven hits in 26 at-bats for a .269 batting average and steal six bases, but it took him a long time to find his batting eye.

- In the four games that Darrel Chaney played in the Series, he was 0-for-7 at the plate with two strikeouts.
- César Gerónimo's .158 batting average in 19 at-bats has to be classified as a disappointment.
- Jim McGlothlin was knocked around for a 12.00 ERA in his three innings of work.
- Denis Menke uniquely gets both cheers and jeers. While Menke's defensive play was stellar, his offensive contributions were minimal. He got just two hits in 24 official at-bats for an .083 batting average.

## Oakland's Studs

- Gene Tenace was only known to hardcore baseball fans before the 1972 World Series. However, Tenace became the talk of the sports world with his MVP performance. Not only did his four home runs in the Series put him in the same elite company as Ruth, Gehrig, Snider and Bauer, Tenace also drove in nine of the 16 runs his team scored in the Series. He was obviously the star—and an unexpected one—of the Fall Classic.
- Rollie Fingers appeared in six of the seven Series games. His sneaky whiff of Johnny Bench was the most memorable strikeout of the 1972 World Series—perhaps of any World Series! Fingers' numbers were excellent: He pitched 10⅓ innings, struck out 11 batters, compiled a 1.74 ERA, and got credit for the A's win in Game Four. Lawrence M. Stolle accurately wrote that "Fingers was as troublesome to Cincinnatians as a bill collector."[22]
- In the 1972 Fall Classic, Gonzalo Márquez was marvelous as a pinch hitter—arguably the toughest job in baseball. The Venezuelan succeeded three times in five World Series at-bats for a .600 batting average.
- In three Series games, Ken Holtzman picked up a victory in Game One, pitched 12⅔ innings, and compiled a 2.13 ERA. It was a very workmanlike and competent performance.
- On the mound, Catfish Hunter compiled a 2–0 record in the three games in which appeared. He had two starts in the Series, but his relief appearance got him a Game Seven win. In those three games, Hunter notched 11 strikeouts. Offensively, Hunter batted .200. He had an RBI single and drew two walks.

## Oakland's Duds

- Mike Epstein was an awful 0-for-16 in the World Series with three strikeouts. Epstein's batting slump was so noticeable that manager Dick Williams finally ran out of patience and benched him for Game Seven.

- Bert Campaneris did not make the most of Commissioner Bowie Kuhn's very generous and forgiving ruling that allowed him to play in the World Series. After getting hits in his first two plate appearances in Game One, Campaneris' bat went cold. He batted just .179 (5-for-28) as the A's leadoff hitter and scored just one run. Campaneris had led the AL in stolen bases in 1972, but he did not have a single steal in the Series.
- Matty Alou was a late season pickup by Oakland. In the seven Series games, Alou got exactly one hit in 24 at-bats. His miserable .042 batting average was an embarrassment for the former NL batting champion. Desperately searching for anything positive to say about Alou's offensive stats, late in Game Seven Jim Simpson of NBC Radio noted that Alou was the only regular player on either team to have not struck out in the Series. One other trivial high note: Alou had the A's only stolen base in the World Series.
- George Hendrick was the man assigned to replace the injured Reggie Jackson in center field. He did not succeed. Hendrick was basically benched after the fifth game because he had managed just two hits in his 15 at-bats.
- Relief pitcher Dave Hamilton recorded a godawful 27.00 ERA in 1⅓ innings over two games.

# Chapter Notes

## Introduction

1. Bob Hertzel, "Another Look: The 1972 World Series," Baseballprospectus.com, October 12, 2010.

## Chapter 1

1. "1972: Labor Pains," Thisgreatgame.com.
2. Jack Hugerich, *Schenectady Gazette*, April 8, 1972, 20.
3. "March 31, 1972: The Day the Players Took Control of Their Union," MLB news, March 31, 2016.
4. "Baseball Players' Strike Begins Today," *Schenectady Gazette*, April 1, 1972, 18.
5. *Ibid.*
6. Herschel Nessenson, "Talks Prove Fruitless in Baseball Strike," *Schenectady Gazette*, April 3, 1972, 33.
7. "Jim Murray," *Schenectady Gazette*, April 4, 1972, 20.
8. "1972: Labor Pains," Thisgreatgame.com.
9. Oscar Kahan, "Salary for Strikers Becomes New Issue," *The Sporting News*, April 22, 1972, 3.
10. Joel Zoss and John S. Bowman, *The National League* (London: Bison Books, 1986), 144.

## Chapter 2

1. Greene, Chip, ed., *Mustaches and Mayhem: Charlie O's Three-Time Champions the Oakland Athletics, 1972–74* (Phoenix, AZ: Society for American Baseball Research, 2015), 1.

2. *Ibid.*
3. Ken Burns, *Baseball* (PBS Documentary), PBS Home Video, 1994.
4. Jim Hunter and Armen Keteyian, *Catfish: My Life in Baseball* (New York: McGraw Hill, 1988), 3.
5. Bob Hertzel, "Another Look: The 1972 World Series," Baseballprospectus.com, October 12, 2010.
6. Mickey Mantle, Quote.webcircle.com.
7. Ron Fimrite, "They're Just Mad About Charlie," *Sports Illustrated*, May 21, 1979, 38.
8. Eric Aron, "Manager Dick Williams," SABR biography, September 1, 2015.
9. Ron Bergman, "A's Harmony and Unity to Depend on Finley," *The Sporting News*, October 24, 1970, 25.
10. Dick Williams and Bill Plaschke, *No More Mr. Nice Guy* (New York: Harcourt Brace Jovanovich, 1990), 20.
11. Glenn Dickey, "Saluting Finley's champs," *San Francisco Chronicle*, July 14, 2002.
12. Ray Ratto, *The Swingin' A's* (MLB-TV documentary), 2017.
13. Vida Blue segment, *CBS Evening News*, June 26, 1971.
14. Jim Hunter and Armen Keteyian, *Catfish: My Life in Baseball* (New York: McGraw Hill, 1988), 90.
15. Gayle Montgomery, "A's Dream Is Ended, But the Fans Die Hard," *Oakland Tribune*, October 6, 1971, 1.
16. Gene Tenace, *The Swingin' A's* (MLB-TV documentary), 2017.
17. "Odom Shot Trying to Prevent Burglary," *The Sporting News*, January 22, 1972, 33.

18. Ron Bergman, "GIs in Vietnam Cheer Blue-Bob Hope Comedy Battery," *The Sporting News*, January 22, 1972, 33.

19. Jim Hunter and Armen Keteyian, *Catfish: My Life in Baseball* (New York: McGraw Hill, 1988), 90.

## Chapter 3

1. Matt Rothenberg, "150 Years Ago, Pro Baseball Began in Cincinnati," Baseballhall.org.

2. Joe Posnanski, *The Machine* (New York: HarperCollins, 2009), 10–11.

3. Ken Burns, *Baseball* (PBS Documentary), PBS Home Video, 1994.

4. Jon Wertheim, "Johnny Bench is Already a Hall of Famer, But He's Looking for a New Distinction," *Sports Illustrated* online archives, July 5, 2018.

5. Cindy Thomson, "Sparky Anderson," SABR biography, 2010.

6. Sparky Anderson (with Dan Ewald), *They Call Me Sparky* (Chelsea, MI: Sleeping Bear Press, 1998), 36.

7. Earl Lawson, "Bristol, Deposed Red Boss, Victim of Pitching Letdown," *The Sporting News*, October 25, 1969, 27.

8. *Ibid.*

9. *Ibid.*

10. Sparky Anderson (with Dan Ewald), *They Call Me Sparky* (Chelsea, MI: Sleeping Bear Press, 1998), 99.

11. Ralph Bernstein, "Memories of '70 keeping Sparky Anderson silent," *Fredericksburg Free Lance-Star*, October 13, 1972, 8.

12. Charley Feeney, "Playing Games," *Pittsburgh Post-Gazette*, October 10, 1972, 17.

13. *Ibid.*

14. Joe Posnanski, *The Machine* (New York: HarperCollins, 2009), 42.

15. Earl Lawson, "Relaxed Reds Set Sights on Individual Goals," *The Sporting News*, September 30, 1972, 10.

16. Sparky Anderson (with Dan Ewald), *They Call Me Sparky* (Chelsea, MI: Sleeping Bear Press, 1998), 98.

## Chapter 4

1. Christopher D. Chavis, "October 3, 1972: The Fenway Faithful are Left Wondering, What If We Had One More Game?" SABR online article.

2. Cait Murphy. *Crazy '08: How a Cast of Cranks, Rogues, Boneheads, and Magnates Created the Greatest Year in Baseball History* (New York: HarperCollins/Smithsonian Books), 2007, 224.

3. "Bowie and Marvin May Cost Red Sox Flag," *Pittsburgh Press*, October 2, 1972, 33.

4. "Tigers Grab East Lead by Beating Red Sox, 4–1," *Schenectady Gazette*, October 3, 1972, 24.

5. Harold Kaese, "Lefties Coming Up, Sox Gambled on Kaline," *Boston Globe*, October 4, 1972, 61.

6. Jim Hawkins, "Kaline's the Hero, 3–1," *Detroit Free Press*, October 4, 1972, 2D.

7. Larry Paladino, "Tigers Nip Red Sox Again to Win AL East Crown," *Schenectady Gazette*, October 4, 1972, 46.

## Chapter 5

1. Todd Masters, *The 1972 Detroit Tigers: Billy Martin and the Half-Game Champs* (Jefferson, NC: McFarland, 2010).

2. Bill Dow, "How Billy Martin and Umpire John Rice Cost the Tigers the 1972 Pennant," Vintagedetroit.com, October 1, 2011.

3. Larry Claflin, "Story of Year in Boston: Red Sox Hill Revolution," *The Sporting News*, October 14, 1972, 3.

4. "Insiders Say," *The Sporting News*, August 23, 1975, 4.

5. Curt Gowdy, NBC-TV broadcast of Game One of the 1972 ALCS, October 7, 1972.

6. Tony Kubek, NBC-TV broadcast of Game Two of the 1972 ALCS, October 8, 1972.

7. Joe Bigham, "Billy Sees Suspension for Campy," *Schenectady Gazette*, October 9, 1972, 46.

8. Tony Kubek, NBC-TV broadcast of Game Two of the 1972 ALCS, October 8, 1972.

9. Joe Bigham, "Billy Sees Suspension for Campy," *Schenectady Gazette*, October 9, 1972, 46.

10. *Ibid.*

11. *Ibid.*

12. *Ibid.*

13. *Ibid.*

14. *Ibid.*

15. Bruce Markusen, *A Baseball Dynasty* (Haworth, NJ: St. Johann Press, 2002), 133.

16. *Ibid.*

17. Bill Dow, "When Campy Campaneris Tossed His Bat at Tiger pitcher LaGrow in the '72 Playoffs," Vintage detroit.com, October 13, 2011.

18. Joe Bigham, "Billy Sees Suspension for Campy," *Schenectady Gazette*, October 9, 1972, 46.

19. *Ibid.*

20. *Ibid.*

21. Ralph Ray, "Swinging A's Put Tigers Down for Two Count," *The Sporting News*, October 21, 1972, 4.

22. Hal Bock, "Coleman Job Keeps Tigers Alive," *Schenectady Gazette*, October 11, 1972, 44.

23. Hal Bock, "Tigers' 10th-Inning Rally Stuns Oakland," *Schenectady Gazette*, October 12, 1972, 34.

24. *Ibid.*

25. *Ibid.*

26. "Tigers Nip A's in 10th," Montreal Gazette, October 12, 1972, 25.

27. Piet Bennett, "Relievers Didn't Do Job Says Disappointed Dick," *Schenectady Gazette*, October 12, 1972, 34.

28. Monte Moore, NBC Radio broadcast of Game Four of the 1972 ALCS, October 11, 1972.

29. "Tigers Suddenly in Driver's Seat," *Calgary Herald*, October 12, 1972, 43.

30. Hal Bock, "Athletics Edge Tigers for Series Berth," *Schenectady Gazette*, October 13, 1972, 28.

31. Ray Lane, Detroit Tigers Radio broadcast of Game Five of the 1972 ALCS, October 12, 1972.

32. Ernie Harwell, *ibid.*

33. Monte Moore, NBC Radio broadcast of Game Four of the 1972 ALCS, October 11, 1972.

34. Harry Atkins, "Cash, Howard Unhappy Over Disputed Decision," *Schenectady Gazette*, October 13, 1972, 28.

35. *Ibid.*

36. *Ibid.*

37. *Ibid.*

38. *Ibid.*

39. Red Smith, "Tiger Fans Left Stands for Lions," *Bangor Daily News*, October 13, 1972. 10.

40. "Williams Claims Victory Was 'Biggest in Career,'" *Schenectady Gazette*, October 13, 1972, 28.

41. *Ibid.*

42. "A's Charge Into World Series with 2–1 Win," *Bangor Daily News*, October 13, 1972, 10.

43. "Williams Claims Victory Was 'Biggest in Career,'" *Schenectady Gazette*, October 13, 1972, 28.

44. Larry Paladino, "A's Win First Title Since 1931," *Fredericksburg Free Lance-Star*, October 13, 1972, 8.

## Chapter 6

1. William Leggett, "Simply Call It the National Pastime," *Sports Illustrated*, October 9, 1972, 47.

2. Curt Gowdy, NBC-TV broadcast of Game Five of the 1972 NCLS, October 11, 1972.

3. William Leggett, "Simply Call It the National Pastime," *Sports Illustrated*, October 9, 1972, 47.

4. Steve Blass (with Erik Sherman), *A Pirate for Life* (New York: Triumph Books, 2012).

5. Ron Fimrite, "Mad About the Game," *Sports Illustrated*, October 16, 1972, 31.

6. Bob Smizik, "Pirate Lefties Manhandle Reds," *Pittsburgh Press*, October 8, 1972, D1.

7. Bob Smizik, "Reds Get to Pirates, Moose Real Fast," *Pittsburgh Press*, October 9, 1972, 25.

8. Charley Feeney, "Playing Games," *Pittsburgh Post-Gazette*, October 11, 1972, 27.

9. D. Byron Yake, "Tolan, Teammates Feel Win Provides an Edge," *Schenectady Gazette*, October 9, 1972, 38.

10. *Ibid.*

11. Gary Mihoces, "Bucs Cry 'Foul' on Tolan Hit," *Schenectady Gazette*, October 9, 1972, 38.

12. *Ibid.*

13. Roy McHugh, "Clemente Not Raising Storm Over Playoff Doldrums," *Pittsburgh Press*, October 9, 1972, 2.

14. *Ibid.*

15. Gary Mihoces, "Bucs Cry 'Foul' on Tolan Hit," *Schenectady Gazette*, October 9, 1972, 38.

16. *Ibid.*

17. Ken Rappoport, "Sanguillén Helps Pirates to 3–2 Squeeze of Reds," October 10, 1972, 23.

18. *Ibid.*

19. Earl Lawson, "Wild Pitch Sets Off Reds' NL Pennant Party," *The Sporting News*, October 28, 1972, 9.

20. "Ross Credits Crowd for Sterling Chore," *Schenectady Gazette*, October 11, 1972, 44.

21. Charley Feeney, "Today's a Must Day for Bucs," *Pittsburgh Post-Gazette*, October 11, 1972, 1.

22. "Ross Credits Crowd for Sterling Chore," *Schenectady Gazette*, October 11, 1972, 44.

23. *Ibid.*

24. *Ibid.*

25. Ian MacDonald, "Roused Reds tame Pirates," *Montreal Gazette*, October 11, 1972, 33–34.

26. Al Michaels, NBC Radio broadcast of Game Five of the 1972 NLCS, October 11, 1972.

27. Ian MacDonald, "Bench Listens to Mother and Reds Win It," *Montreal Gazette*, October 12, 1972, 25.

28. Bill Winter, "Mother Knew Best for Cincinnati Hero Bench," *Schenectady Gazette*, October 12, 1972, 33.

29. *Ibid.*

30. *Ibid.*

31. Al Michaels, NBC Radio broadcast of Game Five of the 1972 NLCS, October 11, 1972.

32. *Ibid.*

33. "Johnny Bench Relives the 9th Inning of the '72 NLCS," MLB YouTube Channel, October 11, 2018.

34. Floyd Johnson, "Bob Moose," SABR biography.

35. George Strode, "Sanguillén Says Decisive Wild Pitch Hit Something," *Schenectady Gazette*, October 12, 1972, 33.

36. *Ibid.*

37. *Ibid.*

38. *Ibid.*

39. *Ibid.*

40. "The Strike That Bounced," *Pittsburgh Post-Gazette*, October 12, 1972, 20.

41. *Ibid.*

42. Bob Broeg, "Broeg on Baseball," *The Sporting News*, November 4, 1972, 4.

43. "Reds Bench Erupts with Johnny," *Pittsburgh Post-Gazette*, October 12, 1972, 20.

44. Earl Lawson, "Wild Pitch Sets Off Reds' NL Pennant Party," *The Sporting News*, October 28, 1972, 9.

45. *Ibid.*

46. Ian MacDonald, "Bench Listens to Mother and Reds Win It," *Montreal Gazette*, October 12, 1972, 25.

47. *Ibid.*

48. *Ibid.*

49. *Ibid.*

50. *Ibid.*

51. Bob Smizik, "Bucs Lived, Died by Bats," *Pittsburgh Press*, October 13. 1972, 31.

52. "Pirates Act Professional Despite Painful Defeat," *Schenectady Gazette*, October 13, 1972, 28.

53. *Ibid.*

54. *Ibid.*

55. Pat Livingston, "Pirates Go Out with Their Heads High," *Pittsburgh Press*, October 12, 1972, 42.

56. Al Abrams, "Sidelights on Sports: Baseball's Big Day," *Pittsburgh Post-Gazette*, October 13, 1972, 13.

57. "Cincinnatians Loud But 'Not Too Bad,'" *Fredericksburg Free Lance-Star*, October 12, 1972, 10.

58. *Ibid.*

59. Kipp Martin, "Reds Memory: 1972 NLCS, Game Five, 9th Inning," Redscontentplus.com, April 19, 2020.

## Chapter 7

1. Ian MacDonald, "Giants on Mays: We've Lost Our Leader," *Montreal Gazette*, May 13, 1972, 19.

2. Warren Corbett, "Milt Pappas," SABR biography.

3. "Bruce Froemming," Alchetron.com, August 29, 2018.

4. Ron Bergman, "Banquet Requests Pour In; Rudi Prefers Home Hearth," *The Sporting News*, December 16, 1972, 51.

## Chapter 8

1. Ron Fimrite, "A Big Beginning for the Little League," *Sports Illustrated*, October 23, 1972, 26.

2. Matt Kelly, "A's Shut Down Big Red Machine in Thrilling Game 7," Baseball-hall.org.

3. Ron Fimrite, "A Big Beginning for the Little League," *Sports Illustrated*, October 23, 1972, 26.

4. *Ibid.*

5. Hal Bock, "Nolan Face Holtzman in Series Opener," *Schenectady Gazette*, October 14, 1972, 20.

6. *Ibid.*

7. Anderson, Sparky (with Dan Ewald), *They Call Me Sparky* (Chelsea, MI: Sleeping Bear Press, 1998), 56–57.

8. Greene, Chip (editor). *Mustaches and Mayhem: Charlie O's Three-Time Champions the Oakland Athletics, 1972–74* (Phoenix, AZ: Society for American Baseball Research, 2015).

9. Pete Rose, *The Swingin' A's* (MLB-TV documentary), 2017.

10. Charley Feeney, "Playing Games," *Pittsburgh Post-Gazette*, October 13, 1972, 14.

11. "Reds, Pirates Toughest Two Teams: Pete Rose," *Schenectady Gazette*, October 13, 1972, 29.

12. Terry Flynn, "Bench Minds His Mom," *Windsor Star*, October 12, 1972, 39.

13. Ken Rappaport, "Blue Not Happy with A's Treatment," *Schenectady Gazette*, October 14, 1972, 20.

14. Ian MacDonald, "Campaneris Back, Jackson Out," *Montreal Gazette*, October 14, 1972, 27.

15. Ed Levitt, "Joyland for A's," *Oakland Tribune*, October 15, 1972, 53.

16. "Jim McKay," *Windsor Star*, October 14, 1972, 20.

17. Joe Falls, "Enough Brainwashing," *The Sporting News*, November 4, 1972, 4.

18. *Ibid.*

19. George Hostetter, "Gone from A's, Valley Gets Moore," *Fresno Bee*, February 16, 1993.

20. Matt Bohn, "Monte Moore," SABR biography.

## Chapter 9

1. Hal Bock, "Nolan Faces Holtzman in Series Opener," *Schenectady Gazette*, October 14, 1972, 20.

2. Bob Addie, "Addie's Atoms," *The Sporting News*, November 11, 1972, 14.

3. Hal Bock, "Nolan Faces Holtzman in Series Opener," *Schenectady Gazette*, October 14, 1972, 20.

4. Ron Fimrite, "A Big Beginning for the Little League," *Sports Illustrated*, October 23, 1972, 26–27.

5. Hal Bock, "Nolan Faces Holtzman in Series Opener," *Schenectady Gazette*, October 14, 1972, 20.

6. "Jackson on Crutches for Opener," *Schenectady Gazette*, October 14, 1972, 20.

7. Ian MacDonald, "Campaneris back, Jackson Out," *Montreal Gazette*, October 14, 1972, 27.

8. Austin Gisriel, "Darold Knowles," SABR biography, March 10, 2021.

9. Hal Bock, "Nolan Faces Holtzman in Series Opener," *Schenectady Gazette*, October 14, 1972, 20.

10. *Ibid.*

11. Ian MacDonald, "Campaneris back, Jackson Out," *Montreal Gazette*, October 14, 1972, 27.

12. Milton Richman, "Campy: The Last Days Was a Terrible Feeling for Me," *Windsor Star*, October 14, 1972, 20.

13. Hal Bock, "Nolan Faces Holtzman in Series Opener," *Schenectady Gazette*, October 14, 1972, 20.

14. Jim Simpson, NBC Radio broadcast of Game One of the 1972 World Series, October 14, 1972.

15. *Ibid.*, Monte Moore.

16. Joe Falls, "Something Is Bugging Blue," *The Sporting News*, May 27, 1972, 2.

17. *Ibid.*

18. Monte Moore, NBC Radio broadcast of Game One of the 1972 World Series, October 14, 1972.

19. "Reds' Study Key to Win by Oakland," *Spokane Spokesman-Review*, October 15, 1972, S3.

20. *Ibid.*

21. Ron Bergman, "A's Sock It to Reds," *Oakland Tribune*, October 15, 1972, 53.

22. "Reds' Study Key to Win by Oakland," *Spokane Spokesman-Review*, October 15, 1972, S3.

23. Ron Bergman, "A's Sock It to Reds," *Oakland Tribune*, October 15, 1972, 53.

24. George Ross, "Tenace Powers A's Win; Series in Oakland Tuesday," *Oakland Tribune*, October 15, 1972, 1.

25. "Actions Louder, Finley Asserts,"

*Spokane Spokesman-Review*, October 15, 1972, S3.

26. *Ibid.*

## Chapter 10

1. Bob Smizik, "Rudi's Bat, Glove, Put A's 2 Up," *Pittsburgh Press*, October 16, 1972, 27.
2. Ian MacDonald, "Williams Compares Rudi's Catch to Gi's, Amorós' and Mays,'" *Montreal Gazette*, October 16, 1972, 13.
3. Jim Simpson, NBC Radio's broadcast of Game Two of the 1972 World Series, October 15, 1972.
4. "Tribute Paid to Jackie Robinson on 25th Anniversary of Debut," *Montreal Gazette*, October 16, 1972, 14.
5. Curt Gowdy, NBC-TV broadcast of Game Two of the 1972 World Series, October 15, 1972.
6. Al Michaels, *ibid.*
7. Curt Gowdy, *ibid.*
8. Al Michaels, *ibid.*
9. Curt Gowdy, *ibid.*
10. *Ibid.*
11. *Ibid.*
12. *Ibid.*
13. Jim Simpson, NBC Radio broadcast of Game Two of the 1972 World Series, October 15, 1972.
14. Monte Moore, *ibid.*
15. Curt Gowdy, NBC-TV broadcast of Game Two of the 1972 World Series, October 15, 1972.
16. Charles Feeney, "Rudi's Catch Bets of All—Williams," *Pittsburgh Post-Gazette*, October 16, 1972, 22.
17. *Ibid.*
18. Roger Angell, *Five Seasons* (New York: Simon & Schuster, 1977), 55.
19. Jim Hunter and Armen Keteyian, *Catfish: My Life in Baseball* (New York: McGraw Hill, 1988), 104.
20. Lowell Reidenbaugh, "Rudi's Bat and Glove Help Hunter to Shoot Down Reds," *The Sporting News*, October 28, 1972, 5.
21. Al Abrams, "Spotlights on Sports," *Pittsburgh Post-Gazette*, October 16, 1972, 22.
22. *Ibid.*
23. *Ibid.*
24. Charley Feeny, "Joe HRs, Saves It with Grab," *Pittsburgh Post-Gazette*, October 16, 1972, 23.
25. Ron Bergman, "Catfish Will Seek $80,000 in 1973," *The Sporting News*, October 7, 1972, 5.
26. *Ibid.*
27. Ian McDonald, "Fischer, Spassky Together Would Still Be No Match for Williams the Strategist, Says His Buddy Mauch," *Montreal Gazette*, October 17, 1972, 33.
28. *Ibid.*
29. Al Abrams, "One More for Hair," *Pittsburgh Post-Gazette*, October 16, 1972, 22.
30. *Ibid.*
31. Ian MacDonald, "The 'Other Catcher' Leads A's," *Montreal Gazette*, October 16, 1972, 14.
32. "Cincy 'Steamed Up' After Trip to Coast," *Schenectady Gazette*, October 17, 1972, 25.
33. *Ibid.*
34. Ken Rappaport, "Oakland's Rudi Rocks Reds," *Windsor Star*, October 16, 1972, 27.
35. Gene Caddes, "Joe Rudi Latest Oakland Hero," *Beaver County Times*, October 16, 1972, C-2.
36. Lawrence M. Stolle, "Tanner Seen as Leading Candidate for Top Honors," *Youngstown Vindicator*, October 18, 1972, 36.
37. Lawrence M. Stolle, "A's Go Two Up on Stumbling Reds; Series Shifts to Oakland Tuesday Night," *Youngstown Vindicator*, October 16, 1972, 18.

## Chapter 11

1. Red Smith, "Tiger Fans Left Stands for Lions," *Bangor Daily News*, October 13, 1972, 10.
2. Harold Friend, "Baseball History: Dick Williams Embarrassed Johnny Bench," Bleacherreport.com, August 19, 2010.
3. Jim Hunter and Armen Keteyian, *Catfish: My Life in Baseball* (New York: McGraw Hill, 1988), 104.
4. Ian McDonald, "Fischer, Spassky Together Would Still Be No Match for Williams the Strategist, Says His Buddy Mauch," *Montreal Gazette*, October 17, 1972, 33.

5. Hal Bock, "Rain, Hailstorm, KO's 3rd Game of Series," *Schenectady Gazette,* October 18, 1972, 50.

6. *Ibid.*

7. John G. Griffin, "Oakland, Reds Try Again Tonight," *Beaver County Times,* October 18, 1972, C-23.

8. Richard Paloma, "1972 Oakland Athletics Championship: You Never Forget Your First," Whitecleatbeat.com, October 7, 2015.

9. John G. Griffin, "Oakland, Reds Try Again Tonight," *Beaver County Times,* October 18, 1972, C-23.

10. Joseph Durso, "Storm Wipes Out Third World Series Contest," *New York Times* (online archives), October 18, 1972.

11. Bob Hertzel, "Another Look: The 1972 World Series," Baseballprospectus.com, October 12, 2010.

12. Milton Richman, "Bench, Jackson Break Age-Old Rule," *Beaver County Times,* October 18, 1972, C-24.

13. Samuel J. Skinner, Jr., "On the Way Back," *Black Sports,* June/July 1972.

14. Ron Bergman, "Blue Moon Mystery—Fast Ball That Sinks," *The Sporting News,* May 31, 1969, 10.

15. Al Michaels, NBC Radio broadcast of Game Three of the 1972 World Series, October 18, 1972.

16. *Ibid.*

17. Jim Simpson, *ibid.*

18. Al Michaels, *ibid.*

19. Ian MacDonald, "Reds Win One on Pitching 1–0 as Billingham, Carroll Do Job," *Montreal Gazette,* October 19, 1972, 35.

20. *Ibid.*

21. Bert Campaneris, *1972 World Series,* Major League Baseball Promotion Corp., 1972.

22. Al Michaels, NBC Radio broadcast of Game Three of the 1972 World Series, October 18, 1972.

23. Johnny Bench, *1972 World Series,* Major League Baseball Promotion Corp., 1972.

24. Ian MacDonald, "Reds Win One on Pitching 1–0 as Billingham, Carroll Do Job," *Montreal Gazette,* October 19, 1972, 35.

25. Jim Simpson, NBC Radio broadcast of Game Three of the 1972 World Series, October 18, 1972.

26. Al Michaels, *ibid.*

27. Curt Gowdy, *1972 World Series,* Major League Baseball Promotion Corp., 1972.

28. Milton Richman, "Fingers Bluffs Out Bench," *Pittsburgh Press,* October 19, 1972, 43.

29. Joe Falls, "Enough Brainwashing," *The Sporting News,* November 4, 1972, 4.

30. Harold Friend, "Baseball History: Dick Williams Embarrassed Johnny Bench," Bleacherreport.com, August 19, 2010.

31. Al Michaels, NBC Radio broadcast of Game Three of the 1972 World Series, October 18, 1972.

32. "Reds are Riled Up," *Sarasota Journal,* October 19, 1972, D1.

33. "Reds Take Third Game In 'Twilight' with Single Run," *Sarasota Journal,* October 19, 1972, D1.

34. *Ibid.*

35. *Ibid.*

36. *Ibid.*

37. *Ibid.*

38. Ian MacDonald, "Reds Win One on Pitching 1–0 as Billingham, Carroll Do Job," *Montreal Gazette,* October 19, 1972, 35.

39. *Ibid.*

40. *Ibid.*

41. Milton Richman, "Fingers Bluffs Out Bench," *Pittsburgh Press,* October 19, 1972, 43.

42. Ian MacDonald, "Reds Win One on Pitching 1–0 as Billingham, Carroll Do Job," *Montreal Gazette,* October 19, 1972, 35.

43. *Ibid.*

44. Milton Richman, "Fingers Bluffs Out Bench," *Pittsburgh Press,* October 19, 1972, 43.

45. *Ibid.*

46. Ian MacDonald, "Reds Win One on Pitching 1–0 as Billingham, Carroll Do Job," *Montreal Gazette,* October 19, 1972, 35.

47. "1972 World Series," Baseball-reference.com.

48. Charley Feeney, "Playing Games," *Pittsburgh Post-Gazette,* October 19, 1972, 25.

49. *Ibid.*

50. *Ibid.*

51. *Ibid.*

## Chapter 12

1. Bob Smizik, "'Little Clemente' Puts A's One Win Away from Title," *Pittsburgh Press*, October 20, 1972, 29.
2. Al Michaels, NBC Radio broadcast of Game Four of the 1972 World Series, October 19, 1972.
3. *Ibid.*
4. *Ibid.*
5. *Ibid.*
6. Jim Simpson, *ibid.*
7. Al Michaels, *ibid.*
8. *Ibid.*
9. Monte Moore, NBC-TV broadcast of Game Four of the 1972 World Series, October 19, 1972.
10. Al Michaels, NBC Radio broadcast of Game Four of the 1972 World Series, October 19, 1972.
11. Jim Simpson, *ibid.*
12. *Ibid.*
13. Curt Gowdy, NBC-TV broadcast of Game Four of the 1972 World Series, October 19, 1972.
14. Bob Smizik, "'Little Clemente' Puts A's One Win Away from Title," *Pittsburgh Press*, October 20, 1972, 29.
15. *Ibid.*
16. *Ibid.*
17. *Ibid.*
18. Gordon Sakamoto, "As Carroll Crumbles, Reds' Hopes Bog Down," *Windsor Star*, October 20, 1972, 30.
19. *Ibid.*
20. Bob Smizik, "'Little Clemente' Puts A's One Win Away from Title," *Pittsburgh Press*, October 20, 1972, 29.
21. "Booed and Pelted, Rose Strikes Back in Anger," *Schenectady Gazette*, October 21, 1972, 22.
22. Bob Smizik, "'Little Clemente' Puts A's One Win Away from Title," *Pittsburgh Press*, October 20, 1972, 29.
23. Will Grimsley, "Tenace Heroics Setting World Right on 'Tennis,'" *Schenectady Gazette*, October 20, 1972, 18.
24. Bob Smizik, "Gaining Respect," *Pittsburgh Press*, October 20, 1972, 29.
25. *Ibid.*
26. Ralph Bernstein, "Not Much Different Say Umps on 'Zone,'" *Schenectady Gazette*, October 20, 1972, 18.
27. *Ibid.*
28. *Ibid.*
29. *Ibid.*

30. Larry Shepard, NBC-TV broadcast of Game Five of the 1972 World Series, October 20, 1972.
31. Bob Smizik, "'Little Clemente' Puts A's One Win Away from Title," *Pittsburgh Press*, October 20, 1972, 29.
32. "Jim Murray," *Schenectady Gazette*, October 20, 1972, 19.
33. *Ibid.*
34. *Ibid.*
35. *Ibid.*
36. Lawrence M. Stolle, "Major League Moguls Push for Inter-League Play," *Youngstown Vindicator*, October 20, 1972, 21.

## Chapter 13

1. "Booed and Pelted, Rose Strikes Back in Anger," *Schenectady Gazette*, October 21, 1972, 22.
2. "Jim Murray," *Calgary Herald*, October 21, 1972, 29.
3. "Booed and Pelted, Rose Strikes Back in Anger," *Schenectady Gazette*, October 21, 1972, 22.
4. *Ibid.*
5. *Ibid.*
6. Monte Moore, NBC-TV broadcast of Game Five of the 1972 World Series, October 20, 1972.
7. Jim Murray, "When Popped Bunt Fell, A's Fell with It," *Oakland Tribune*, October 21, 1972, 25-E.
8. Charles F. Faber, "Jim McGlothlin," SABR biography.
9. *Ibid.*
10. Curt Gowdy, NBC-TV broadcast of Game Five of the 1972 World Series, October 20, 1972.
11. Ken Burns, *Baseball* (PBS Documentary), PBS Home Video, 1994.
12. Jim Simpson, NBC Radio broadcast of Game Five of the 1972 World Series, October 20, 1972.
13. Al Michaels, *ibid.*
14. Bill Plaschke, "The Memories Linger: 20 Years Ago, Series Star Tenace Was Threatened by a Gun-Toting Man in the Stands," *Los Angeles Times* (online archives), October 20, 1992.
15. Al Michaels, NBC Radio broadcast of Game Five of the 1972 World Series, October 20, 1972.
16. *Ibid.*

17. *Ibid.*

18. *Ibid.*

19. *Ibid.*

20. Curt Gowdy, NBC-TV broadcast of Game Five of the 1972 World Series, October 20, 1972.

21. Tony Kubek, NBC-TV broadcast of Game Five of the 1972 World Series, October 20, 1972.

22. Al Michaels, NBC Radio broadcast of Game Five of the 1972 World Series, October 20, 1972.

23. Bob Smizik, "Fingers All Thumbs, Muffs Double Play," *Pittsburgh Press*, October 21, 1972, 6.

24. *Ibid.*

25. Tony Kubek, NBC-TV broadcast of Game Five of the 1972 World Series, October 20, 1972.

26. Curt Gowdy, NBC-TV broadcast of Game Five of the 1972 World Series, October 20, 1972.

27. *Ibid.*

28. Jim Simpson, NBC Radio broadcast of Game five of the 1972 World Series, October 20, 1972.

29. Al Michaels, *ibid.*

30. "Booed and Pelted, Rose Strikes Back in Anger," *Schenectady Gazette*, October 21, 1972, 22.

31. Ralph Bernstein, "Apples, Oranges Don't Bother Rose," *Fredericksburg Free Lance-Star*, October 21, 1972, 8.

32. "Jim Murray," *Calgary Herald*, October 21, 1972, 29.

33. Eric Prewitt, "Final Out Gamble by A's Failed," *Schenectady Gazette*, October 21, 1972, 22.

34. *Ibid.*

35. *Ibid.*

36. *Ibid.*

37. *Ibid.*

38. *Ibid.*

39. "Rose Strikes Out at Tenace," *Pittsburgh Press*, October 21, 1972, 6.

40. *Ibid.*

41. "Melvin Durslag," *The Sporting News*, November 4, 1972, 4.

42. Lawrence M. Stolle, "Inspired Reds Confident They Will Win It All Now," *Youngstown Vindicator*, October 21, 1972, 13.

43. Bill Winter, "Anderson Gives Williams Edge," *Fredericksburg Free Lance-Star*, October 21, 1972, 8.

44. *Ibid.*

45. Lawrence M. Stolle, "Inspired Reds Confident They Will Win It All Now," *Youngstown Vindicator*, October 21, 1972, 13.

46. Ed Levitt, "Too Often for Vida?" *Oakland Tribune*, October 21, 1972, 23-E.

47. "Rose's Hit in 9th Ruins A's Bid for Clincher, 5–4," *Youngstown Vindicator*, October 21, 1972, 12.

48. "Jim Murray," *Calgary Herald*, October 21, 1972, 29.

## Chapter 14

1. William Leggett, "Mustaches All the Way," *Sports Illustrated*, October 30, 1972, 22.

2. Bob Smizik, "Reds Clobber A's, 8–1, Even Series," *Pittsburgh Press*, October 22, 1972, D1.

3. William Leggett, "Mustaches All the Way," *Sports Illustrated*, October 30, 1972, 22.

4. Monte Moore, NBC Radio broadcast of Game Six of the 1972 World Series, October 21, 1972.

5. Bob Smizik, "Reds Clobber A's, 8–1, Even Series," *Pittsburgh Press*, October 22, 1972, D2.

6. Monte Moore, NBC Radio broadcast of Game Six of the 1972 World Series, October 21, 1972.

7. *Ibid.*

8. *Ibid.*

9. Jim Simpson, *ibid.*

10. Bob Smizik, "Reds Clobber A's, 8–1, Even Series," *Pittsburgh Press*, October 22, 1972, D1.

11. Monte Moore, NBC Radio broadcast of Game Six of the 1972 World Series, October 21, 1972.

12. Hal Bock, "Cincy Convinces A's Williams, 8–1," *San Bernardino County Sun*, October 22, 1972, E-1.

13. "1972 World Series," Baseball-reference.com.

14. "Suspect, Pistol Reported Seized," *New York Times* online archives, October 22, 1972.

15. "Gunman, Reds Worry Tenace," *Pittsburgh Press*, October 22, 1972, D1.

16. Andrew Shinkle, "Not-So-Great Moment in Reds Fan History: October 15, 1972," Redreporter.com, November 15, 2014.

17. Bob Smizik, "Reds Clobber A's, 8–1, Even Series," *Pittsburgh Press*, October 22, 1972, D2.

18. *Ibid.*

19. *Ibid.*

20. Monte Moore, NBC Radio broadcast of Game Six of the 1972 World Series, October 21, 1972.

21. "Suspect, Pistol Reported Seized," *New York Times* online archives, October 22, 1972.

## Chapter 15

1. "It's a Beautiful Thing," *Fredericksburg Free Lance-Star*, October 23, 1972, 6.

2. "Jim Murray," *Calgary Herald*, October 23, 1972, 14.

3. Bob Hertzel, "Another Look: The 1972 World Series," Baseballprospectus.com, October 12, 2010.

4. Monte Moore, NBC Radio broadcast of Game Seven of the 1972 World Series, October 22, 1972.

5. *Ibid.*

6. Bill Winter, "Tolan Takes the Blame," *Bowling Green Daily News*, October 23, 1972, 6.

7. Monte Moore, NBC Radio broadcast of Game Seven of the 1972 World Series, October 22, 1972.

8. *Ibid.*

9. *Ibid.*

10. Jim Hunter and Armen Keteyian, *Catfish: My Life in Baseball* (New York: McGraw Hill, 1988), 104.

11. *Ibid.*, 105.

12. Jim Simpson, NBC Radio broadcast of Game Seven of the 1972 World Series, October 22, 1972.

13. William Leggett, "Mustaches All the Way," *Sports Illustrated*, October 30, 1972, 22.

14. Vito Stellino, "Tenace, Bando, Star in 7th Game of Thrilling Battle," *Youngstown Vindicator*, October 23, 1972, 16.

15. Jim Hunter and Armen Keteyian, *Catfish: My Life in Baseball* (New York: McGraw Hill, 1988), 105.

16. "Melvin Durslag," *The Sporting News*, November 4, 1972, 4.

17. Neal Russo, "The Hollingsworth Report: It Helped A's Conquer Reds," *The Sporting News*, November 11, 1972, 36.

18. Joe Rudi, *The Swingin' A's* (MLB-TV documentary), 2017.

19. Bob Hertzel, "Another Look: The 1972 World Series," Baseballprospectus.com, October 12, 2010.

20. Dick Williams, NBC Radio broadcast of Game Seven of the 1972 World Series, October 22, 1972.

21. Lowell Reidenbaugh, "Amazin' A's Reign as World Champs," *The Sporting News*, November 4, 1972, 3.

22. *Ibid.*

23. *Ibid.*

24. "The Gang that Won the Series: Just 19 Mustaches and a Mule," *Calgary Herald*, October 23, 1972, 14.

25. Eric Prewitt, "Dick Changed His Mind in 'Overmanaging' Job," *Schenectady Gazette*, October 23, 1972, 39.

26. *Ibid.*

27. *Ibid.*

28. Bill Winter, "Tolan Takes the Blame," *Bowling Green Daily News*, October 23, 1972, 6.

29. *Ibid.*

30. Bob Weston, "Oakland Never Quit...'Best in Baseball,'" *Middlesboro Daily News*, October 23, 1972, 8.

31. *Ibid.*

32. "The Gang That Won the Series: Just 19 Mustaches and a Mule," *Calgary Herald*, October 23, 1972, 14.

33. Sparky Anderson (with Dan Ewald), *They Call Me Sparky* (Chelsea, MI: Sleeping Bear Press, 1998).

34. *Ibid.*

35. "Reds Let the Sunshine In," *Calgary Herald*, October 21, 1972, 29.

36. The Gang That Won the Series: Just 19 Mustaches and a Mule," *Calgary Herald*, October 23, 1972, 14.

37. *Ibid.*

38. Jim Hunter and Armen Keteyian, *Catfish: My Life in Baseball* (New York: McGraw Hill, 1988), 102.

39. *Ibid.*

40. Al Abrams, "Spotlights on Sports," *Pittsburgh Post-Gazette*, October 23, 1972, 31.

41. Lowell Reidenbaugh, "Amazin' A's Reign as World Champs," *The Sporting News*, November 4, 1972, 3.

42. Ed Levitt, "Meet the Champs," *Oakland Tribune*, October 23, 1972, E-37.

43. "Reagan Sends Congratulations," *Oakland Tribune*, October 23, 1972, E-38.

44. Lowell Reidenbaugh, "Amazin' A's Reign as World Champs," *The Sporting News*, November 4, 1972, 3.

45. Al Abrams, "Spotlights on Sports," *Pittsburgh Post-Gazette*, October 23, 1972, 26.

## Chapter 16

1. Hal Bock, "Color Baseball's World Champions Green and Gold," *Schenectady Gazette*, October 24, 1972, 25.

2. *Ibid.*

3. *Ibid.*

4. *Ibid.*

5. *Ibid.*

6. *Ibid.*

7. *Ibid.*

8. Dave Condon, "Charlie O.: Amazing Sports Maverick," *The Sporting News*, January 6, 1973, 32.

9. Charles O. Finley, *Finley's Heroes* (Revere, MA: Fleetwood Recording, 1972).

## Chapter 17

1. Al Michaels, *Bench*, MLB documentary, 2019.

2. *Ibid.*

3. "Outlook Bright for Bench After Lung Lesion Surgery," *Montreal Gazette*, December 12, 1972, 38.

4. *Ibid.*

5. Johnny Bench, *Bench*, MLB documentary, 2019.

## Chapter 18

1. Pete Rose, *The Swingin' A's* (MLB-TV documentary), 2017.

2. John Ring, "The Enigma of Bobby Tolan," Redlegnation.com, April 2, 2017.

3. *Ibid.*

4. Joe Garagiola, NBC-TV broadcast of Game Four of the 1976 World Series, October 20, 1976.

5. Joe Morgan, *ibid.*

6. Ron Fimrite, "Ah, How Great It Is," *Sports Illustrated*, November 1, 1976, 18.

7. Sparky Anderson (with Dan Ewald), *They Call Me Sparky* (Chelsea, MI: Sleeping Bear Press, 1998).

8. *Ibid.*

9. Ron Bergman, "Epstein Exit Traced to Tenace Shoulder Ailment," *The Sporting News*, December 23, 1972, 37.

10. Mike Shatzkin (editor), *The Ballplayers* (New York: William Morrow, 1990), 312–313.

11. "Phillies Get First Selection," *New Castle News*, November 27, 1972, 22.

12. Rory Costello, "Allan Lewis," SABR Biography.

13. Mark Armour, "Charlie Finley," SABR Biography, 2015.

14. Ron Bergman, "Andrews Case 'the Last Straw' for Williams," *The Sporting News*, November 3, 1973, 5.

15. Dink Carroll, "Charlie Finley of the A's: Not Your Usual Baseball Man," *Montreal Gazette*, October 16, 1973, 41.

16. Ron Bergman, "Andrews Case 'the Last Straw' for Williams," *The Sporting News*, November 3, 1973, 5.

17. Ron Bergman, "Finley Finds a Skipper in A's Dark-Ened Past," *The Sporting News*, March 9, 1974, 29.

18. Ed Levitt, "Accent on Sports," *Oakland Tribune*, December 8, 1976, 37.

19. *Ibid.*

20. Ron Bergman, "Moore's Loyalty Receives Its Reward—Finley's Ax," *The Sporting News*, December 25, 1976, 50.

21. Ron Fimrite, "They're Just Mad About Charlie," *Sports Illustrated*, May 21, 1979, 38.

22. Tom Weir, "Page Prods A's Awake … Fans Snooze On," *The Sporting News*, May 5, 1979, 16.

23. Ron Fimrite, "They're Just Mad About Charlie," *Sports Illustrated*, May 21, 1979, 38.

24. Tom Weir, "Page Prods A's Awake … Fans Snooze On," *The Sporting News*, May 5, 1979, 16.

25. Ron Fimrite, "They're Just Mad About Charlie," *Sports Illustrated*, May 21, 1979, 38.

26. *Ibid.*, 40.

27. *Ibid.*, 38.

28. *Ibid.*, 39.

29. Kit Stier, "New Owners to Keep A's in Oakland," *The Sporting News*, September 6, 1980, 57.

30. "Oakland A's Owner Charlie O. Finley Dies," *Washington Post* (online archives), February 20, 1996.

31. Mark Armour, "Charlie Finley," SABR Biography, 2015.

32. *Ibid.*

33. Vida Blue, *The Swingin' A's* (MLB-TV documentary), 2017.

## Chapter 19

1. Royse Parr, "Jerry Adair," SABR Biography.

2. Jeff English, "Catfish Hunter," SABR Biography, February 21, 2021.

3. *Ibid.*

4. Mike Dyer, "One of the Saddest Moments in Reds' History, 40 Years Later," Cincinnati.com, December 24, 2015.

## Chapter 20

1. "Melvin Durslag," *The Sporting News*, November 4, 1972, 3.

2. Sam Miller, "Ranking Every World Series in MLB History," ESPN.com, October 30, 2020.

## Appendix B

1. Pete Rose, *The Swingin' A's* (MLB-TV documentary), 2017.

2. Lawrence M. Stolle, "Ohioans Play Leading Roles as Oakland Captures Series," *Youngstown Vindicator*, October 23, 1972, 16.

# Bibliography

## Books

Allen, Lee. *The National League Story.* Revised edition. New York: Hill & Wang, 1965.

Anderson, Sparky, with Dan Ewald. *They Call Me Sparky.* Chelsea, MI: Sleeping Bear, 1998.

Angell, Roger. *Five Seasons.* New York: Simon & Schuster, 1977.

Blass, Steve, with Erik Sherman. *A Pirate for Life.* New York: Triumph, 2012.

Clavin, Tom, and Danny Peary. *Gil Hodges.* New York: New American Library, 2012.

Cosell, Howard. *Cosell.* Richmond Hill, ON: Pocket Books, 1974.

Dykes, Jimmie, and Charles O. Dexter. *You Can't Steal First Base.* New York: J.B. Lippincott, 1967.

Erardi, John. *Tony Pérez: From Cuba to Cooperstown.* Wilmington, OH: Orange Frazer, 2018.

Finoli, David, and Bill Ranier. *The Pittsburgh Pirates Encyclopedia.* Champaign, IL: Sports Publishing, 2003.

Greene, Chip, ed. *Mustaches and Mayhem: Charlie O's Three-Time Champions the Oakland Athletics, 1972–74* (e-book). Phoenix: Society for American Baseball Research, 2015.

Honig, Donald. *Baseball America.* New York: Macmillan, 1985.

Hunter, Jim, and Armen Keteyian. *Catfish: My Life in Baseball.* New York: McGraw-Hill, 1988.

Jackson, Reggie, with Mike Lupica. *Reggie: The Autobiography.* New York: Random House, 1984.

Kashatus, William C. *The Philadelphia Athletics.* Mount Pleasant, SC: Arcadia, 2002.

Koppett, Leonard. *Koppett's Concise History of Major League Baseball.* Philadelphia: Temple University Press, 1998.

Libby, Bill. *Charlie O and the Angry A's.* New York: Doubleday, 1975.

Lieb, Frederick G. *Connie Mack: Grand Old Man of Baseball.* Kent, OH: The Kent State University Press, 2012; first published by G.P. Putnam's Sons, 1945.

_____. *The Detroit Tigers.* Mattituck, NY: Amereon, 1946.

Markusen, Bruce. *A Baseball Dynasty.* Haworth, NJ: St. Johann Press, 2002.

_____. *Roberto Clemente: The Great One.* Champaign, IL: Sports Publishing, 2001.

_____. *The Team That Changed Baseball: Roberto Clemente and the 1971 Pittsburgh Pirates.* Yardley, PA: Westholme, 2006.

Masters, Todd. *The 1972 Detroit Tigers: Billy Martin and the Half-Game Champs.* Jefferson, NC: McFarland, 2010.

McCollister, John. *The Bucs! The Story of the Pittsburgh Pirates.* Lenexa, KS: Addax, 1998.

Michelson, Herbert. *Charlie O.* New York: Bobbs-Merrill, 1975.

Murphy, Cait. *Crazy '08: How a Cast of Cranks, Rogues, Boneheads, and Magnates Created the Greatest Year in Baseball History.* New York: HarperCollins, 2007.

Okrent, Daniel, and Steve Wulf. *Baseball Anecdotes.* New York: Oxford University Press, 1989.

Posnanski, Joe. *The Machine.* New York: HarperCollins, 2009.

Reichler, Joseph L., ed. *The World Series: A 75th Anniversary.* New York: Simon & Schuster, 1978.

Rosenburg, John M. *They Gave Us Baseball*. Harrisburg, PA: Stackpole, 1989.

Shatzkin, Mike, ed. *The Ballplayers*. New York: William Morrow, 1990.

Ward, Geoffrey C., and Ken Burns. *Baseball: An Illustrated History*. New York: Alfred A. Knopf, 2010.

Williams, Dick, and Bill Plaschke. *No More Mr. Nice Guy*. New York: Harcourt Brace Jovanovich, 1990

Zoss, Joel, and John S, Bowman. *The American League*. New York: Bison Books, 1986.

———, and ———. *The National League*. London: Bison Books, 1986.

## Newspaper Archives

*Baltimore Afro-American*
*Bangor Daily News*
*Beaver County Times*
*Boston Globe*
*Bowling Green Daily News*
*Calgary Herald*
*Cincinnati Enquirer*
*Cleveland Plain Dealer*
*Detroit Free Press*
*Dubuque Telegraph-Herald*
*Ellensburg Daily Record*
*Fredericksburg Free Lance-Star*
*Fresno Bee*
*Los Angeles Times*
*Middlesboro Daily News*
*Montreal Gazette*
*New Castle News*
*New York Times*
*Oakland Tribune*
*Pittsburgh Post-Gazette*
*Pittsburgh Press*
*San Bernardino County Sun*
*San Francisco Chronicle*
*Sarasota Journal*
*Schenectady Gazette*
*Spokane Spokesman-Review*
*The Sporting News*
*Syracuse Post-Standard*
*Washington Post*
*Windsor Star*
*Youngstown Vindicator*

## Online Reference Sources

Baseball-Almanac.com
Baseball-Reference.com
Cincinnati.com
ESPN.com
MLB.com
NBCSports.com
Redlegnation.com
Redreporter.com
Retrosheet.org
SABR.org
SI.com
Thisgreatgame.com
Vintagedetroit.com
Whitecleatbeat.com

## Video Sources

*Baseball* (produced by Ken Burns). PBS Home Video, 1994.

*Bench*. MLB Network documentary, 2019.

*1972 World Series*. Major League Baseball Promotion Corp., 1972.

*The Philadelphia Athletics*, Alpha Home Entertainment, 2003.

*The Swingin' A's*. MLB Network documentary, 2017.

# Index